Middle East Conflict
Primary
Sources

Middle East Conflict
Primary Sources

Tom and Sara Pendergast
Ralph G. Zerbonia

U·X·L
An imprint of Thomson Gale,
a part of The Thomson Corporation

THOMSON
──────✳──────
GALE

terville, Maine • London • Munich

Middle East Conflict: Primary Sources

Tom and Sara Pendergast

Project Editor
Ralph G. Zerbonia

Editorial
Sarah R. Hermsen, Nancy Matuszak

Rights and Acquisitions
Shalice Shah-Caldwell, Kim Smilay,
Andrew Specht

Imaging and Multimedia
Lezlie Light, Mike Logusz,
Christine O'Bryan, Denay Wilding

Product Design
Michelle Dimercurio

Composition
Evi Seoud

Manufacturing
Rita Wimberly

For permission to use material from
this product, submit your request via
the Web at http://www.gale-edit.com/
permissions, or you may download our
Permissions Request form and submit
your request by fax or mail to:

Permissions Department
Thomson Gale
27500 Drake Rd.
Farmington Hills, MI 48331-3535
Permissions Hotline:
248-699-8006 or 800-877-4253, ext. 8006
Fax: 248-699-8074 or 800-762-4058

Cover photographs reproduced by
permission of AP/Wide World Photos;
and the Library of Congress.

While every effort has been made to
ensure the reliability of the information presented in this publication,
Thomson Gale does not guarantee the
accuracy of the data contained herein.
Thomson Gale accepts no payment for
listing; and inclusion in the publication
of any organization, agency,
institution, publication, service, or
individual does not imply endorsement
by the editors or publisher. Errors
brought to the attention of the
publisher and verified to the
satisfaction of the publisher will be
corrected in future editions.

LIBRARY OF CONGRESS CATALOGING-IN-PUBLICATION DATA

Pendergast, Tom.
The Middle East conflict. Primary sources / Tom and Sara Pendergast ; project editor, Ralph Zerbonia.
p. cm. – (Middle East conflict reference library)
Includes bibliographical references and index.
ISBN 0-7876-9458-4 (hardcover : alk. paper)
1. Arab-Israeli conflict–Sources–Juvenile literature.
2. Arab-Israeli conflict–Juvenile literatur
I. Pendergast, Sara. II. Zerbonia, Ralph. III. Title. IV. Series.
DS119.7.P4446 2005
956.9405–dc22
2005012551

This title is also available as an e-book.
1414406088
Contact your Thomson Gale sales representative for ordering information.

Printed in the United States of America
10 9 8 7 6 5 4 3 2 1

Contents

Reader's Guide

From the middle of the twentieth century up to the present, no region in the world has been so torn by conflict as the Middle East. From Saudi Arabia in the south to Turkey in the north, and from Egypt in the west to Iran in the east, every nation in the region has been involved in some form of political, social, or military turmoil. What is most striking about the many conflicts that have occurred in the Middle East is their complexity. In almost every case, differences over religion, cultural identity, and political philosophy combine with personal, family, and ethnic biases to fan the flames of conflict. Untangling these numerous and overlapping motivations presents a challenge to even the most experienced scholars and diplomats.

To understand the conflicts that have shaped the Middle East in the twentieth century and beyond, one must keep in mind a variety of important forces that have shaped the region. The oldest and most enduring force is that of religion: the Middle East is home to three of the world's great monotheistic (belief in one god) religions—Judaism, Christianity, and Islam. Each of these religions places great importance on the Middle

East, and on religious shrines and temples that continue to exist in the region, especially in the fiercely contested city of Jerusalem. Religious differences, both those between the religions and among followers of the Sunni and Shiite sects of Islam, continue to play a hugely important role in the Middle East.

Since the seventh century CE, Islam has been the dominant religion in the region, yet since the seventeenth century CE, Muslims (followers of Islam) have felt themselves to be at a disadvantage in relation to the predominantly Christian West, especially Europe and later the United States. Because of the superior economic and military power of Western countries (such as Britain, France, Germany, Canada, and the United States), the West has often forced the mostly Muslim Middle East to accept its influence in the region. During the Cold War (1945–91;) political factions in Egypt, Syria, Iraq, and other nations sought to ally themselves with either the United States or the Soviet Union in order to gain advantage in their countries. But many in the Middle East deeply resent the intrusion of Western power and Western values in their region, and this anti-Western sentiment, combined with religious differences, has often fueled conflict.

In addition to the enduring influence of religion and Western power, other hostilities have contributed to conflict in the Middle East. Ethnic differences have often begun wars, as Arabs have fought against Persians in Iran and Muslim Turks in Turkey, and ethnic Kurds (Non-Arabic muslims) and Armenians (Christian Turks) have sought to establish rule over their own territories. In ethnically diverse Lebanon, a shifting array of groups have formed and broken numerous agreements as they have attempted to create governments that will serve all people.

The flashpoint for so much of the conflict in the Middle East since the end of World War II (1939–45; war in which Great Britain, France, the Soviet Union, the United States, and their allies defeated Germany, Italy, and Japan) has been Israel. Founded by Jews as an independent nation in 1948, Israel has been the spot where all of the various issues in the Middle East have come together. Muslims, Jews, and Christians all seek to control sites in Jerusalem, an Israeli city all three religions consider to be holy. In Israel, Arabs fight against the country that they view as an expression of Western dominance, and they find in that fight a shared identity. Palestinians fight Israelis with rocks and sticks to claim land that they believe was stolen from them by an occupying power, and they seek various means—including terrorism—to express their political will. In Israel, countries from around the world seek to use their influence to bring about peace. For these reasons, Israel has been the focal point for the majority of world attention in the region.

The last great issue driving conflicts in the Middle East in the last century has been oil. Oil has dramatically increased the wealth of those countries that produce it—especially Iran, Iraq, Kuwait, and Saudi Arabia—but it has not brought those countries peace or political stability. In each of these countries, oil wealth has been controlled by a select few who hold power in the government. Foreign powers have worked aggressively to ensure that the oil-producing countries behaved in ways that did not threaten foreign access to oil. Tensions created between various parties vying for control of oil in these countries causes ongoing conflict.

Features and Format

Middle East Conflict: Primary Sources provides readers with firsthand contact with some of the influential documents relating to conflict in the Middle East. The primary sources have been divided into seven thematically organized chapters. The first four chapters provide official documents, proclamations, and resolutions relating to the dominant conflict in the region. Included are those documents that are most essential to understanding this complex issue, from the Balfour Declaration of 1917, which provided the basis for European support for a Jewish state in Palestine, through the United Nations Security Council Resolutions of 1967 and 1973 that attempted to provide a structure for peace, to the Israeli government's Disengagement Plan of 2004 that provided hope that Palestinians might secure control over their own land. The remaining chapters offer alternative approaches to understanding conflict in the region, from the philosophies of competing political programs to personal accounts of individuals caught up in terrorism, warfare, and military occupation, as well as a look at how the conflicts have influenced artists. While the primary documents themselves are the main component of each chapter, introductory and concluding material that are designed to help the reader understand the contexts in which the primary sources have meaning have been included. Each primary source section also has questions to prompt further reflection on the meaning of the document. Numerous sidebars highlight interesting information that enhances each entry, as do over sixty black and white images. The volume includes a timeline, a Words to Know section, and a subject index.

The Middle East Conflict Reference Library

The Middle East Conflict: Primary Sources is one of three volumes in the *The Middle East Conflict Reference Library* intended to aid readers who wish to understand the history of conflict in the Middle East. The set also includes one almanac volume and one volume of primary sources:

- *Middle East Conflict: Almanac* explores the motivations and historical events that have contributed to the conflicts in the Middle East since the end of World War I in 1918. Because history and religion have been such an important source of difference, this volume explores the historical roots of religious conflict and the shifting tides of world powers as they impacted the region. Included are chapters on the rise and fall of the Ottoman Empire, the British and French Mandates in the region, the creation of Israel in 1948, and the various wars that occurred in the region during the twentieth century, such as the Lebanese civil war and the Iran-Iraq war. This volume also traces the path that foreign powers have played in the Middle East and how the international community, as well as the Middle Eastern countries, continue to work towards a permanent peace in the Middle East in the twenty-first century.

- *Middle East Conflict: Biographies* presents biographical essays on twenty-six of the most influential and controversial figures involved in conflict in the Middle East. Included are figures from throughout the region and from throughout the historical period featured in the collection. The earliest entrant featured in this volume is Theodor Herzl, who in the late nineteenth century popularized the idea that Jews should create a national homeland in Palestine; the latest entrant covered is Mahmoud Abbas, who was elected as the leader of the Palestinian people early in 2005. The volume provides coverage of kings and terrorists, poets and presidents. Because Middle Eastern culture has traditionally been dominated by men, there are only two women featured in this collection: Golda Meir, an Israeli political leader, and Hanan Ashrawi, a prominent Palestinian activist.

Acknowledgements

Scarcely a week went by in the process of creating this collection that we two primary authors did not remark to each other about the amazing complexity of the issues we were attempting to explain. We know of no area of human interaction in which the tug of conflicting loyalties—religious, ethnic, national, political, tribal—is so strong and so multi-faceted. The strain of navigating these conflicting loyalties must be immense, and we have tried to approach this collec-tion with a great respect for the difficulties faced by the people who have tried and who still try to achieve meaningful social and political solutions to the problems of the Middle East. We truly believe that there are no easy judgments to make as to who is right or wrong in these conflicts. We sincerely hope that our portrayal of issues in the Middle East has been reasonably objective, though we acknowledge that true objectivity is an impossible ideal.

History did not stop for the writing of this book: during the course of our work, longtime Palestinian political leader Yasser Arafat died and Mahmoud Abbas was elected in his place, creating real hope that Palestinians and Israelis might make meaningful progress toward peace; Syria withdrew its troops from Lebanon, ending a nearly thirty-year occupation; and in Iraq the promise of democratic elections was tempered by the ongoing violence of a determined insurgency. We have tried to present reasonable interpretations of these ongoing events, but have come to the conclusion that when it comes to the Middle East, one must be prepared for sudden and dramatic change.

Our goal has been to present this immensely complex set of conflicts in a manner that is comprehensible to the reading level, and we have been ably assisted in that effort by our son, seventh-grader Conrad Pendergast, who read and commented on several of the chapters in this collection. We would also like to extend our sincere thanks to Ralph Zerbonia, whose clear-headed approach to the various tangles of creating this work has been invaluable.

We Thank our Advisors:

- Dr. Thabit A.J. Abdullah, Professor of History and the Arts, York University, Toronto, Ontario, Canada. Dr. Abdullah is the author of *A Short History of Iraq: From 636 to the Present* and *Merchants, Mamluks and Murder: The Political Economy of Commerce in Eighteenth Century Basara*.

- Dr. Bernard Reich, Professor of Political Science and International Affairs, George Washington University, Washington, D.C. Dr. Reich is the author of a number of books on the Middle East such as *Quest for Peace: United States-Israel Relations and the Arab-Israeli Conflict* and *Arab-Israeli Conflict and Conciliation: A Documentary History*.

Comments and Suggestions

We welcome any comments on the *Middle East Conflict: Primary Sources*. Please write: Editors, *Middle East Conflict Reference Library*, U•X•L, Gale Group, 27500 Drake Road, Farmington Hills, Michigan, 48331; call toll-free: 800-877-4253; fax to: 248-699-8097; or e-mail via www.gale.com.

Timeline of Events

970–931 BCE The First Temple of Solomon, a holy site for Jews, is built in the modern-day city of Jerusalem.

587–586 BCE The First Temple of Solomon is destroyed by the Babylonians along with the Southern Kingdom of Judah.

538 BCE**–70** CE King Cyrus of Persia conqtuers the Babylonians and allows exiled Jews to return to Jerusalem.

520–515 BCE The Second Temple of Solomon is built on the site of the First Temple.

166–160 BCE Restrictions on the practice of Judaism and the destruction of Second Temple lead to Jewish revolt.

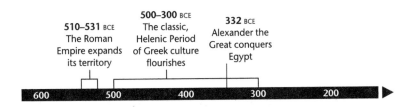

510–531 BCE
The Roman Empire expands its territory

500–300 BCE
The classic, Helenic Period of Greek culture flourishes

332 BCE
Alexander the Great conquers Egypt

600 500 400 300 200

146 BCE–476 CE Most of the Mediterranean region comes under the control of the Roman Empire.

4 BCE–c. 30 CE Jesus, the central figure of Christianity, lives.

30–311 Christianity develops as a religious faith.

66–73 Jews revolt against Roman rule.

c. 380 Christianity becomes the official religion of the Roman Empire.

632 Muhammad of Mecca dies after founding the religion of Islam.

638 Jews are permitted to return to Jerusalem under Muslim rule.

691 Muslims build the Dome of the Rock on the Temple Mount, or al-Haram al-Sharif as the Muslims call it, the site of the First and Second Temples of the Jews. Nearby, Muslims also construct the Al-Aqsa Mosque.

750–1258 The Golden Age of Islamic culture is experienced under the Abbasid Dynasty, based in Baghdad, Iraq.

969 Cairo, Egypt, is founded by the Islamic Shiite Fatimid Dynasty.

1095–1291 The Crusades, or Christian warfare, against the followers of Islam sweeps through the Middle Eastern region and Europe.

1099 Crusaders capture Jerusalem.

1187 Saladin, a Muslim leader of Egypt, wins Jerusalem from the Crusaders.

14th Century The Ottoman Muslim Dynasty rules Turkey and begins the Ottoman Empire.

1516–17 The Ottoman Empire expands from Turkey to rule most of the Middle East.

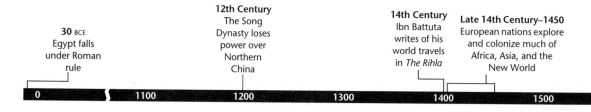

30 BCE Egypt falls under Roman rule

12th Century The Song Dynasty loses power over Northern China

14th Century Ibn Battuta writes of his world travels in *The Rihla*

Late 14th Century–1450 European nations explore and colonize much of Africa, Asia, and the New World

0   1100   1200   1300   1400   1500

1869   Construction is completed on Egypt's Suez Canal, linking the Mediterranean Sea to the Red Sea.

1882   British troops enter Egypt to protect the Suez Canal and take virtual control of the country.

1882–1903 Russian Jews immigrate to Palestine in the First Aliyah.

1896   Theodor Herzl publishes *The Jewish State,* thus popularizing Zionism.

1897   The World Zionist Organization is founded at a Jewish Zionist congress held in Basel, Switzerland.

1904–14 The Second Aliyah brings thousands of Jewish immigrants to Palestine, mainly from Russia and Poland.

1906   Iran creates its first constitution and elected parliament.

1908   The British discover oil in Iran.

1909   Degania, the first kibbutz or communal farm, is founded in Palestine.

1914   At the outbreak of World War I (1914–1918), Britain declares Egypt to be a protectorate of the British Empire.

1915–1923 The population of Armenians (Christian Turks) living within the Ottoman Empire's provinces in modern-day Turkey are systematically killed or forced into concentration camps, where they suffer greatly; an estimated 1.5 million die.

1916   Arabs begin their struggle for independence from Ottoman rule during the Arab Revolt.

November 2, 1917 British foreign secretary Lord Arthur Balfour releases the "Balfour Declaration," a statement written by Herbert Samuel and other prominent

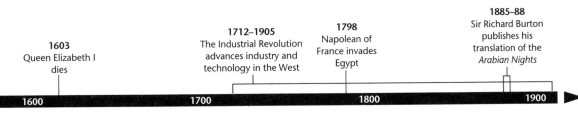

1603
Queen Elizabeth I
dies

1712–1905
The Industrial Revolution
advances industry and
technology in the West

1798
Napolean of
France invades
Egypt

1885–88
Sir Richard Burton
publishes his
translation of the
Arabian Nights

1600   1700   1800   1900

Zionists that promises British support for the Zionist cause.

1917   Britain takes control of Iraq when the Ottoman Empire falls.

1918   Turkey emerges as an independent country at the end of World War I.

1919–23 The Third Aliyah brings more Russian Jews into Palestine.

1920   The League of Nations grants France control of Syria and Lebanon, and Britain control of Palestine, Transjordan, and Iraq under the mandate system.

1922   Egypt gains independence from Britain, though it remains under British influence.

1923   Britain declares Abdullah I as emir of Transjordan.

1924–32 The Fourth Aliyah brings Jewish immigrants from Poland to Palestine.

1929   The Muslim Brotherhood, an Islamic fundamentalist group, is established in Egypt by Sheikh Hassan el-Banna.

1932   King Abd al Aziz ibn Saud unites the various regions of the Arabian Peninsula into the country of Saudi Arabia.

1932   Iraq declares independence from British rule.

1932   A census conducted this year reveals Christians to be a majority in Lebanon; this remains the document by which the Lebanese divide political power for decades to come, even as the number of Muslims in Lebanon surpasses that of Christians.

1933–39 The Fifth Aliyah brings Jewish immigrants, mainly from Germany, to Palestine.

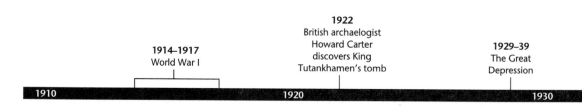

1914–1917
World War I

1922
British archaelogist Howard Carter discovers King Tutankhamen's tomb

1929–39
The Great Depression

1910   1920   1930

1936–39 The Arab Revolt in Palestine calls for an end to Jewish immigration, a stop to Jewish ownership of land in Palestine, and self-governance for Palestinians.

1937 **The Palestine Royal (Peel) Commission Report** makes the first recommendation for two separate independent nations on Palestinian land, one for Jews and one for Arabs.

1939 The British White Paper limits Jewish immigration into Palestine.

1941 The Baath Party is formed in Syria to promote the ideals of socialism and Arab unity.

1942 With the horrors of the Holocaust being revealed, **The Biltmore Program**, a statement created by American Zionists, pressures world powers to support an independent Jewish state in Palestine.

1943 Lebanon becomes independent from the mandate system supervised by France.

1944 **The Alexandria Protocol** creates the framework for the League of Arab States (better known as the Arab League), a group formed in 1945 to unite Arab social, economic, and political interests without the loss of self-rule by individual Arab countries. The headquarters are in Cairo, Egypt.

1945 Turkey becomes one of the founding members of the United Nations, an international organization formed after World War II to regulate peace and relations between countries.

1946 Syria gains independence from French mandate.

1946 Transjordan declares independence as the Hashemite Kingdom of Transjordan.

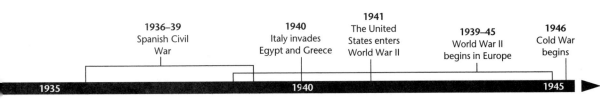

1936–39
Spanish Civil War

1940
Italy invades Egypt and Greece

1941
The United States enters World War II

1939–45
World War II begins in Europe

1946
Cold War begins

1935   1940   1945

1947 The United Nations proposes a division of Palestine into separate Arab and Jewish states.

May 14, 1948 The British mandate over Palestine ends and the **Declaration of the Establishment of the State of Israel** creates an independent Jewish state on Palestinian land.

May 15, 1948 Following the **Statement Issued by the Governments of the Arab League States on the Occasion of the Entry of the Arab Armies in Palestine**, five Arab states—Egypt, Syria, Transjordan, Iraq, and Lebanon—invade Israel. Saudi Arabia provides economic support for Arab nations who go to war to block the formation of the nation of Israel.

1948 Transjordan and Lebanon takes in more than one million Palestinian refugees after Israel claims its independence.

1948–52 Large numbers of Jews from European and Arab countries immigrate to Israel, which opens its borders to Jews, no matter their national origins.

1949 The Arab-Israeli War of 1948 (known as the War of Independence in Israel) ends with Israel as the victor.

1949 The city of Jerusalem is divided into Israeli and Jordanian ruled sections.

1949–57 Syria leans toward a political alliance with the Soviet Union, the world's major supporter of communist and socialist governments.

1950 Transjordan is renamed Jordan.

1951–53 Nationalist prime minister Mohammad Mossadegh seizes power in Iran and nationalizes the oil industry until he is removed from power with assistance from the U.S. Central Intelligence Agency.

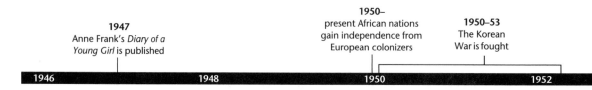

1947
Anne Frank's *Diary of a Young Girl* is published

1950–
present African nations gain independence from European colonizers

1950–53
The Korean War is fought

1946   1948   1950   1952

1952 Egypt's Gamal Abdel Nasser leads a revolt against King Farouk. Nasser is named president and Egypt gains complete independence from British rule.

1953 King Hussein I ascends to the throne in Jordan.

1956 Egyptian president Nasser seizes control of the Suez Canal from the British and the French.

July 1958 King Faisal of Iraq is murdered and replaced by a revolutionary Baathist nationalist group.

1958 Lebanon engages in a brief civil war over whether or not the country should join the Pan-Arab state called the United Arab Republic.

1958–61 Egypt unites with Syria in the United Arab Republic, a short-lived effort to form a Pan-Arab government that will unite all Arab states.

1959 Egyptian president Nasser makes his **Speech to the Officers' Club** where he stress the need for a united group of Arab countries and for the military of these countries to pursue common goals.

1960 Palestinian poet **Mahmoud Darwish** publishes his first collection of poetry, *Asafir bila ajnihah* (*Sparrows without Wings*) and is promptly jailed by the Israeli police.

1963 The Palestine Liberation Organization (PLO) is formed.

1963 A military coup places Baath Party forces in control of the Syrian government. The Baath Party supports a secular (non-religious), socialist form of government, and remains in power through 2005.

1964 Palestinian poet Mahmoud Darwish publishes his second collection of poetry, *Awraq al-zaytun* (*Olive Branches*), which earns him a reputation as one of the

1954–75
The United States becomes involved in the Vietnam War

1958
The European Economic Community is founded

1963
The Organization of African Unity is formed

1954 1956 1958 1960 1962 1964

leading poets of the growing Palestinian resistance movement—and immediate arrest.

June 4–10, 1967 The Six-Day War between Israel and neighboring Arab countries ends with an Israeli victory. At the end of the war, Israel occupies territories in the Golan Heights, the West Bank, the Sinai Peninsula, and the Gaza Strip.

November 22, 1967 UN Security Council Resolution 242 outlines the principles that will guide Arab-Israeli negotiations after the war.

1967 King Faisal ibn Abd al Aziz ibn Saud of Saudi Arabia organizes the first meeting of all the leaders of Islamic nations.

1967 Meir Kahane founds the Jewish Defense League to support Zionism from its headquarters in New York.

1968 The Palestine Liberation Organization revises **The Palestinian National Charter** to declare the purpose of warfare against Israel and to solidify the PLO's right to represent the Palestinian people.

1968 Israel bombs Arab planes at the Beirut airport in Lebanon in retaliation for a Palestinian attack on an Israeli commercial flight.

1968–70 Egypt wages its War of Attrition against Israel, but gains little of the land back that was lost in the Six-Day War.

1969 Supporters of the National Movement in Lebanon call for a new census that would reshuffle political power in the country, giving more power to the Muslim majority. Their efforts are denied by the Christian-led government.

1966–76
China experiences the
Cultural Revolution

1967
Race riots are
held in the U.S.

1969
Two U.S. astronauts
are the first to walk
on the moon

1966

1968

1969　Lebanon grants the Palestine Liberation Organization the authority to govern the Palestinian refugee camps within its borders.

1970　Jordan's King Hussein calls on his military to expel rebel Palestinians from Jordan in an action known as Black September; the Palestinian militants relocate to Lebanon.

1970　Ethnic Kurds (non-Arabic Muslims), having spent 15 years fighting for their independence from Iraq, agree to stop their rebellion and sign a peace plan with the Iraqi government.

1970　Egyptian president Gamal Abdel Nasser dies and is succeeded in office by Anwar Sadat.

1971　Hafez Assad becomes president of Syria. He dominates Syrian politics until his death in 2000.

1971　Palestinian poet Mahmoud Darwish resolves that it is impossible to live in Israel and write his poetry without suffering arrest or intimidation. He begins an exile that will last twenty-five years.

1972　Eleven Israeli athletes are murdered at the Olympic Games in Munich.

1972　Iraq forms the Iraqi Petroleum Company and the Iraq National Oil Company.

October 1973 The Yom Kippur War, also known as the Arab-Israeli War of 1973, between Egypt, Syria, and Israel is launched during an important Jewish holiday.

1973　Menachem Begin and Ariel Sharon create the Likud Party in hopes of winning enough seats in the Knesset (the legislative body of the Israeli government) to disrupt the power of the Labor Party, the political party

1970
Egypt completes the
Aswan Dam

1971
The Nasdeq stock market
index begins

1972–74
The Watergate
scandal erupts in
the United States

1970　　　　　　　　　　　　　　　　　　　　　　　　1972

whose views had dominated Israel since its independence in 1948.

1973   In reaction to Western support for Israel in the Yom Kippur War, Saudi Arabia leads a boycott of oil to the United States, thus starting a world oil crisis.

1974   Saudi Arabia ends the oil boycott and enters into an agreement with the United States that trades a steady oil supply for American military protection.

1974   Turkish troops occupy the Mediterranean island of Cyprus, and maintain control of the northeastern third of the island.

1975   Civil war breaks out in Lebanon.

1976   Syria intervenes in the civil war in Lebanon on the side of the Christians. From this point forward, Syria plays a major role in Lebanese politics.

1976   An Arab summit officially ends the Lebanese civil war with the Riyadh Accords, but fighting continues over the next decade and a half.

1976   The city of Beirut, Lebanon, is divided into separate Christian and Muslim sections by the Green Line.

November 19, 1977 Accepting the invitation of Israeli prime minister Menachem Begin, Egyptian president Anwar Sadat becomes the first Arab leader to visit Jerusalem since the creation of Israel. Both give **Speeches to the Knesset**, which speak on their plans for peace between the two countries.

September 1978 The Camp David Accords held between Egypt and Israel create a plan for peace in the Middle East and self-government for Palestine.

1975	1976	1977
Pol Pot becomes prime minister of Kampuchea	North and South Vietnam unite	AIDS is first diagnosed

1974   1976   1978

1978   Israeli prime minister Menachem Begin and Egyptian president Anwar Sadat share the Nobel Peace Prize.

1978   Israeli troops invade southern Lebanon in an attempt to remove the Palestinians from that region, but most soon withdraw under the supervision of the United Nations Interim Forces In Lebanon (UNIFIL).

January–February 1979 An Islamic Revolution led by Ayatollah Ruhollah Khomeini removes the shah from power and reshapes Iran as an Islamic Republic, with ultimate power held in the hands of the highest ranking Islamic clerics. Iran soon becomes an enemy of the West.

March 1979 Israel signs a peace treaty with Egypt; the League of Arab States ejects Egypt from its membership in protest and moves its headquarters from Cairo, Egypt, to Tunis, Tunisia.

July 17, 1979 Saddam Hussein becomes the president of Iraq, as well as secretary general of the Baath Party Regional Command, chairman of the Revolutionary Command Council, prime minister, and commander of the armed forces.

1979   Armed religious militants capture the Grand Mosque in the city of Mecca, Islam's holiest site. In response, the Saudi royal family increases its adherence to Islamic holy law, or Sharia.

1980s Sumaya Farhat-Naser begins her search for peaceful solutions to the Palestinian-Israeli conflict, which she documents in **Daughter of the Olive Trees.**

1980–88 Iran and Iraq fight a bitter war, which ends with neither side making significant gains.

1979
A nuclear accident occurs
at Three Mile Island

1979
The Soviet Union invades
Afghanistan

1979

June 2, 1980 A bomb planted by Era Rapaport destroys the legs of Bassam Shaka, the mayor of Nablus, a town about thirty miles north of Jerusalem. Rapaport would serve prison time for his attack on the Palestinian and would write about his views on Israeli-Palestinian relations in **Letter from Tel Mond Prison: An Israeli Settler Defends His Act of Terror.**

October 6, 1981 Egyptian president Anwar Sadat is assassinated and succeeded in office by Hosni Mubarak.

1981 Israel destroys an Iraqi nuclear reactor.

June 6–August, 1982 Israel's invasion of Lebanon prompts Lebanon to expel the Palestine Liberation Organization.

September 16–19, 1982 In the Palestinian refugee camps of Sabra and Shatila in Lebanon, some 200 Phalangist militiamen massacre approximately 800 Palestinians.

1982 Israel completely withdraws from the Sinai Peninsula, giving the land back to Egypt.

1982 Hezbollah, the Shiite Muslim group formed to fight Israel in Lebanon, organizes with support from Iran.

1982 U.S. Marines enter Lebanon to help evacuate Israeli and Syrian troops from Lebanon.

1983 Two hundred forty-one U.S. Marines are killed by a suicide bomber in Beirut.

1984 Unable to remove most of the Syrian troops and some Israeli troops, U.S. Marines leave Lebanon.

1984 Meir Kahane's Kach Party wins seats in the Israeli Knesset, but his controversial politics trouble many Israelis, including his book **They Must Go,** which

1980
The United States fails
to free hostages in Iran

1982
Falkland War

1985–87
The Iran-Contra scandal
is revealed as an arms for
hostages play

1980   1982   1984

demands that all Palestinians must be deported from any lands that Israelis live on.

March 16, 1985 Journalist Terry Anderson is kidnapped by Hezbollah activists in Lebanon. His seven years as a hostage are documented in **Den of Lions.**

December 1987 A Palestinian uprising against Israeli rule in the occupied territories (land taken during the Six-Day War of 1967) starts the First Intifada.

January 8, 1988 The first **Communiqué of the Intifada** is released, telling Palestinians to revolt against Israeli occupation of Palestinian land.

July 1988 Jordan renounces its claim to the West Bank, opening the way for this to be considered Palestinian territory.

November 7, 1988 Soha Bechara is arrested by the South Lebanon Army for her activities against Israeli forces. She would document these actions and her time in prison in her book **Resistance: My Life for Lebanon.**

December 1988 The United States recognizes the Palestine Liberation Organization as a legitimate representative of the Palestinian people.

1988 The intensity of conflicts between supporters and opponents of Syrian intervention in Lebanon prevents presidential elections from being held.

1988 Meir Kahane's Kach Party is banned from Israeli politics on the grounds that it is racist and anti-democratic.

October 22, 1989 The Taif Accord restructures the Lebanese government to include more representatives from different religious groups.

1985 Widespread Famine hits Ethiopia

1986 The worst nuclear disaster occurs at Chernobyl

1987 Black Monday: Stocks full sharply around the world

1986

1988

1989 Soviet Jews immigrate to Israel in great numbers.

1989 The League of Arab States readmits Egypt to its membership and moves its headquarters back to Cairo.

1989 Syria lacks a major political ally following the collapse of the Soviet Union. Relations with the West are strained as Western leaders criticize Syria's lack of democracy and its alleged support for terrorist activities. Syria becomes isolated, both politically and economically, from the rest of the world.

1990s Popular protests against Iran's restrictive government bring few changes to a regime considered as one of the world's most repressive.

August 2, 1990 Iraq invades Kuwait, threatening to take control of nearly half the world's oil reserves.

August 1990 The League of Arab States condemns Iraq for invading Kuwait.

May 1991 The Lebanese government grants Syria control of Lebanon's internal affairs, foreign policy, and security.

1991 The Cold War ends with the fall of the Soviet Union, and the United States emerges as the sole world superpower.

1991 A U.S.-led coalition, including Jordan, Syria, Egypt, and many Western nations liberates Kuwait from Iraqi control in the first Gulf War. The United Nations imposes sanctions limiting Iraq's trade with other nations until such time as Iraq reveals and destroys its weapons of mass destruction.

1991 Iraqi president Saddam Hussein remains in control of Iraq after the Persian Gulf War and brutally punishes

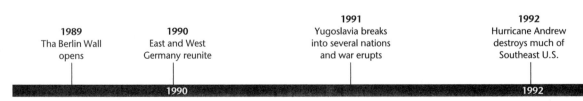

1989
Tha Berlin Wall
opens

1990
East and West
Germany reunite

1991
Yugoslavia breaks
into several nations
and war erupts

1992
Hurricane Andrew
destroys much of
Southeast U.S.

1990

1992

Iraqis who helped the coalition forces, killing hundreds of thousands of Shiites in southern Iraq and Kurds in the north.

1992 The United Nations creates an autonomous region in northern Iraq to provide protection for Kurds living there.

September 13, 1993 Palestinian leader Yasser Arafat and Israeli prime minister Yitzhak Rabin shake hands on the lawn of the White House in Washington, D.C., in celebration of the **Israeli-PLO Declaration of Principles** signed at the Oslo Accords, which provides a framework for further peace negotiations and creates the Palestinian Authority, the main governing body of the Palestinian people.

1993 Joe Sacco publishes his first comic book about his time in the Middle East and his experiences with the Israeli-Palestinian conflicts. This and other comics would be grouped in a graphic novel called **Palestine.**

May 1994 Independent Palestinian governments are started in the Gaza Strip and the city of Jericho (near Jerusalem).

1994 King Hussein of Jordan and Israeli prime minister Yitzhak Rabin sign a peace agreement that officially ends the state of war that had lasted between their countries since 1948.

September 28, 1995 Oslo 2, the interim agreement to further peace between Palestinians and Israel, is signed. The agreement extends Palestinian self-government to portions of the West Bank and details the structure of an elected Palestinian Council.

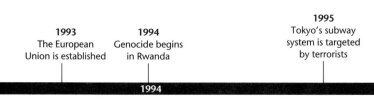

1993
The European
Union is established

1994
Genocide begins
in Rwanda

1995
Tokyo's subway
system is targeted
by terrorists

1994

1996

November 4, 1995 100,000 Israelis gather in support of Israel's "land for peace" plan, which calls for Israel to withdraw from some of the lands it acquired during the Six-Day War in 1967 and allows Palestinians to govern themselves. After speaking to the crowd, Israeli prime minister Yitzhak Rabin is assassinated.

January 1996 The first Palestinian Authority elections are held.

1996 Turkey begins the process of becoming a part of the European Union.

1996 Terrorists blow up a U.S. military facility within Saudi Arabia, killing 19 Americans.

February 23, 1998 Osama bin Laden and the World Islamic Front issue their **"Jihad Against Jews and Crusaders,"** which demands that all influences that do not support the Islamic faith must be removed from Arabic Middle Eastern countries and that Israel must be destroyed.

2000 A Camp David summit, which attempts to find peace between Israel and the Palestinians, is aborted when the Second Intifada (al-Aqsa Intifada) begins and Yasser Arafat appears unwilling to stop the violence.

2000 Hezbollah and its supporters finally prompt a complete Israeli evacuation from the security zone Israel had maintained in southern Lebanon since 1982.

September 11, 2001 The World Trade Center and the Pentagon are attacked by Muslim terrorists led by Osama bin Laden.

2001 U.S. president George W. Bush outlines a plan for a Palestinian state at the United Nations.

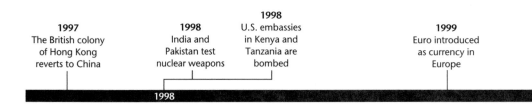

1997
The British colony of Hong Kong reverts to China

1998
India and Pakistan test nuclear weapons

1998
U.S. embassies in Kenya and Tanzania are bombed

1999
Euro introduced as currency in Europe

1998

2000

2001 Ariel Sharon becomes Israeli prime minister and announces his willingness to negotiate with Palestinians.

March 19, 2003 A U.S.-led coalition that includes troops from Great Britain and Australia initiates a second Gulf War against Iraq.

March 19, 2003 Mahmoud Abbas is named prime minister of the Palestinian Authority.

March 24, 2003 Twenty-one of the Arab League's twenty-two member states vote to call for the immediate withdrawal of U.S. and British troops from Iraq.

December 13, 2003 Iraqi president Saddam Hussein is captured by coalition forces.

June 2004 U.S. forces turn over Saddam Hussein to Iraqi officials.

June 28, 2004 The Iraqi interim government takes control of the country but international military forces remain to help Iraq transition to full self-governance.

November 11, 2004 Palestinian leader Yasser Arafat dies.

2004 Israeli prime minister Ariel Sharon announces **Israel's Revised Disengagement Plan**, under which Israel agrees to withdraw Jewish settlements from the West Bank and the Gaza Strip.

January 9, 2005 Mahmoud Abbas is elected to the presidency of the Palestinian Authority.

April 26, 2005 The last Syrian troops leave Lebanon, marking the first time in close to thirty years that foreign troops have not been on Lebanese soil.

2005 Iran hosts the International Conference on Islamic Unity and warns that U.S. foreign policy is harmful to Muslim states.

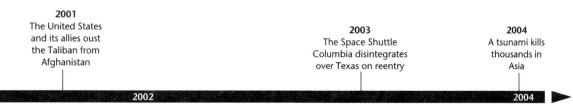

2001
The United States and its allies oust the Taliban from Afghanistan

2002

2003
The Space Shuttle Columbia disintegrates over Texas on reentry

2004
A tsunami kills thousands in Asia

2004

The Arab League, also known as the League of Arab States, was formed in 1945 to promote political, military, and economic cooperation within the Arab world.

Arabs: People of the Middle East and North Africa who speak the Arabic language, or who live in countries in which Arabic is the dominant language.

Autonomy: In the Israeli-Palestinian conflict, autonomy is a form of Palestinian self-governance within Israeli-controlled territories that falls short of political independence.

B

Baath Party: A secular (non-religious) political movement founded in Syria in the 1940s with the goal of uniting the Arab world and creating one powerful Arab state. The party became powerful in Syria as well as in Iraq, but the divisions between members kept the parties from each country from coordinating efforts. In Iraq, the Baath Party was long controlled by dictator Saddam Hussein.

Bilateral: Of or relating to two nations in international politics. A bilateral agreement affects two nations.

C

Caliph: The spiritual, political, and military leader of the world's Muslims from the death of Muhammad until the caliphate was abolished in 1924.

Caliphate: The office or authority of the caliph.

Camp David: A U.S. presidential retreat in the mountains of Maryland, this protected camp has been the site of several key negotiating sessions in the Israeli-Palestinian conflict.

Christian: A believer of any of the religions derived from the teachings of Jesus Christ and based on the Bible as sacred scripture. Eastern Orthodox, Roman Catholic, and Protestant faiths are considered Christian religions.

Coalition: A temporary alliance of countries working toward a common goal.

Cold War: A period of political tension and military rivalry between the United States and the Soviet Union, based on ideological differences between democracy and communism, that lasted from 1945 to 1991.

D

Diplomacy: The act of negotiating between countries.

F

Fatah: A Palestinian militant group, founded in 1957 by Yasser Arafat, long dedicated to the destruction of Israel and the unification of Arab states in the Middle East.

Fatwa: A statement of religious law issued by an Islamic cleric.

Fedayeen: An Arabic term meaning one who sacrifices for a cause; by the late 1940s Palestinians calling themselves fedayeen organized attacks on Israeli targets and secured funding and support from Egypt. Opponents to the fedayeen use the term to describe members of Arab terrorist groups. Fedayeen groups have formed several times in the twentieth century.

Fundamentalism: A movement stressing adherence to a strict or literal interpretation of religious principles.

G

Gaza Strip: A narrow strip of land along the eastern shore of the Mediterranean, west of Israel and bordering Egypt in the southwest. Occupied by Egypt in 1948, then captured by Israel in 1967, the region is largely controlled by the Palestinian Authority, with key population centers controlled by Israel.

Guerilla warfare: Combat tactics used by a smaller, less well-equipped fighting force against a more powerful foe.

H

Haganah: The underground defense force established in 1920 by Zionists in Palestine as a military group independent of foreign authority. Haganah operated until 1948 when Israel transformed it into the new country's standing army, called the Israel Defense Forces.

Hamas: An Islamic fundamentalist group, founded in 1987, that is opposed to the existence of Israel in any form. Hamas has sponsored violent actions that have led it to be considered a terrorist organization by Israel, the United States, and many other Western countries. The term Hamas is an acronym of Harakat al-Muqawamah al-Islamiyyah, also known as the Islamic Resistance Movement.

Hebrew: The ancient language of the Jewish people that has been revived as the official language of Israel.

Hezbollah: A militant Shiite political party, based in Lebanon, which fought against Israeli occupation in southern Lebanon in the 1970s and 1980s, and continues to oppose Israeli occupation of land in northern Israel. Hezbollah has been designated a terrorist organization by the United States and several other Western countries, though others claim that it is a political organization that does not conduct terrorist acts.

Holocaust: The slaughter of millions of European civilians, primarily Jews, by the Nazis during World War II (1939–45).

I

Insurgency: A revolt against a political authority that falls short of revolution.

Intifada: The armed and violent popular uprising of Palestinians against Israeli occupation in the West Bank and Gaza Strip. The Intifada has been sporadic, with periodic surges in popular unrest; the First Intifada started in 1987 and lasted until 1993. The Intifada beginning in 2000 and continuing through 2005 is known as the al-Aqsa, or Second, Intifada.

Intrafada: The popular uprising of Palestinians against other Palestinians suspected of supporting the activities of the Israeli occupation or the Israeli army. Occurred in parallel to the First Intifada.

Irgun Zvai Leumi: A militant underground group founded in 1931 that worked to secure Israeli independence by staging violent attacks on British and Arab targets. Also known simply as Irgun.

Islam: The religious faith followed by Muslims based on a belief in Allah as the sole God and in Muhammad as his prophet.

Islamic Fundamentalism: See Islamism.

Islamism: The ideology that a conservative interpretation of the Islamic faith, including the rule of Sharia, should provide the basis for the political, social, and cultural life in every Muslim nation.

J

Jerusalem: The capital of the ancient kingdoms of Israel and Judah; home of holy sites for Christian, Jewish, and Muslim religions. It was divided in 1948 with separate sections ruled by Jordan and Israel until 1967. Since 1967 Israel has controlled the entire city and claimed it as its capital.

Jew: A believer in Judaism, the faith started by the ancient Hebrews, that is based on the belief in one God and the teachings of Abraham, Moses, and the Hebrew prophets.

Jihad: A holy war waged on behalf of Islamic religious duty.

K

Kibbutz: A communal settlement in Israel where settlers share all property and work collaboratively together.

Knesset: The legislative branch, or parliament, of the Israeli government. The Knesset is composed of 120 members elected to four-year terms.

Koran: The holy book of Islam, also called the Quran.

L

League of Nations: A loose confederation of sixty states, formally organized on January 10, 1920, with the goal of aiding the peaceful resolution of conflicts between nations. The League of Nations disbanded in 1946 and was succeeded by the United Nations.

M

Mandate: A form of rule over a conquered territory, granted by the League of Nations following World War I, that gave Great Britain and France control over much of the Middle East.

Mufti: Islamic religious leader.

Mujahideen: Islamic holy warriors.

Muhammad: The prophet of the religion Islam.

Muslim Brotherhood: An Islamic fundamentalist group organized in opposition to Western influence and power, with branches in every country in the Middle East.

Muslims: People who practice the religion of Islam.

N

Nationalism: The belief that a people with shared ethnic, cultural, and/or religious identities had the right to form their own nation; in established nations, nationalism takes the form of extreme pride and loyalty to a defined nation and its culture.

Normalize: To restore or repair the conditions and relations between countries.

O

Occupation: The physical and political control of an area seized by a foreign military force.

Occupied territories: The name Palestinians have given to territories under the political and military control of Israel, though containing Palestinian majority populations, especially the West Bank and Gaza Strip.

Organization of Petroleum Exporting Countries (OPEC): An organization formed in the 1960s by the world's major oil-producing nations to coordinate policies and ensure stable oil prices in world markets.

Orthodox Judaism: The main branch of the Jewish faith, based on a historical faith to the teachings of the Torah, the Jewish holy scriptures.

Oslo Accords: A set of agreements forged in 1993 between Israel and the Palestinians that gave Palestinians limited self-rule in the Gaza Strip and the West Bank under the governance of the newly-created Palestinian Authority.

Ottoman Empire: A powerful political entity, led by Turkish sultans, that exerted control over much of the Middle East from 1516 until 1918.

P

Palestine: A region in the Middle East on the eastern shore of the Mediterranean Sea, roughly defined as within the greatest claimed borders of the modern nation of Israel. The State of Palestine, proclaimed in 1988, is represented by the Palestinian Authority, though it controls no actual territory.

Palestinian Authority: The recognized governing institution for Palestinians, created by the Oslo Accords in 1993, with control in the Gaza Strip and West Bank. Also known as the Palestinian National Authority.

Palestine Liberation Organization (PLO): A political organization representing displaced Palestinians. The main goals of the PLO included reclaiming lost territory from Israel and establishing an independent Palestinian state. Also known as the Palestinian Liberation Organization.

Palestinians: An Arab people whose ancestors lived in the region of Palestine, now the Jewish state of Israel, and who continue to lay claim to that land.

Pan-Arabism: A movement for the unification of Arab peoples. Pan-Arabism has been promoted at various times in the Middle East as a way of uniting Arab countries against Israel and the West. It is the official policy of the Baath Party.

Passover: A Jewish holiday beginning on the 14th of Nisan in the Hebrew calendar and commemorating the Hebrews' liberation from slavery in Egypt.

Peace process: Negotiations between countries or warring parties designed to establish peaceful relations. The term is frequently used to refer specifically to the Israeli-Palestinian peace process.

Pogroms: A Yiddish term for organized attacks on a weaker group; used to describe attacks on Jews.

R

Rabbi: The spiritual leader of a Jewish synagogue.

Ramadan: The sacred ninth month of the Islamic year, during which Muslims fast from dawn to sunset.

Refugees: People who flee their country to escape violence or persecution. Often used to refer to Palestinians who fled Israel after the 1948 Arab-Israeli War or the Six-Day War of 1967, but also used to refer to those who live in Israeli-occupied territories.

Right of return: The right, claimed by a dispossessed people, to return to their historic homeland. This right has been claimed by both Jews and Palestinians, the former to refer to their right to claim citizenship in Israel, no matter the country of their birth; the latter to refer to the right of Palestinian refugees to return to lands claimed by Israel after the 1948 Arab-Israeli War and the Six-Day War of 1967.

S

Self-determination: The right of a people within a territory to define their own political status.

Self-rule: A group's political control of their own lives; self-governance.

Settlements: Villages established and inhabited in order to claim land. In the Middle East, these typically refer to Jewish settlements established in the occupied territories against the wishes of the Palestinian inhabitants.

Sharia: A system of Islamic law based on the Koran. Sharia attempts to create the perfect social order, based on God's will and justice, and covers a wide range of human activities, including acts of religious worship, the law of contracts and obligations, personal status law, and public law.

One of the best known provisions of Sharia is the rule that women should keep themselves covered at all times.

Shiite: A branch of the Islamic religion practiced by 15 percent of the world's Muslims. Shiites believe that only direct descendents of the prophet Muhammad are qualified to lead the Islamic faith. Shiites are in the majority in Iraq and Iran.

Socialism: The theory or system of social organization by which the major means of production and distribution are owned, managed, and controlled by the government, by an association of workers, or the community as a whole.

Sultan: A ruler of a Muslim state, especially the Ottoman Empire.

Sunni: A branch of the Islamic religion practiced by 85 percent of the world's Muslims. Sunnis believe that elected officials, regardless of their heritage, are qualified to lead the Islamic faith. Sunnis are in the majority in every Arab nation except Iran and Iraq.

T

Taliban: An Islamic group that took over the government of Afghanistan in 1996 and was displaced in 2002.

Talmud: The authoritative, ancient body of Jewish teachings and tradition.

Temple Mount: A contested religious site in the old city of Jerusalem. Known in Hebrew as Har HaBayit and in Arabic as al-Haram al-Sharif, it is the site of ancient Jewish temples and, since the seventh century, the home to the Dome of the Rock and the Al-Aqsa Mosque, two Muslim shrines. The Temple Mount is the holiest site in Judaism, the third holiest site in Islam, and also important to the Christian faith.

Terrorism: Premeditated, politically motivated violence carried out against noncombatant targets.

Torah: A Hebrew word meaning teaching or instruction, it literally refers to the first five books of the Hebrew bible. In common usage, however, the term Torah is often used to refer to the body of wisdom held in Jewish scriptures and sacred literature.

U

Unilateral: An act or decision initiated by one side in a conflict, especially by one powerful nation.

United Nations: An association of countries set up in 1945 to promote peace, security, and cooperation between nations.

W

Weapons of mass destruction: Any nuclear, chemical, or biological weapons capable of killing or injuring great numbers of people.

West Bank: A geographic area west of the Jordan River that has been a source of contention between Israel, Jordan, and the Palestinians. Annexed by Jordan in 1948, and captured by Israel in 1967, by 2004 the region was under joint Israeli-Palestinian control.

Y

Yeshiva: A school for the study of the Torah, or Jewish holy books. Yeshivas were a training ground for Orthodox Jewish rabbis, though not all students became rabbis.

Yiddish: A form of the German language written in the Hebrew alphabet and used by Jews.

Yom Kippur: One of the most important Jewish holidays, also called the Day of Atonement, which begins at nightfall on the tenth day of the month of Tishri on the Hebrew calendar. (Tishri falls between September and October on the Gregorian calendar.)

Z

Zionism: An international political movement, originating in the late nineteenth century, that called for the creation of an independent Jewish state in Palestine. Following the creation of that state, Israel, in 1948, Zionism has been devoted to the support of Israel.

1

Vying for Power: Dividing Palestine

In the years leading up to World War I (1914–18; war in which Great Britain, France, the United States, and their allies defeated Germany, Austria-Hungary, and their allies), the Ottoman Empire (a vast Turkish empire of southwest Asia, northeast Africa, and southeast Europe that reigned from the thirteenth century to the early twentieth century) held control over much of what is known today as the Middle East. The modern nations of the Middle East were then territories within the empire, their populations loosely governed and not overly prosperous in this time before oil wealth transformed the region. World War I brought sweeping change to the region. The Ottoman Empire was defeated by Allied forces led by Britain and France, and after the war those two European powers began the process of rewriting the map of the region. Under the authority of the League of Nations (a loose confederation of sixty states, formed in 1919, whose goal was to peacefully resolve conflicts between nations), Britain and France divided much of the former Ottoman territory into regions ruled under their mandate, or administrative control. The areas operating under French mandate were Lebanon and Syria; those under British control were Palestine (later known as Israel), Transjordan (later known as Jordan), and Iraq.

Arthur Balfour addresses the issue of Zionism in Palestine, the root of many conflicts between Palestinians and Jews. *(© Bettmann/Corbis.)*

The area known as Palestine lay on the eastern shore of the Mediterranean Sea, and it stretched inland about fifty miles to the banks of the Jordan River and the Dead Sea. Much of the area was desert, and only one-third of the territory could then support agriculture. But the area was home to some of the holiest sites in the Jewish, Christian, and Muslim religions, especially in the city of Jerusalem. In the mid-nineteenth century, Palestine had been home to about 500,000 people, approximately 80 percent of them Arab Muslims, 10 percent Christians, 4 percent Jews, and 1 percent Druze (a Muslim religious sect).

In the 1880s a new force began to reshape Palestine. That force was known as Zionism, a movement by Jews to establish an independent Jewish state in Palestine. Zionists declared that Jews had a claim to land in Palestine, where the twelve ancient tribes of the Jewish faith had ruled thousands of years before, and they encouraged Jews to move to Palestine. In the mid-nineteenth century, small numbers of Jews fleeing discrimination and persecution because of their religious beliefs in Europe and Russia began to settle in Palestine. In the late 1890s, Theodor Herzl (1860–1904), author of *The Jewish State,* created the World Zionist Organization to promote increased Jewish immigration to Palestine, and the number of immigrants increased. Zionism attracted the support of wealthy and influential Jews in Europe and the United States, including Herbert Samuel (1870–1963), a British politician. By 1917 Samuel and other supporters of Zionism had urged the British government to express its qualified support for Zionism. That support came in the form of a letter, known as the Balfour Declaration, that expressed the British position.

The Balfour Declaration, named after British foreign secretary Lord Arthur Balfour (1848–1930), is perhaps the single most important document in the history of the century-long conflict between Jews and Arabs in the Middle East, yet it is just one sentence long. It reads:

> *"His Majesty's Government view with favour the establishment in Palestine of a national home for the Jewish people, and will use their best endeavours to facilitate the achievement of this object, it being understood that nothing shall be done which may prejudice the civil and religious rights of the existing non-Jewish communities in Palestine, or the rights and political status enjoyed by Jews in any other country."*

The dual promise implied in this declaration—the promise that Britain would support both Jewish and Arab interests in Palestine—proved nearly impossible to fulfill, as successive British administrations discovered through the 1920s, 1930s, and 1940s. Jews and the Arabs who lived in Palestine—or Palestinians—fought regularly and sometimes violently over control of land and access to holy sites in Jerusalem. Increasingly, both sides became committed to the idea that the other was the enemy, and that they must fight to remove the enemy's influence from Palestine.

The documents that make up this section show how the various players in this conflict—the British, the Zionists, and the Arabs—struggled to develop policies and strategies to address their interests in Palestine. The Palestine Royal Commission Report, often called the Peel Commission Report, was issued in 1937 by the British in an attempt to provide a framework for cooperation between Jews and Arabs in Palestine. (It proved so unpopular that a "White Paper," issued in 1939, reversed several of its suggestions.) The Biltmore Program was an argument made by American Zionists that Palestine should attain independence as a Jewish state, and it argued against British policy. Finally, the Alexandria Protocol, issued in 1944 during the midst of World War II (1939–45; war in which Great Britain, France, the Soviet Union, the United States, and their allies defeated Germany, Italy, and Japan), was the founding document of the League of Arab States, a coalition of Arab nations that joined together to oppose Zionism and to argue that Palestine should attain independence as an Arab state.

The Peel Commission

Excerpts from the Palestine Royal (Peel) Commission Report
(July 7, 1937)
Reprinted in *Palestine and the Arab-Israeli Conflict*
Edited by Charles D. Smith
Published in 2001

In 1917, in the midst of World War I (1914–18; war in which Great Britain, France, the United States, and their allies defeated Germany, Austria-Hungary, and their allies), the British government issued the Balfour Declaration, changing the lives of many of the people in Palestine. The Balfour Declaration, issued in the form of a letter from diplomat Arthur Balfour (1848–1930), tried to clarify Britain's official position toward two groups who were vying for power in Palestine. These groups were the native Arabs, primarily farmers and small-scale traders, and Zionist Jews, recent immigrants whose mission was to build up an independent Jewish state in Palestine. Britain believed that the two groups could live alongside one another. Therefore, the Balfour Declaration stated that Britain would favor "the establishment in Palestine of a national home for the Jewish people, and [would] use their best endeavours to facilitate the achievement of this object, it being understood that nothing shall be done which may prejudice the civil and religious rights of the existing non-Jewish communities in Palestine." It was a dual promise that proved impossible to keep.

After World War I, British and French troops who had ventured into the Middle East to fight against the

"Manifestly the problem cannot be solved by giving either the Arabs or the Jews all they want. The answer to the question 'Which of them in the end will govern Palestine?' must surely be 'Neither'."

Ottoman Empire (a vast empire of southwest Asia, northeast Africa, and southeast Europe that reigned from the thirteenth century to the early twentieth century) remained in the region. They divided the land into new territories, based upon historical precedents, and worked with the League of Nations, a loose confederation of sixty states, formed in 1919, whose goal was to peacefully resolve conflicts between nations, to establish a system of governance in the region. The system they devised was called the mandate system, for it gave Britain and France a mandate, or authorization, to provide governance for these new territories until such time as they could become independent nations. Britain took control of Palestine, and in 1920 Herbert Samuel (1870–1963) was named the first High Commissioner for Palestine.

From the very beginning, Palestine proved a difficult place to rule. The native Arabs—called Palestinians—resented the way that wealthy Zionists established settlements on Arabic land. They accused the Zionists of using their superior wealth to buy up large tracts of land and force Palestinian peasants to leave the lands they had tended for generations. They also resented the newcomers' claims to rights to visit holy sites. Zionists, on the other hand, were single-minded in their desire to give Palestine a Jewish identity. They created their own school systems and labor unions, and gave preferential treatment to Jews over Palestinians. Zionists argued that the Arabs could move to other nearby countries that had an Arab character, such as Transjordan or Syria. Palestine, they believed, was fated to be a Jewish state.

These competing claims to control in Palestine led to nearly constant conflict between Jews and Arabs. In May 1921, anti-Jewish riots broke out in the town of Jaffa and surrounding villages, leaving forty-seven Jews and forty-eight Arabs dead. In 1929 riots broke out over access to a holy site called the Western Wall (or Wailing Wall; surviving section of a wall of an ancient temple). This time, 133 Jews and at least 113 Arabs died. Neither Arab leader Grand Mufti Al-Hajj Amin al-Husayni (1895–1974) nor a string of Jewish leaders could stop the violence. By 1936 Arabs had decided that the only way to protect their rights was to rise up in a general revolt against both the British and the Jews. This Arab Revolt lasted until 1939. The British were forced to send large numbers of troops to Palestine during the revolt to keep order, but changing politics in Europe—especially the rise of the Nazis in Germany—made Palestine seem like an unwanted diversion, and the British government began to look for a way to peacefully give up control of Palestine.

Late in 1936 the British appointed a commission, headed by William Robert Wellesley (1867–1937), the first Earl of Peel, to investigate the situation in Palestine and make recommendations to the British government. The commission, often known as the Peel Commission, issued its report on July 7, 1937, after nearly six months of lengthy investigations and hearings, including interviews with people on all sides of the conflict. Their report, technically called Command Paper 5479, is best known as the Palestine Royal Commission, or Peel Commission, Report, and it is reproduced below.

William Robert Wellesley, the first Earl of Peel, who headed the Royal Peel Commission. *(© Hulton-Deutsch Collection/Corbis.)*

Things to remember while reading excerpts from the "Palestine Royal (Peel) Commission Report"

- Both Jews and Arabs made historical claims to Palestine. Jews claimed that their ancestors had roots to Palestine that dated from ancient times up to 70 CE, when Romans destroyed a Jewish temple and drove Jews from the region. Arabs had lived in Palestine for centuries, and could point to hundreds of years of history living and farming in the region.

- One of the key ideas to come out of this document was the idea of partition. Partition meant the division of Palestine into two independent states. Try to gain an understanding of what the Commission means by partition.

- The events in Palestine were deeply influenced by the rise of the Nazi Party in Germany. When Adolf Hitler (1889–1945), the head of the Nazi Party, came to power in 1933, he immediately passed laws that discriminated against Jews. Many Jews escaped this persecution by immigrating to Palestine.

Excerpts from the Palestine Royal (Peel) Commission Report (July 7, 1937)

1. Before submitting the proposals we have to offer for its drastic treatment we will briefly restate the problem of Palestine.

2. Under the stress of the World War the British Government made promises to Arabs and Jews in order to obtain their support. On the strength of those promises both parties formed certain expectations.

*3. The application to Palestine of the **Mandate System** in general and of the specific mandate in particular implied the belief that the obligations thus undertaken towards the Arabs and the Jews respectively would prove in course of time to be mutually compatible owing to the **conciliatory** effect on the Arab Palestinians of the material prosperity which Jewish immigration would bring in Palestine as a whole. That belief has not been justified, and we see no hope of its being justified in the future. . . .*

5. What are the existing circumstances?

*An irrepressible conflict has arisen between two national communities within the narrow bounds of one small country. About 1,000,000 Arabs are in strife, open or **latent**, with some 400,000 Jews. There is no common ground between them. The Arab community is predominantly **Asiatic** in character, the Jewish community predominantly European. They differ in religion and in language. Their cultural and social life, their ways of thought and conduct, are as incompatible as their national aspirations. These last are the greatest bar to peace. Arabs and Jews might possibly learn to live and work together in Palestine if they would make a genuine effort to reconcile and*

Mandate System: Form of rule over a conquered territory, granted by the League of Nations following World War I, that gave Great Britain and France control over much of the Middle East.

Conciliatory: Letting go of emotions such as anger or distrust.

Latent: Hidden.

Asiatic: Non-Western.

combine their national ideals and so build up in time a joint or dual nationality. But this they cannot do. The War and its sequel have inspired all Arabs with the hope of reviving in a free and united Arab world the traditions of the Arab golden age. The Jews similarly are inspired by their historic past. They mean to show what the Jewish nation can achieve when restored to the land of its birth. National **assimilation** between Arabs and Jews is thus ruled out. In the Arab picture the Jews could only occupy the place they occupied in Arab Egypt or Arab Spain. The Arabs would be as much outside the Jewish picture as the **Canaanites** in the old land of Israel. The National Home, as we have said before, cannot be half-national. In these circumstances to maintain that Palestinian citizenship has any moral meaning is a mischievous pretence. Neither Arab nor Jew has any sense of service to a single State.

6. This conflict was inherent in the situation from the outset. The terms of the mandate tended to confirm it. If the Government had adopted a more rigorous and consistent policy it might have repressed the conflict for a time, but it could not have resolved it.

7. The conflict has grown steadily more bitter. It has been marked by a series of five Arab outbreaks, culminating in the rebellion of last year. In the earlier period hostility to the Jews was not widespread among the **fellaheen**. It is now general. The first three outbreaks, again, were directed only against the Jews. The last two were directed against the Government as well.

8. This intensification of the conflict will continue. The **estranging** force of conditions inside Palestine is growing year by year. The educational systems, Arab and Jewish, are schools of **nationalism**, and they have only existed for a short time. Their full effect on the rising generation has yet to be felt. And patriotic "youth-movements," so familiar a feature of present-day politics in other countries of Europe or Asia, are afoot in Palestine. As each community grows, moreover, the rivalry between them deepens. The more numerous and prosperous and better-educated the Arabs become, the more insistent will be their demand for national independence and the more bitter their hatred of the obstacle that bars the way to it. As the Jewish National Home grows older and more firmly rooted, so will grow its self-confidence and political ambition.

9. The conflict is primarily political, though the fear of economic **subjection** to the Jews is also in Arab minds. The mandate, it is supposed, will terminate sooner or later. The Arabs would hasten the day, the Jews retard it, for obvious reasons in each case. Meanwhile the

Assimilation: Being brought into one nation.

Canaanites: Ancient tribe of non-Jews.

Fellaheen: Arab peasants.

Estranging: Increasingly hostile.

Nationalism: Devotion to the ideas and culture of a specific nation.

Subjection: Control taken by force or domination.

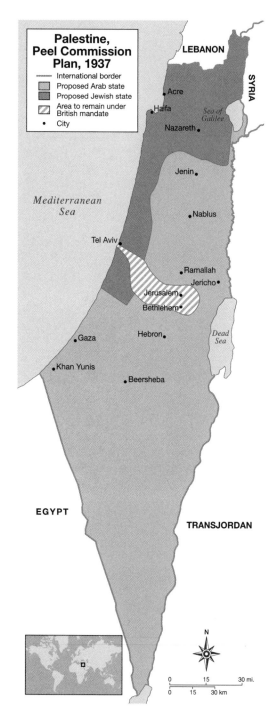

Palestine, Peel Commission Plan, 1937

International border
Proposed Arab state
Proposed Jewish state
Area to remain under British mandate
• City

LEBANON

SYRIA

Acre

Haifa

Sea of Galilee

Nazareth

Jenin

Mediterranean Sea

Nablus

Tel Aviv

Ramallah

Jericho

Jerusalem

Bethlehem

Gaza

Hebron

Dead Sea

Khan Yunis

Beersheba

EGYPT

TRANSJORDAN

N

0   15   30 mi.
0   15   30 km

A map showing the Peel Commission's plan for separating Palestine into two states, one for Arabs and one for Jews. *(Map by XNR Productions, Inc. The Gale Group.)*

whole situation is darkened by uncertainty as to the future. The conflict, indeed, is as much about the future as about the present. Every intelligent Arab and Jew is forced to ask the question "Who in the end will govern Palestine?" This uncertainty is doubtless aggravated by the fact that Palestine is a mandated territory; but, in the light of nationalist movements elsewhere, we do not think the situation would be very different if Palestine had been a British Colony.

10. Meantime the "external factors" will continue to play the part they have played with steadily increasing force from the beginning. On the one hand, Saudi Arabia, the Yemen, Iraq and Egypt are already recognized as sovereign states, and Trans-Jordan as an "independent government." In less than three years' time Syria and the Lebanon will attain their national sovereignty. The claim of the Palestine Arabs to share in the freedom of all Asiatic Arabia will thus be reinforced. Before the War they were linked for centuries past with Syria and the Lebanon. They already exceed the Lebanese in numbers. That they are as well qualified for self-government as the Arabs of neighbouring countries has been admitted.

11. On the other hand, the hardships and anxieties of the Jews in Europe are not likely to grow less in the near future. The pressure on Palestine will continue and might at any time be accentuated. The appeal to the good faith and humanity of the British people will lose none of its force. The Mandatory will be urged unceasingly to admit as many Jews into Palestine as the National Home can provide with a livelihood and to protect them when admitted from Arab attacks.

12. Thus, for internal and external reasons, it seems probable that the situation, bad as it now is, will grow worse. The conflict will go on, the gulf between Arabs and Jews will widen. . . .

14. In these circumstances, we are convinced that peace, order and good government can only be

maintained in Palestine for any length of time by a rigorous system of repression. Throughout this Report we have been careful not to overstate the facts as we see them: but understatement is no less reprehensible; and we should be failing in our duty if we said anything to encourage a hopeful outlook for the future peace of Palestine under the existing system or anything akin to it. . . .

To put it in one sentence, we cannot—in Palestine as it now is—both concede the Arab claim to self-government and secure the establishment of the Jewish National Home. And this conflict between the two obligations is the more unfortunate because each of them, taken separately, accords with British sentiment and British interest. On the one hand, the application of the mandate System to Arab Palestine as a means of advancement to self-government was in harmony with British principles—the same principles as have been put into practice since the War in different circumstances in India, Iraq and Egypt. British public opinion is wholly sympathetic with Arab aspirations towards a new age of unity and prosperity in the Arab world. Conversely, the task of governing without the consent or even the acquiescence of the governed is one for which, we believe, the British people have little heart. On the other hand, there is a strong British tradition of friendship with the Jewish people. Nowhere have Jews found it easier to live and prosper than in Britain. Nowhere is there a more genuine desire to do what can be done to help them in their present difficulties. Nowhere, again, was Zionism better understood before the War or given such practical proofs of sympathy. And British interest coincides with British sentiment. From the earliest days of the British **connexion** with India and beyond, the peace of the Middle East has been a cardinal principle of our foreign policy; and for the maintenance of that peace British statesmanship can show an almost unbroken record of friendship with the Arabs. . . .

A continuance or rather an aggravation—for that is what continuance will be—of the present situation cannot be contemplated without the gravest misgivings. It will mean constant unrest and disturbance in peace and potential danger in the event of war. It will mean a steady decline in our prestige. . . .

19. **Manifestly** the problem cannot be solved by giving either the Arabs or the Jews all they want. The answer to the question "Which of them in the end will govern Palestine?" must surely be "Neither." We do not think that any fair-minded statesman would suppose, now that the

Connexion: Connection.

Manifestly: Clearly.

hope of harmony between the races has proved **untenable**, that Britain ought either to hand over to Arab rule 400,000 Jews, whose entry into Palestine has been for the most part facilitated by the British Government and approved by the League of Nations; or that, if the Jews should become a majority, a million or so of Arabs should be handed over to their rule. But, while neither race can justly rule all Palestine, we see no reason why, if it were practicable, each race should not rule part of it. . . .

Partition seems to offer at least a chance of ultimate peace. We can see none in any other plan. . . .

1. Treaty System

. . .

6. Treaties of Alliance should be negotiated by the Mandatory with the Government of Trans-Jordan and representatives of the Arabs of Palestine on the one hand and with the Zionist Organisation on the other. These Treaties would declare that, within as short a period as may be convenient, two sovereign independent States would be established—the one an Arab State, consisting of Trans-Jordan united with that part of Palestine which lies to the east and south of a frontier such as we suggest in Section 3 below; the other a Jewish State consisting of that part of Palestine which lies to the north and west of that frontier. . . .

2. The Holy Places

. . .

12. We regard the protection of the **Holy Places** as a permanent trust, unique in its character and purpose, and not contemplated by Article 22 of the Covenant of the League of Nations. We submit for consideration that, in order to avoid misunderstanding, it might frankly be stated that this trust will only terminate if and when the League of Nations and the United States desire it to do so, and that, while it would be the trustee's duty to promote the well-being and development of the local population concerned, it is not intended that in course of time they should stand by themselves as a wholly self-governing community. . . .

10. Exchange of Land and Population

. . .

35. We have left to the last the two-fold question which, after that of the **Frontier**, is the most important and most difficult of all the questions which Partition in any shape involves.

Untenable: Not capable of being maintained.

Partition: Dividing Palestine into two independent states.

Holy Places: Religious sites located in the city of Jerusalem.

Frontier: Borders.

36. If Partition is to be effective in promoting a final settlement it must mean more than drawing a frontier and establishing two States. Sooner or later there should be a transfer of land and, as far as possible, an exchange of population. . . .

CONCLUSION

1. "Half a loaf is better than no bread" is a peculiarly English proverb; and, considering the attitude which both the Arab and the Jewish representatives adopted in giving evidence before us, we think it improbable that either party will be satisfied at first sight with the proposals we have submitted for the adjustment of their rival claims. For Partition means that neither will get all it wants. It means that the Arabs must acquiesce in the exclusion from their sovereignty of a piece of territory, long occupied and once ruled by them. It means that the Jews must be content with less than the Land of Israel they once ruled and have hoped to rule again. But it seems to us possible that on reflection both parties will come to realize that the drawbacks of Partition are outweighed by its advantages. For, if it offers neither party all it wants, it offers each what it wants most, namely freedom and security. . . .

What happened next . . .

As the authors of the report predicted, neither side was happy with the recommendations of the Commission. The Jews, represented by a government-like organization called the Jewish Agency, accepted the idea of partition, but they believed that the portion of Palestine allotted to the Jews should be much larger, and they wanted Britain to pay to evict Palestinians from what would become Jewish territory. The Arabs, however, rejected the idea of partition altogether. They argued that since 70 percent of the population was Arabic, and 90 percent of the land was owned by Arabs, that the state should be Arab. The Arab Higher Committee, which spoke for the Arabs at the time, rejected the idea that a Jewish state should be forced upon Palestinians and called for the British to restrict Jewish immigration to Palestine. Riots and protests continued, and the situation did not improve.

Soon even the British agreed that partition was impossible and that they could not create a Jewish national home without the consent of the Arabs. Over the next several years, the British backtracked in their policy. As early as 1938 they issued another Command Paper, number 5893, that called the creation of independent Arab and Jewish states impractical. They also placed limits on Jewish immigration, despite the increased oppression that Jews faced in Germany and elsewhere in Europe. Finally, the British officially reversed parts of their policy when they issued a document known as the 1939 White Paper.

The White Paper rejected the idea of partition, instead calling for the creation of an "independent Palestine state" in "which the two peoples in Palestine, Arabs and Jews, share authority in government in such a way that the essential interests of each are secured." Hoping to appease Arab anger at the growth in the Jewish population, the White Paper restricted Jewish immigration to Palestine for the next ten years and made future immigration subject to the consent of the Arabs. The White Paper pleased the Arabs enough to stop the organized uprising against British rule, but it angered the Jews. They felt that Britain had betrayed them by limiting immigration and backtracking on their support for a Jewish "national home," which many Jews were beginning to think of as an independent state. Despite all the diplomacy, the situation in Palestine improved very little in the 1940s. Arabs and Jews continued to build separate cultures and to fight against each other for control of the land they both claimed. Meanwhile, the rest of the world became absorbed in the fighting of World War II (1939–45; war in which Great Britain, France, the Soviet Union, the United States, and their allies defeated Germany, Italy, and Japan).

Though the Peel Commission Report and the White Paper seemed to cancel each other out, the Peel Report has become a very important historical document. It is the first official document to acknowledge the possibility that Palestine might be divided into two independent states, one Jewish and the other Arab. In the early 2000s, this remained the most widely accepted solution to the enduring conflict over control of the region. In fact, the

Jewish state of Israel has acknowledged the rights of Palestinians to form an independent state, and negotiations continue over exactly what borders that state will take.

Did you know ...

- The population of Palestine doubled over the course of the British mandate, jumping from 750,000 to 1.8 million from 1922 to 1946. In 1922, 89 percent of the population was Arab and 11 percent Jewish. By 1946, just 69 percent was Arab and 31 percent Jewish.

- It is estimated that in the mid-1930s, over 90 percent of Jews in Palestine were literate, while only 30 percent of Arabs were literate.

- In 1936, per household income for Jews in Palestine was 44 Palestinian pounds, while that of Arabs was 17 Palestinian pounds.

- Jewish immigration into Palestine increased steadily until 1935, then dropped off for a number of years. According to statistics compiled by the British, 4,075 Jewish immigrants entered Palestine in 1931; 9,553 in 1932; 30,327 in 1933; 42,359 in 1934; and 61,584 in 1935. From there, the numbers fell: 29,727 entered in 1936; 10,536 in 1937; 12,868 in 1938; 16,405 in 1939; and 4,547 in 1940.

Consider the following ...

- Based on the conflicting claims to regions of Palestine in the 1930s, what would have been the best recommendation for Jews and Arabs to resolve their differences? How would this recommendation provide for the very different needs and perceived injustices of each side?

- Were the recommendations made by the Peel Commission fair? Explain why or why not.

- Diplomatic papers such as the Peel Commission Report are often dry and impersonal. What is the tone of this report? Do the writers sympathize with either side in the conflict? Use quotations to make a case for either side.

For More Information

Books

Encyclopedia of the Modern Middle East. 4 vols. New York: Macmillan Reference USA, 1996.

Farsoun, Samih K., with Christina E. Zacharia. *Palestine and the Palestinians.* Boulder, CO: Westview Press, 1997.

Smith, Charles D., ed. *Palestine and the Arab-Israeli Conflict: A History with Documents.* 4th ed. Boston and New York: Bedford/St. Martin's, 2001.

Web Sites

"The Origins and Evolution of the Palestine Problem: 1917–1988." *United Nations Information System on the Question of Palestine.* http://domino.un.org/UNISPAL.NSF/561c6ee353d740fb8525607d00581829/aeac80e740c782e4852561150071fdb0!OpenDocument (accessed on June 24, 2005).

"Report of the Palestine Royal Commission." *United Nations Information System on the Question of Palestine.* http://domino.un.org/unispal.nsf/cf02d057b04d356385256ddb006dc02f/08e38a718201458b052565700072b358!OpenDocument (accessed on June 24, 2005).

The Biltmore Program

The Biltmore Program (May 11, 1942)
**Reprinted in *The Arab States and the Arab League*
Edited by Muhammad Khalil
Published in 1962**

E ver since 1917, the year that Britain had pledged in the Balfour Declaration to "use [its] best endeavours to facilitate the . . . establishment in Palestine of a national home for the Jewish people," Jewish supporters of this idea, called Zionists, looked to Britain to defend their cause. Throughout the 1920s and into the 1930s, the British government, which controlled Palestine, allowed Jewish immigrants to enter Palestine where they helped build farms, businesses, and communities, thus creating a distinct Jewish society that existed alongside—but separate from— the Arab community in Palestine. British support for the Zionist cause weakened considerably in the late 1930s, however, after protests, riots, and violent attacks by Arabs on both Jews and British officials made it clear that Palestinians, Arabs living in Palestine, did not intend to give control of Palestine to the growing Jewish population. In 1939 the British released a new statement of policy, called the White Paper, that placed numerical limits on Jewish immigration to Palestine and promised Arabs the leading role in a future independent Palestine.

"The Conference declares that the new world order that will follow victory cannot be established on foundations of peace, justice and equality, unless the problem of Jewish homelessness is finally solved."

The Biltmore Hotel in New York was the site of the meeting in 1942 where the Biltmore Program was drafted. *(© Bettmann/Corbis.)*

The White Paper enraged Zionists, who charged that the British had abandoned their support for a Jewish national home in Palestine. After 1939, Zionists began to look beyond Britain for support for their ultimate goal of making Palestine a secure site for the development of a Jewish homeland. European countries were out of the question, for most of them were caught up in the fighting of World War II (1939–45; war in which Great Britain, France, the Soviet Union, the United States, and their allies defeated Germany, Italy, and Japan). Increasingly, Zionist leaders looked to the United States for support. The United States had a sizable Jewish population, including many wealthy supporters of Zionist causes, and it did not have a history of persecuting Jews. Moreover, the entry of the United States into World War II late in 1941 placed that country in a position to speak out against those countries who did persecute Jews, such as Germany.

During World War II, Germany was controlled by the Nazi Party leader Adolf Hitler (1889–1945), who in the 1930s had increased anti-Semitism (hostility toward Jews) in Germany, including laws restricting Jewish activities. By 1939, German soldiers began to round up Jews in Germany and in conquered territories and send them to concentration camps, places where prisoners of war are held and often made to work. By the early 1940s, rumors began to circulate that Jews were being killed in great numbers as part of Hitler's plan, known as the "Final Solution," to rid Europe of Jews. At the time, however, these remained rumors; it was not until November of 1942 that hard evidence of mass killings began to emerge. Still, these rumors contributed to the sense that something must be done to open Palestine to greater immigration of Jews.

Under these circumstances, about six hundred American Zionists and numerous Zionist leaders from Europe and from Palestine itself gathered at the Biltmore Hotel in New York City from May 6 to May 11, 1942. The result of their meeting was the creation of the Biltmore Program, an eight-part statement of goals for the Zionist movement.

Things to remember while reading the "Biltmore Program"

- Zionists had long spoken of a Jewish homeland in Palestine, but the political status of that homeland was often left unstated. Some Zionists felt that a homeland could exist in an independent, non-Jewish nation that recognized and accepted Jewish immigrants. Others believed that the only safe homeland would be in an independent Jewish nation.

- Among the participants at the conference were Dr. Chaim Weizmann (1874–1952), the head of the World Zionist Organization and a moderate who wanted to seek cooperation with the British, and David Ben-Gurion (1886–1973), the leader of the Jewish Agency (the government-like organization of Jews in Palestine) who wanted to break decisively with the British and seek an independent Jewish state.

The Biltmore Program (May 11, 1942)

*1. American Zionists assembled in this Extraordinary Conference reaffirm their **unequivocal** devotion to the cause of democratic freedom and international justice to which the people of the United States, allied with the other United Nations, have dedicated themselves, and give expression to their faith in the ultimate victory of humanity and justice over lawlessness and brute force.*

2. This Conference offers a message of hope and encouragement to their fellow Jews in the Ghettos and concentration camps of

Unequivocal: Clear and without misunderstanding.

Hitler-dominated Europe and prays that their hour of liberation may not be far distant.

3. The Conference sends its warmest greetings to the Jewish Agency Executive in Jerusalem, to the Va'ad Leumi, and to the whole Yishuv in Palestine, and expresses its profound admiration for their steadfastness and achievements in the face of peril and great difficulties. The Jewish men and women in field and factory, and the thousands of Jewish soldiers of Palestine in the Near East who have acquitted themselves with honor and distinction in Greece, Ethiopia, Syria, Libya and on other battlefields, have shown themselves worthy of their people and ready to resume the rights and responsibilities of nationhood.

4. In our generation, and in particular in the course of the past twenty years, the Jewish people have awakened and transformed their ancient homeland; from 50,000 at the end of the last war their numbers have increased to more than 500,000. They have made the waste places to bear fruit and the desert to blossom. Their pioneering achievements in agriculture and in industry, embodying new patterns of cooperative endeavor, have written a notable page in the history of colonization.

5. In the new values thus created, their Arab neighbors in Palestine have shared. The Jewish people in its own work of national redemption welcomes the economic, agricultural and national development of the Arab peoples and states. The Conference reaffirms the stand previously adopted at Congresses of the World Zionist Organization, expressing the readiness and the desire of the Jewish people for full cooperation of their Arab neighbors.

6. The Conference calls for the fulfillment of the original purpose of the Balfour Declaration and the mandate which "recognizing the historical connection of the Jewish people with Palestine" was to afford them the opportunity, as stated by President Wilson, to found there a Jewish Commonwealth.

The Conference affirms its unalterable rejection of the White Paper of May 1939 and denies its moral or legal validity. The White Paper seeks to limit, and in fact to nullify Jewish rights to immigration and settlement in Palestine, and, as stated by Mr. Winston Churchill in the House of Commons in May 1939, constitutes a "breach and repudiation of the Balfour Declaration." The policy of the White Paper is cruel and indefensible in its denial of sanctuary to Jews fleeing from Nazi persecution; and at a time when Palestine has become a focal point in the war front of the United Nations, and the Palestine Jewry must provide all available manpower for farm and factory and camp, it is in direct conflict with the interests of the allied war effort.

Va'ad Leumi: Executive body of the elected Jewish assembly in Palestine.

Yishuv: Jewish community.

World Zionist Organization: Group devoted to promoting Jewish settlement in Palestine.

President Wilson: U.S. president Woodrow Wilson (1856–1924; served 1913–21).

Winston Churchill: British politician and writer and later prime minister of Great Britain (1874–1965; served 1940–45).

7. *In the struggle against the forces of aggression and* **tyranny**, *of which Jews were the earliest victims, and which now menace the Jewish National Home, recognition must be given to the right of the Jews of Palestine to play their full part in the war effort and in the defense of their own country, through a Jewish military force fighting under its own flag and under the high command of the United Nations.*

8. *The Conference declares that the new world order that will follow victory cannot be established on foundations of peace, justice and equality, unless the problem of Jewish homelessness is finally solved.*

The Conference urges that the gates of Palestine be opened; that the Jewish Agency be vested with control of immigration into Palestine and with the necessary authority for **upbuilding** *the country, including the development of its unoccupied and uncultivated lands; and that Palestine be established as a Jewish Commonwealth integrated in the structure of the new democratic world.*

Then and only then will the age-old wrong to the Jewish people be righted.

What happened next . . .

Despite the fact that the group assembled at the Biltmore Hotel had no official status and did not represent a single identifiable organization, the Biltmore Program had a significant impact on events in the United States and, eventually, in Palestine. As a means of increasing American support for Zionism, wrote Charles D. Smith, author of *Palestine and the Arab-Israeli Conflict*, "the Biltmore declarations were extraordinarily successful, especially once news of the Holocaust [the mass killing of European Jews and others by the Nazis during World War II] began to spread in the latter half of 1942. Membership in Zionist organizations increased substantially. Publicity for the Zionist cause was pursued, including books published and distributed with Jewish financial aid." As a result, American politicians and the public became increasingly sympathetic to the idea of increasing immigration to Palestine and creating a Jewish

Tyranny: Absolute power, especially when exercised unjustly or cruelly.

Upbuilding: Building up.

Pasachoff, Naomi. *Links in the Chain: Shapers of the Jewish Tradition.* New York: Oxford University Press, 1997.

Raider, Mark A. *The Emergence of American Zionism.* New York: New York University Press, 1998.

Shpiro, David H. *From Philanthropy to Activism: The Political Transformation of American Zionism in the Holocaust Years, 1933–1945.* New York: Pergamon Press, 1994.

Smith, Charles D., ed. *Palestine and the Arab-Israeli Conflict: A History with Documents.* 4th ed. Boston and New York: Bedford/St. Martin's, 2001.

Urofsky, Melvin I. *American Zionism from Herzl to the Holocaust.* Lincoln: University of Nebraska Press, 1995.

The Alexandria Protocol

The Alexandria Protocol (October 7, 1944)
Issued by representatives of Egypt, Iraq, Lebanon, Syria, and Transjordan
Reprinted in *The Arab States and the Arab League*
Edited by Muhammad Khalil
Published in 1962

When the British took control of Palestine—first with a military government following the end of World War I (1914–18; war in which Great Britain, France, the United States, and their allies defeated Germany, Austria-Hungary, and their allies) in 1920, then with a civilian government authorized by the League of Nations after 1922—they did so with the intention of creating a society that would eventually be self-supporting. In their vision for the future, first proposed in the Balfour Declaration of 1917, Jewish capital and ingenuity would be joined with Arab labor to create a successful multicultural, democratic society. Though both Jews and Palestinians (Arabs living in Palestine) sometimes said that they shared this vision, that was not the way they acted. Jews embraced Zionism, the belief that Palestine should be a national home for Jewish people from around the world, and they did all they could to encourage Jews to populate the region; Palestinians believed that Palestine was their land, and they did not welcome the Jews who came in growing numbers, buying land and building homes and businesses. From the 1920s onward, Jews and Arabs clashed over control of Palestine.

"A League will be formed of the independent Arab States which consent to join the League. . . . The object of the League will be . . . to insure their [Arab States] cooperation, and protect their independence and sovereignty against every aggression by suitable means."

By the 1930s, clashes between Jews and Arabs had become frequent and increasingly violent. Both sides wanted to extend their range of control and both sides felt that the British administrators in the country were favoring their enemies. Arab revolts held between 1936 and 1939, which killed and wounded hundreds on both sides, brought open fighting between Arabs, Jews, and British forces. Years of conflict in Palestine, combined with the entry of Britain into World War II (1939–45; war in which Great Britain, France, the Soviet Union, the United States, and their allies defeated Germany, Italy, and Japan) in 1939, had overextended British forces, and in the early 1940s they prepared to leave Palestine. It was not yet clear in the mid-1940s what would happen in Palestine once the British left.

The doubtful future of Palestine in the early and mid-1940s had sharpened the organization and focus of Zionist groups in Palestine. Jews had built well-disciplined militias (amateur military forces) and had systems in place to provide water, power, education, and other services to their communities. No such organization and infrastructure existed within the Palestinian community. The Grand Mufti Al-Hajj Amin al-Husayni (1895–1974) had been the dominant political and religious leader among Palestinians in the 1930s, but his exile from the country in 1939 left a vacuum of power that no one else was prepared to fill. Political groups in Palestine were more involved in fighting each other than joining together to combat Zionism. Moreover, Arab communities were generally poor, with inadequate social systems. Palestinians were ill-prepared to govern in the absence of the British administration.

The leaders of neighboring Arab countries recognized that there was no organized Palestinian plan to take control of Palestine in the event of British withdrawal. Moreover, many Arab leaders felt that the end of World War II might provide Arab countries with an opportunity to assert greater political independence from the Western countries that had once claimed them as colonies. As the war went on, all of the Arab countries began frequent talks aimed at increasing cooperation among Arab nations and at supporting Palestine's efforts to resist Zionist domination. In the fall of 1944 representatives of five of these nations—Egypt, Iraq, Lebanon, Syria, and Transjordan—met in Alexandria, Egypt, and took the initial steps to organize themselves into a political union and establish a clear position on the question of Palestine. The document they signed on October 7, 1944, was called the Alexandria Protocol.

Things to remember while reading the "Alexandria Protocol"

- Like the **Biltmore Program** (see entry), which called for Palestine to become an independent Jewish state, the Alexandria Protocol calls for Palestine to become an independent Arab state.

- The Alexandria Protocol was written with the events of World War II in mind. Look for the ways that the document reflects the uncertain shape of the postwar world.

The Alexandria Protocol (October 7, 1944)

Anxious to strengthen and consolidate the ties which bind all Arab countries and to direct them toward the welfare of the Arab world, to improve its conditions, insure its future, and realize its hopes and aspirations,

And in response to Arab public opinion in all Arab countries,

*Have met at Alexandria from **Shawwal 8, 1363** (September 25, 1944) to Shawwal 20, 1363 (October 7, 1944) in the form of a Preliminary Committee of the General Arab Conference, and have agreed as follows:*

1. LEAGUE OF ARAB STATES

A League will be formed of the independent Arab States which consent to join the League. It will have a council which will be known as the "Council of the League of Arab States" in which all participating states will be represented on an equal footing.

The object of the League will be to control the execution of the agreements which the above states will conclude; to hold periodic meetings which will strengthen the relations between those states; to coordinate their political plans so as to insure their cooperation, and

Shawwal 8, 1363: Dates in this document are from the Islamic calendar.

While the Arab League started with only five members, it has grown over time to include many countries and organizations. *(© Mona Sharaf/ Reuters/Corbis.)*

protect their independence and sovereignty against every aggression by suitable means; and to supervise in a general way the affairs and interests of the Arab countries.

The decisions of the Council will be binding on those who have accepted them except in cases where a disagreement arises between two member states of the League in which the two parties shall refer their dispute to the Council for solution. In this case the decision of the Council of the League will be binding.

In no case will resort to force to settle a dispute between any two member states of the League be allowed. But every state shall be free to conclude with any other member state of the League, or other powers, special agreements which do not contradict the text or spirit of the present dispositions.

In no case will the adoption of a foreign policy which may be prejudicial to the policy of the League or an individual member state be allowed.

The Council will intervene in every dispute which may lead to war between a member state of the League and any other member state or power, so as to reconcile them.

A subcommittee will be formed of the members of the Preliminary Committee to prepare a draft of the statutes of the Council of the League and to examine the political questions which may be the object of agreement among Arab States.

2. COOPERATION IN ECONOMIC, CULTURAL, SOCIAL, AND OTHER MATTERS

A. The Arab States represented on the Preliminary Committee shall closely cooperate in the following matters:

(1) Economic and financial matters, i.e., commercial exchange, customs, currency, agriculture, and industry.

(2) Communications, i.e., railways, roads, aviation, negation, posts and telegraphs.

(3) Cultural matters.

(4) Questions of nationality, passports, visas, execution of judgments, extradition of criminals, etc.

(5) Social questions.

(6) Questions of public health.

B. A subcommittee of experts for each of the above subjects will be formed in which the states which have participated in the Preliminary Committee will be represented. This subcommittee will prepare draft regulations for cooperation in the above matters, describing the extent and means of that collaboration.

C. A committee for coordination and editing will be formed whose object will be to control the work of the other subcommittees, to coordinate that part of the work which is accomplished, and to prepare drafts of agreement which will be submitted to the various governments.

D. When all the subcommittees have accomplished their work, the Preliminary Committee will meet to examine the work of the subcommittees as a preliminary step toward the holding of a General Arab Conference.

3. CONSOLIDATION OF THESE TIES IN THE FUTURE

While expressing its satisfaction at such a happy step, the Committee hopes that Arab States will be able in the future to consolidate that step by other steps, especially if post-war events should result in institutions which will bind various Powers more closely together.

4. SPECIAL RESOLUTION CONCERNING LEBANON

The Arab States represented on the Preliminary Committee emphasize their respect of the independence and sovereignty of Lebanon in its present frontiers, which the governments of the above States have already recognized in consequence of Lebanon's adoption of an independent policy, which the Government of that country announced in its program of October 7, 1943, unanimously approved by the Lebanese Chamber of Deputies.

5. SPECIAL RESOLUTION CONCERNING PALESTINE

A. The Committee is of the opinion that Palestine constitutes an important part of the Arab World and that the rights of the Arabs in Palestine cannot be touched without prejudice to peace and stability in the Arab World.

The Committee also is of the opinion that the pledges binding the British Government and providing for the **cessation** of Jewish immigration, the preservation of Arab lands, and the achievement of independence for Palestine are permanent Arab rights whose prompt implementation would constitute a step toward the desired goal and toward the stabilization of peace and security.

The Committee declares its support of the cause of the Arabs of Palestine and its willingness to work for the achievement of their legitimate aims and the safeguarding of their just rights.

The Committee also declares that it is second to none in regretting the woes which have been inflicted upon the **Jews of Europe** by European dictatorial states. But the question of these Jews should not be confused with Zionism, for there can be no greater injustice and aggression than solving the problem of the Jews of Europe by another injustice, i.e., by inflicting injustice on the Arabs of Palestine of various religions and denominations.

B. The special proposal concerning the participation of the Arab Governments and peoples in the "Arab National Fund" to safeguard the lands of the Arabs of Palestine shall be referred to the committee of financial and economic affairs to examine it from all its angles and to

Cessation: Stopping.

Jews of Europe: European Jews were being persecuted and systematically murdered by German Nazi forces.

submit the result of that examination to the Preliminary Committee in its next meeting.

In faith of which this protocol has been signed at Faruq I University at Alexandria on Saturday, Shawwal 20, 1363 (October 7, 1944).

What happened next . . .

The signing of the Alexandria Protocol represented the first time that Arab nations had joined together to further their political interests, and it expressed the hope that in the future those nations could work together to address the political and economic issues that faced them. Less than a year later, the League of Arab States called for by the Alexandria Protocol came into being. On March 22, 1945, Yemen and Saudi Arabia joined the five Protocol states in signing the Covenant of the League of Arab States, which mirrored the Protocol in most areas.

The League of Arab States, often called simply the Arab League, has been a durable organization, if not a terribly effective one. Though it continues to exist—in 2005 it had twenty-two members in the Middle East and Northern Africa—the Arab League has never succeeded at encouraging the kinds of economic and political cooperation achieved by such regional organizing bodies as the Organization of American States (in South and Central America and the Caribbean) or the European Union. Though the reasons behind the failure of Arab states to cooperate are a matter of substantial dispute, observers point to the fact that most Arab states are led by authoritarian figures, or people favoring absolute obedience to authority, accustomed to dictating policy, and this might be a key obstacle to effective joint action.

One thing that Arab nations agreed on, however, was their desire that Palestine achieve independence as an Arab nation. The Arab League Covenant strengthened the call for Palestinian independence, declaring that Palestine's "existence and *de jure* [by right] national independence is a matter on which there is no doubt as there is no doubt about the independence of the other Arab countries." Just as the Zionists had used the Biltmore Program to stake a claim for an independent Jewish Palestine, Arab countries used the Alexandria Protocol and the Covenant of the League of Arab States to stake a similar claim for an Arab Palestine. Ever since that time, Arab nations have supported the rights of Palestinians to create an independent state. Several times over the years Arab nations have gone to war with Israel—the Jewish state that was created in Palestine in 1948—to try to achieve that goal.

Did you know ...

- The British relinquished their mandate over Palestine in 1947, at which time the United Nations took control. Very quickly, the United Nations proposed a plan to partition Palestine into two independent states, one Arab and one Jewish.

- Violence between Arabs and Jews in Palestine occurred continuously throughout the 1930s and 1940s, but open and organized warfare did not happen until 1948, after Jews declared the independence of the state of Israel and Arab countries joined together to battle the Jews (now called Israelis).

- The Covenant of the League of Arab States declared that its primary purpose was to provide for "the general good of the Arab States, the improvement of their circumstances, the security of their future, and the realization of their hopes and aspirations."

Consider the following ...

- Both the Biltmore Program and the Alexandria Protocol make claims about the right of Palestine to become independent. Compare and contrast these opposing claims. Are the assertions of both sides accurate? How do the documents attempt to discuss history so as to support their position?

- Are there ways that the Alexandria Protocol could have been written that would have encouraged greater Arab cooperation, or assured that Palestinian independence was achieved?

For More Information

Books

Encyclopedia of the Modern Middle East. 4 vols. New York: Macmillan Reference USA, 1996.

Gomaa, Ahmed M. *The Foundation of the League of Arab States: Wartime Diplomacy and Inter-Arab Politics, 1941 to 1945.* New York: Longman, 1977.

Khalil, Muhammad, ed. *The Arab States and the Arab League: A Documentary Record, Vol. II International Affairs.* Beirut, Lebanon: Khayats, 1962.

Web Sites

League of Arab States. http://www.arableagueonline.org/arableague/index_en.jsp (accessed on June 24, 2005).

2

Forming a State: The Birth of Israel and the Arab Response

I n the 1920s, after World War I (1914–18; war in which Great Britain, France, the United States, and their allies defeated Germany, Austria-Hungary, and their allies), an international organization called the League of Nations authorized a mandate, or system of control, for Britain in the Middle Eastern land of Palestine. Under this system, Britain served as the ruling power of Palestine. The British mandate also recognized that Jews had a historical connection to Palestine and had the right to a Jewish state. At that time, Arabs made up the majority of Palestine's population, and they too felt that they had a historical connection to the land. Both Arabs and Jews made claims for the same land, and leaders of the two sides vied for power. Tensions rose, but no solution to the problem was found.

Many Jews adhered to Zionism, the belief in establishing a Jewish state in Palestine. The British mandate initially supported Zionism and Jews began to immigrate to Palestine in larger numbers in the 1920s and 1930s with the goal of settling the land and establishing their nation. The new Jewish settlers clashed with Arab Palestinians over ownership of land and resources. The two sides came into increasing conflict, which the British government was unable to resolve.

Many Jewish people around the world supported the creation of the nation of Israel in 1948. *(© Bettmann/Corbis.)*

During World War II (1939–45; war in which Great Britain, France, the Soviet Union, the United States, and their allies defeated Germany, Italy, and Japan), German leader Adolf Hitler (1889–1945) oversaw the Holocaust, a mass extermination of European Jews and others. Millions of Jews were killed. This persecution made Jews more intent on establishing their own nation. Though the British had restricted the number of Jews who could immigrate to Palestine to appease Arab leaders in the late 1930s, many Jews already there smuggled in those fleeing persecution in Europe. These illegal activities generated hostility between the British government and the Jewish activists, and the rise of Jewish immigrants escalated tensions between Jews and Arabs.

By the end of World War II Jews and Arabs in Palestine were both working to gain independence from British rule. They each wanted their own nation. In 1947 Britain relinquished, or gave up, its mandate in Palestine and turned the problem over to the United Nations, an organization formed in 1945 to find peaceful solutions to international problems. The United Nations drew up a plan to partition, or divide, the land of Palestine into two states, one Jewish and one Arab.

While Jewish leaders in Palestine accepted the plan of the United Nations, Arab Palestinian leaders called for Arab control over all of Palestine. Arabs turned for direction to the Arab League, which formed in 1944 as a body to coordinate the political and economic efforts of Arab member states. The organization resolved to protect Palestine from the threat of Zionism, but infighting between Arab leaders for ultimate control of the league weakened its effectiveness in responding to the issue.

In May 1948, the British officially gave up control of Palestine, and both Jews and Arabs issued documents outlining their plan to create their own states in Palestine. The Declaration of Israel's Independence and the Statement Issued by the Governments of the Arab League States on the Occasion of the Entry of the Arab Armies in Palestine explain in detail each side's perspective on its claims to Palestine. These documents began a war between the newly created Jewish state of Israel and Arab Palestinians supported by various Arab countries. Israel, backed by the United States and other Western European countries, proved to be stronger in the conflict and thousands of Arab Palestinians were forced out of Palestine into surrounding Arab-controlled countries such as Jordan, Syria, and Egypt, creating refugee camps. Yet both of these documents make strong cases for why each group is entitled to the land of Palestine and continue to be the cause of many of the conflicts in the Middle East.

Establishment of the State of Israel

Declaration of the Establishment of the State of Israel (May 14, 1948)

Issued by Israel's Provisional Council of State at Tel Aviv
Reprinted in *Palestine and the Arab-Israeli Conflict*
Edited by Charles D. Smith
Published in 2001

"This right is the natural right of the Jewish people to be masters of their own fate, like all other nations, in their own sovereign state."

The declaration of Israel's statehood on May 14, 1948, served as the culmination of many decades of work on the part of Zionists, those who wanted to create a Jewish state in Palestine, around the world. Before and during World War I (1914–18; war in which Great Britain, France, the United States, and their allies defeated Germany, Austria-Hungary, and their allies), Zionists promoted Jewish settlement in Palestine and coordinated several fund-raising drives in Britain and the United States. Jews realized that to continue their efforts to create a Jewish state in Palestine, they needed to be organized and efficient. To this end, they established the Jewish Agency. The agency started as an effort to link Zionist fund-raising efforts with the governing bodies distributing those funds to Jews in Palestine. After 1929 the agency was redesigned to serve the economic and social needs of Jewish settlement in Palestine, and within a decade the agency had evolved into a fully functioning governing body of the Jewry in Palestine. With its first offices in Jerusalem, the Jewish Agency soon had branch offices in London, Geneva, and New York City. On behalf of the Jewry in Palestine, the agency negotiated with Palestinian leadership, foreign governments, and the United

Nations. By World War II (1939–45; war in which Great Britain, France, the Soviet Union, the United States, and their allies defeated Germany, Italy, and Japan), it also coordinated the efforts of Jewish militias, or amateur military groups.

Throughout the years under the British mandate (1922–47; a form of government where Britain ruled over Palestine), the Jewish Agency spent a great deal of effort developing and maintaining influential contacts in foreign governments, and detailed the impact on Jews of every policy made under the mandate. When the Jewish Agency heard of the British decision to evacuate Palestine and end its mandate, it firmly established itself as the Jewish governing body and quickly seized the opportunity to steer its people's own fate. When the United Nations (an international organization founded in 1945 to promote peace and cooperation between countries around the world) investigated the question of which group should rule in Palestine in 1947, members of the Jewish Agency presented their pleas for an independent state in Palestine, which they would call Israel. Confident that the international community of Europe and the United States would quickly recognize the legitimacy of its claim to independence, the Jews' only concern was how the Arabs would react.

Even before Israel was created, Jewish people in Palestine celebrated Partition Day when the United Nations said that Israel had the right to exist as a separate country.
(© David Rubinger/Corbis.)

Things to remember while reading the "Declaration of the Establishment of the State of Israel"

- The Declaration of Israel's Independence mentions the resolution of the United Nations General Assembly of

November 29, 1947. This resolution called for the partition or dividing of Palestine into separate Jewish and Arab states.

- In February of 1948 the Jewish Agency mobilized its defense forces to seize control over all the territory granted to the Jewish state by the United Nations resolution. The operation sparked a mass evacuation of Arab Palestinians, and nearly 300,000 had fled from these areas by May.

- Note how carefully the document explains why Israel should be an independent state.

- Notice that the declaration of Israel's independence extends an offer of invitation to all Jews wishing to immigrant to the land.

Declaration of the Establishment of the State of Israel (May 14, 1948)

*Eretz-Israel was the birthplace of the Jewish people. Here their spiritual, religious and political identity was shaped. Here they first attained to statehood, created cultural values of national and universal significance and gave to the world the eternal **Book of Books**.*

After being forcibly exiled from their land, the people kept faith with it throughout their dispersion and never ceased to pray and hope for their return to it and for the restoration in it of their political freedom.

*Impelled by this historic and traditional attachment, Jews strove in every successive generation to re-establish themselves in their ancient homeland. In recent decades they returned in their masses. Pioneers, **Ma'apilim** and defenders, they made deserts bloom, revived the Hebrew language, built villages and towns, and created a thriving community controlling its own economy and culture, loving peace but knowing how to defend itself, bringing the blessings of progress to all the country's inhabitants, and aspiring towards independent nationhood.*

*In the year **5657**, at the summons of the spiritual father of the Jewish State, Theodor Herzl, the First Zionist Congress convened and proclaimed the right of the Jewish people to national rebirth in its own country.*

Eretz-Israel: "The land of Isreal"; a historic Jewish name for Palestine.

Book of Books: The Bible.

Ma'apilim: Immigrants coming to Israel in defiance of British policy.

5657: Reference to the Jewish calendar corresponding to the year 1897.

David Ben-Gurion, the first prime minister of Israel, reads the Declaration of the Establishment of Israel to the newly formed Israeli government in May 1948. *(© Bettmann/Corbis.)*

This right was recognized in the Balfour Declaration of 2 November, 1917, and reaffirmed in the mandate of the League of Nations which, in particular, gave international sanction to the historic connection between the Jewish people and Eretz-Israel and to the right of the Jewish people to rebuild its national home.

The catastrophe which recently befell the Jewish people—the massacre of millions of Jews in Europe—was another clear demonstration of the urgency of solving the problem of its homelessness by re-establishing in Eretz-Israel the Jewish State, which would open the gates of the homeland wide to every Jew and confer upon the Jewish people the status of a fully privileged member of the comity of nations.

*Survivors of the Nazi **holocaust** in Europe, as well as Jews from other parts of the world, continued to migrate to Eretz-Israel, undaunted by difficulties, restrictions and dangers, and never ceased to assert their right to a life of dignity, freedom and honest toil in their national homeland.*

In the second world war, the Jewish community of this country contributed its full share to the struggle of the freedom—and peace-loving nations against the forces of Nazi wickedness and, by the blood of its soldiers and its war effort, gained the right to be reckoned among the peoples who founded the United Nations.

*On 29 November, 1947, the United Nations General Assembly passed a resolution calling for the establishment of a Jewish state in Eretz-Israel; the General Assembly required the inhabitants of Eretz-Israel to take such steps as were necessary on their part for the implementation of that resolution. This recognition by the United Nations of the right of the Jewish people to establish their state is **irrevocable**.*

This right is the natural right of the Jewish people to be masters of their own fate, like all other nations, in their own sovereign state.

Accordingly we, members of the People's Council, representatives of the Jewish community of Eretz-Israel and of the Zionist movement, are here assembled on the day of the termination of the British mandate over Eretz-Israel and, by virtue of our natural and historic right and on the strength of the resolution of the United Nations General Assembly, hereby declare the establishment of a Jewish state in Eretz-Israel, to be known as the State of Israel.

*We declare that, with effect from the moment of the termination of the mandate being tonight, the eve of **Sabbath**, the 6th Iyar, 5708 (15 May 1948), until the establishment of the elected, regular authorities of the state in accordance with the constitution which shall be adopted by the elected Constituent Assembly not later than 1 October 1948, the People's Council shall act as a provisional Council of State, and its executive organ, the People's Administration, shall be the Provisional Government of the Jewish state, to be called "Israel".*

*The State of Israel will be open for Jewish immigration and for the ingathering of the exiles; it will foster the development of the country for the benefit of all its inhabitants; it will be based on freedom, justice and peace as envisaged by the Prophets of Israel; it will ensure complete equality of social and political rights to all its inhabitants irrespective of religion, race or sex; it will guarantee freedom of religion, conscience, language, education and culture; it will safeguard the **Holy Places** of all religions; and it will be faithful to the principles of the Charter of the United Nations.*

Holocaust: The slaughter of millions of European civilians, especially Jews, by the Nazis during World War II (1939–45).

Irrevocable: Impossible to take back.

Sabbath: Day of rest and worship; from sundown on Friday to sundown on Saturday for the Jewish people.

Holy Places: Religious sites located in the city of Jerusalem.

The State of Israel is prepared to cooperate with the agencies and representatives of the United Nations in implementing the resolution of the General Assembly of 29 November 1947, and will take steps to bring about the economic union of the whole of Eretz-Israel.

*We appeal to the United Nations to assist the Jewish people in the building-up of its state and to receive the State of Israel into the **comity** of nations.*

We appeal—in the very midst of the onslaught launched against us now for months—to the Arab inhabitants of the State of Israel to preserve peace and participate in the upbuilding of the state on the basis of full and equal citizenship and due representation in all its provisional and permanent institutions.

We extend our hand to all neighboring states and their peoples in an offer of peace and good neighborliness, and appeal to them to establish bonds of cooperation and mutual help with the sovereign Jewish people settled in its own land. The State of Israel is prepared to do its share in a common effort for the advancement of the entire Middle East.

*We appeal to the Jewish people throughout the **diaspora** to rally round the Jews of Eretz-Israel in the tasks of immigration and upbuilding and to stand by them in the great struggle for the realization of the age-old dream—the redemption of Israel.*

Placing our trust in the Almighty, we affix our signatures to this proclamation at this session of the Provisional Council of State, on the soil of the homeland, in the city of Tel-Aviv, on this Sabbath eve, the 5th day of Iyar, 5708 (14th May 1948).

What happened next . . .

Israel did secure the international recognition it had hoped for: the United States and the Soviet Union were the first to recognize Israel's independence, and all the other Western states quickly followed. But just as feared, the Arab states did not. The Arab Palestinians did not have an organized government in place at the time, so the League of Arab States (an organization of several Middle Eastern countries that wanted to unify the Middle East under Arab rule) served as the governing body speaking for the population of Arabs in Palestine.

Comity: Friendship.

Diaspora: The Jewish community living in many countries throughout the world.

The day after Israel declared its independence, the Arab League mobilized forces against the new country.

The Arab military forces from Egypt, Iraq, Jordan, Lebanon, and Syria advanced on Israel in uncoordinated efforts. Although the Arabs had superior weaponry at the beginning of the war, the efficient organization and greater manpower of the Israeli forces prevailed. The Arab-Israeli War of 1948, known as the War of Independence in Israel, ended in 1949 with the defeat of the Arabs. By the end of the war, Israel occupied all the territory the United Nations had assigned to it under the partition plan of 1947, as well as land the United Nations had allotted for the Arab state in Palestine, and parts of Lebanon and Egypt. The Arab Palestinians who had been living in the areas now claimed by Israel found themselves without any land of their own. Half of the population had become refugees in the West Bank and the Gaza Strip, and the other half had fled into neighboring Arab states.

Did you know . . .

- The Arab-Israeli War of 1948 resulted in the division of Jerusalem into Jewish and Arab sectors.

- After the war, Israel immediately began to build itself as a nation, and within twenty years it had become the most technologically advanced country in the Middle East.

- After the Arab-Israeli War the Arab Palestinian government was destroyed, and many Arab Palestinians lost their rights, including the right to own land that had been taken over by Israel. This caused many Arab Palestinians to become refugees without a country or a government.

Consider the following . . .

- The Declaration of Israel's Independence notes that the land was the birthplace of the Jewish people. Why would this fact give the Jewish people a claim to the land? Are there peoples in other countries who might use this same claim for their own purposes?

- The Declaration of Israel's Independence offers a hand of peace to Arabs, but the Jewish Agency had been working for nearly a year to organize military takeovers of several

Arab Palestinian areas. How might Arab Palestinians who had been forced from their homes by the Jews feel about the Declaration of Israel's Independence?

- The Declaration of Israel's Independence states that United Nations' recognition of the right of the Jewish people to establish their state is "irrevocable." Explain why the authors of the Declaration of Israel's Independence made this claim. (Hint to consider: If the United Nations had resolved that the Jewish people did not have the right to establish a self-ruled state, would that particular decision have been "irrevocable" as well?)

For More Information

Books

Louis, W. Roger. *The British Empire in the Middle East, 1945-1951: Arab Nationalism, the United States and Postwar Imperialism.* New York and London: Oxford, 1984.

Miller, Debra A. *The Arab-Israeli Conflict.* San Diego, CA: Lucent Books, 2005.

Smith, Charles D., ed. *Palestine and the Arab-Israeli Conflict: A History with Documents.* 4th ed. Boston and New York: Bedford/St. Martin's, 2001.

Wagner, Heather Lehr. *Israel and the Arab World.* Philadelphia: Chelsea House, 2002.

Web Sites

"Zionism and the Creation of Israel." *MidEast Web.* http://www.mideastweb. org/zionism.htm (accessed June 24, 2005).

Occasion of the Entry of the Arab Armies in Palestine

Statement Issued by the Governments of the Arab League States
on the Occasion of the Entry of the Arab Armies in Palestine
(May 15, 1948)

Reprinted in *The Arab States and the Arab League:*
***A Documentary Record* Vol. II**
Edited by Muhmmad Khalil
Published in 1962

"The events which have taken place in Palestine have unmasked the aggressive intentions and the imperialistic designs of the Zionists. . . ."

As the United Nations (an international organization founded in 1945 to promote peace and cooperation between countries around the world) considered the idea of partitioning, or dividing, Palestine into Jewish and Arab states, Arab Palestinians were living without an organized self-government. The governing body of the Arab Palestinians, the Arab Higher Committee, which had formed in 1936, had been dissolved by the British in 1937 and its leaders had been deported as a result of the ongoing Arab revolts in Palestine.

The Arab Palestinians' political weakness made them dependent on the League of Arab States. The League of Arab States had formed in 1944 as an organization that would enable Arab states to work together while maintaining their separate identities. The first members were Egypt, Saudi Arabia, Yemen, Transjordan (later known as Jordan), Syria, Lebanon, and Iraq. In an attempt to help establish a Arab Palestinian government, the Arab League sponsored the Arab Higher Committee and positioned the exiled Palestinian leaders in

While the Arab League supported the Palestinians and made Palestinian leaders part of the Arab Higher Committee, the Palestinians had little true power in the Arab League. *(© Hulton-Deutsch Collection/Corbis.)*

the top positions. But the Palestinians in the Arab Higher Committee and the leaders of the Arab League could not agree on the future of Palestine, and the Arab Higher Committee was condemned to be an insignificant, powerless part of the Arab League.

When Israel declared its independence on May 14, 1948, the Arab Palestinians were completely reliant on the Arab League, having no government and no unified military of their own. The statement issued on May 15, 1948, by the governments of the Arab League States broadened the Arab-Israeli conflict beyond Palestine to include all the neighboring Arab states.

Things to remember while reading the "Statement Issued by the Governments of the Arab League States on the Occasion of the Entry of the Arab Armies in Palestine"

- A surge of Arab nationalism, or the belief that Arab countries should rule themselves, rose in the early 1900s against the Ottoman Empire (a vast empire of southwest Asia, northeast Africa, and southeast Europe that reigned from the thirteenth century to the early twentieth century), which ruled over much of the area now considered part of the Middle East.

- European domination of the Middle East after World War I (1914–18; war in which Great Britain, France, the United States, and their allies defeated Germany, Austria-Hungary, and their allies) provoked resentment among Arabs, many of whom had been promised autonomy for helping the Europeans overthrow the Ottoman Empire.

- Both Britain and France granted many Arab nations their independence as World War II (1939–45; war in which Great Britain, France, the Soviet Union, the United States, and their allies defeated Germany, Italy, and Japan) came to a close.

- The League of Arab States was united in its opposition to Jewish claims to Palestine.

Statement Issued by the Governments of the Arab League States on the Occasion of the Entry of the Arab Armies in Palestine (May 15, 1948)

*1. Palestine was part of the former Ottoman Empire, subject to its law and represented in its parliament. The overwhelming majority of the population of Palestine were Arabs. There was in it a small minority of Jews that enjoyed the same rights and bore the same responsibilities as the [other] inhabitants, and did not suffer any ill-treatment on account of its religious beliefs. The **holy places** were inviolable and the freedom of access to them was guaranteed.*

Holy places: Religious sites located in the city of Jerusalem.

2. *The Arabs have always asked for their freedom and independence. On the outbreak of the First World War, and when the Allies declared that they were fighting for the liberation of peoples, the Arabs joined them and fought on their side with a view to realizing their national aspirations and obtaining their independence. England pledged herself to recognize the independence of the Arab countries in Asia, including Palestine. The Arabs played a remarkable part in the achievement of final victory and the Allies have admitted this.*

3. *In 1917 England issued a **declaration** in which she expressed her sympathy with the establishment of a national home for the Jews in Palestine. When the Arabs knew of this they protested against it, but England reassured them by affirming to them that this would not prejudice the right of their countries to freedom and independence or affect the political status of the Arabs in Palestine. **Notwithstanding** the legally void character of this declaration, it was interpreted by England to aim at no more than the establishment of a spiritual centre for the Jews in Palestine, and to conceal no ulterior political aims, such as the establishment of a Jewish State. The same thing was declared by the Jewish leaders.*

4. *When the war came to an end England did not keep her promise. Indeed, the Allies placed Palestine under the mandate system and entrusted England with [the task of carrying it out], in accordance with a document providing for the administration of the country, in the interests of its inhabitants and its preparation for the independence which the Covenant of the League of Nations recognized that Palestine was qualified to have.*

5. *England administered Palestine in a manner which enabled the Jews to flood it with immigrants and helped them to settle in the country. [This was so] notwithstanding the fact that it was proved that the density of the population in Palestine had exceeded the economic capacity of the country to absorb additional immigrants. England did not pay regard to the interests or rights of the Arab inhabitants, the lawful owners of the country. Although they used to express, by various means, their concern and **indignation** on account of this state of affairs which was harmful to their being and their future, they [invariably] were met by indifference, imprisonment and oppression.*

6. *As Palestine is an Arab country, situated in the heart of the Arab countries and attached to the Arab world by various ties—spiritual, historical, and strategic—the Arab countries, and even the Eastern ones, governments as well as peoples, have concerned themselves with the problem of Palestine and have raised it to the international level;*

Declaration: The Balfour Declaration.

Notwithstanding: Despite anything to the contrary.

Indignation: Anger aroused by something unjust.

The Arab League met shortly after Israel declared independence to discuss how it would combat the newly formed Jewish state.

(© Bettmann/Corbis)

[they have also raised the problem] with England, asking for its solution in accordance with the pledges made and with democratic principles. The Round Table Conference was held in London in 1939 in order to discuss the Palestine question and to arrive at the just solution thereof. The Governments of the Arab States participated in [this conference] and asked for the preservation of the Arab character of Palestine and the proclamation of its independence. This conference ended with the issue of a White Paper in which England defined her policy towards Palestine, recognized its independence, and undertook to set up the institutions that would lead to its exercise of the characteristics of [this independence]. She [also] declared that her obligations concerning the establishment of a Jewish national home had been fulfilled, since that home had actually been established. But the policy defined in that [White] paper was not carried out. This, therefore, led to the

*deterioration of the situation and the **aggravation of matters** contrary to the interests of the Arabs.*

*7. While the Second World War was still in progress, the Governments of the Arab States began to hold consultations regarding the reinforcement of their co-operation and the increasing of the means of their collaboration and their **solidarity**, with a view to safeguarding their present and their future and to participating in the erection of the **edifice** of the new world on firm foundations. Palestine had its [worthy] share of consideration and attention in these conversations. These conversations led to the establishment of the League of Arab States as an instrument for the co-operation of the Arab States for their security, peace and well-being.*

The Pact of the League of Arab States declared that Palestine has been an independent country since its separation from the Ottoman Empire, but the manifestations of this independence have been suppressed due to reasons which were out of the control of its inhabitants. The establishment of the United Nations shortly afterwards was an event about which the Arabs had the greatest hopes. Their belief in the ideals on which that organization was based made them participate in its establishment and membership.

*8. Since then the Arab League and its [member] Governments have not spared any effort to pursue any course, whether with the Mandatory Power or with the United Nations, in order to bring about a just solution of the Palestine problem: [a solution] based upon true democratic principles and compatible with the provisions of the Covenant of the League of Nations and the [Charter] of the United Nations, and which would [at the same time] be lasting, guarantee peace and security in the country and prepare it for progress and prosperity. But **Zionist** claims were always an obstacle to finding such a solution, [as the Zionists], having prepared themselves with armed forces, strongholds and fortifications to face by force anyone standing in their way, publicly declared [their intention] to establish a Jewish State.*

9. When the General Assembly of the United Nations issued, on 29 November 1947, its recommendation concerning the solution of the Palestine problem, on the basis of the establishment of an Arab State and of another Jewish [state] in [Palestine] together with placing the City of Jerusalem under the trusteeship of the United Nations, the Arab States drew attention to the injustice implied in this solution [affecting] the right of the people of Palestine to immediate independence, as well as democratic principles and the provisions of the Covenant of the League of Nations and [the Charter] of the United Nations. [These States also]

Aggravation of matters: Increasing anger over issues.

Solidarity: Common interests within a group.

Edifice: Bulding of large size.

Zionist: Any person working to create an independent Jewish State.

*declared the Arabs' rejection of [that solution] and that it would not be possible to carry it out by peaceful means, and that its forcible imposition would **constitute** a threat to peace and security in this area.*

The warnings and expectations of the Arab States have, indeed, proved to be true, as disturbances were soon widespread throughout Palestine. The Arabs clashed with the Jews, and the two [parties] proceeded to fight each other and shed each other's blood. Whereupon the United Nations began to realize the danger of recommending the partition [of Palestine] and is still looking for a way out of this state of affairs.

10. Now that the British mandate over Palestine has come to an end, without there being a legitimate constitutional authority in the country, which would safeguard the maintenance of security and respect for law and which would protect the lives and properties of the inhabitants, the Governments of the Arab States declare the following:—

First: That the rule of Palestine should revert to its inhabitants, in accordance with the provisions of the Covenant of the League of Nations and [the Charter] of the United Nations and that [the Palestinians] should alone have the right to determine their future.

*Second: Security and order in Palestine have become disrupted. The Zionist aggression resulted in the **exodus** of more than a quarter of a million of its Arab inhabitants from their homes and in their taking refuge in the neighbouring Arab countries.*

*The events which have taken place in Palestine have unmasked the aggressive intentions and the imperialistic designs of the Zionists, including the atrocities committed by them against the peace-loving Arab inhabitants, especially in **Dayr Yasin, Tiberias and others**. Nor have they respected the inviolability of **consuls**, as they have attacked the consulates of the Arab States in Jerusalem. After the termination of the British mandate over Palestine the British authorities are no longer responsible for security in the country, except to the degree affecting their withdrawing forces, and [only] in the areas in which these forces happen to be at the time of withdrawal as announced by [these authorities]. This state of affairs would render Palestine without any governmental machinery capable of restoring order and the rule of law to the country, and of protecting the lives and properties of the inhabitants.*

Third: This state of affairs is threatening to spread to the neighbouring Arab countries, where feeling is running high because of the events in Palestine. The Governments of the Member States of the

Constitute: Establish.

Exodus: Departure of a large number of people.

Dayr Yasin, Tiberias and others: Arab villages in which Jews attacked and killed numerous Arabs.

Consuls: Government representatives.

Arab League and of the United Nations are exceedingly worried and deeply concerned about this state of affairs.

Fourth: *These Governments had hoped that the United Nations would have succeeded in finding a peaceful and just solution of the problem of Palestine, in accordance with democratic principles and the **provisions** of the Covenant of the League of Nations and [the Charter] of the United Nations, so that peace, security and prosperity would prevail in this part of the world.*

Fifth: *The Governments of the Arab States, as members of the Arab League, a regional organization within the meaning of the provisions of Chapter VIII of the Charter of the United Nations, are responsible for maintaining peace and security in their area. These Governments view the events taking place in Palestine as a threat to peace and security in the area as a whole and [also] in each of them taken separately.*

Sixth: *Therefore, as security in Palestine is a sacred trust in the hands of the Arab States, and in order to put an end to this state of affairs and to prevent it from becoming aggravated or from turning into [a state of] chaos, the extent of which no one can foretell; in order to stop the spreading of disturbances and disorder in Palestine to the neighbouring Arab countries; in order to fill the gap brought about in the governmental machinery in Palestine as a result of the termination of the mandate and the non-establishment of a lawful successor authority, the Governments of the Arab States have found themselves compelled to intervene in Palestine solely in order to help its inhabitants restore peace and security and the rule of justice and law to their country, and in order to prevent bloodshed.*

Seventh: *The Governments of the Arab States recognize that the independence of Palestine, which has so far been suppressed by the British mandate, has become an accomplished fact for the lawful inhabitants of Palestine. They alone, by virtue of their **absolute sovereignty**, have the right to provide their country with laws and governmental institutions. They alone should exercise the attributes of their independence, through their own means and without any kind of foreign interference, immediately after peace, security and the rule of law have been restored to the country.*

At that time the intervention of the Arab states will cease, and the independent State of Palestine will co-operate with the [other member] States of the Arab League in order to bring peace, security and prosperity to this part of the world.

Provisions: Agreement between parties regarding some aspect of a legal matter.

Absolute Sovereignty: Ultimate control over all matters in a specific region.

Emphatically: Forcefully.

The Governments of the Arab States emphasize, on this occasion, what they have already declared before the London Conference and the United Nations, that the only solution of the Palestine problem is the establishment of a unitary Palestinian State, in accordance with democratic principles, whereby its inhabitants will enjoy complete equality before the law, [and whereby] minorities will be assured of all the guarantees recognized in democratic constitutional countries, and [whereby] the holy places will be preserved and the right of access thereto guaranteed.

*Eighth: The Arab States most **emphatically** declare that [their] intervention in Palestine was due only to these considerations and objectives, and that they aim at nothing more than to put an end to the prevailing conditions in [Palestine]. For this reason, they have great confidence that their action will have the support of the United Nations; [that it will be] considered as an action aiming at the realization of its aims and at promoting its principles, as provided for in its Charter.*

What happened next . . .

When the Arab League members mobilized their armies and invaded Israel in May 1948, they had high hopes that they were about to establish the Arab nation of Palestine. Arabs outnumbered the Jewish residents in Palestine by more than two to one, and the Arab military forces outnumbered those of the Jews. But the Arab invaders lacked strong organization. The Arab forces—including Palestinians led by the Grand Mufti of Jerusalem (the religious leader of Arab Palestinians), and forces from Egypt, Iraq, Jordan, Lebanon, Saudi Arabia, and Syria—that were mobilized against Israel were not motivated by a common goal or directed by a centralized command. The Jewish forces were. The Jews had developed a highly organized underground army before declaring independence; that army became the country's official army in 1948. Although the Arabs initially had superior weaponry, Israel soon gained access to weapons from the United States and Western European countries and secured the necessary equipment to overcome its deficiencies.

In addition, Israel remained focused on its task of pushing Arabs out, while Arab infighting led to distracting skirmishes between Arab armies during the war.

By 1949 Israel had won the war and even expanded its territory. Much of the land the United Nations had proposed for the independent Arab state in 1947 had become either part of Israel or annexed to Jordan. Palestine had almost no land available after the war. Nearly one-half million Palestinians had fled out of fear or had been forced off land captured by Israel during the war. Some of these Palestinians moved to neighboring Arab countries, but most gathered in refugee camps in hopes of returning to their homes. The inability of the peoples of Israel and Palestine to find lasting peace kept over one million Palestinians languishing in refugee camps by 2005.

Did you know. . .

- The conflict between the newly declared state of Israel and the Arab nations is known as the Arab-Israeli War of 1948 as well as the War of Independence.

- Of Palestine's 1.3 million Arab inhabitants before the Arab-Israeli War, almost half became refugees, living in refugee camps in the West Bank, the Gaza Strip, or in neighboring Arab countries such as Jordan or Lebanon, by war's end.

- In September 1948 the Arab League announced the formation of an All-Palestine Government, but Arab infighting, especially between Egypt and Jordan, destroyed the power of the new government and it languished as a powerless department of the Arab League until 1959.

- Palestinians refer to the Arab-Israeli War of 1948 as al-Nakbah, or the disaster.

- Neither Israel nor the Arab states agreed to negotiate a lasting peace after the Arab-Israeli War of 1948.

Consider the following . . .

- Could the Arab-Israeli War have been avoided if the Arab states had agreed to the Jewish state's existence? What might Palestine have looked like in this case?

- In what other diplomatic ways might the Arab States have reacted to the declaration of Israel's independence? Was war the only recourse left to them?

- Does the Statement Issued by the Governments of the Arab League States on the Occasion of the Entry of the Arab Armies in Palestine on May 15, 1948, provide any insight into the continued difficulties between Arab countries and Israel?

For More Information

Books

Diller, Daniel, ed. *The Middle East.* 8th ed. Washington, DC: Congressional Quarterly, 1995.

Drummond, Dorothy. *Holy Land Whose Land? Modern Dilemma Ancient Roots.* Seattle, WA: Educare Press, 2002.

Khalil, Muhammad, ed. *The Arab States and the Arab League: A Documentary Record, Vol. II International Affairs.* Beirut, Lebanon: Khayats, 1962.

Web Sites

The Question of Palestine & the United Nations. http://www.un.org/Depts/dpi/palestine/ (accessed on June 24, 2005).

3

Conflict in the Middle East after the Six-Day War of 1967

O n May 14, 1948, the state of Israel declared its independence, thus achieving the long-held goal of the world Jewish community for a national homeland. Israel then fought a war for its existence, decisively defeating the combined forces of the Arab nations of Egypt, Iraq, Jordan, Lebanon, and Syria. The end of this war in 1949 did not bring peace to the Middle East, however. It drove approximately 700,000 of the native Arab inhabitants of Israel—known as Palestinians, for their claim to the territory formerly known as Palestine—out of Israel and into neighboring countries, especially Lebanon and Jordan. (In turn, some 600,000 Jews living in Arab nations relocated to Israel.) These Palestinians were deeply angered at what they perceived to be the Jewish theft of their nation. The neighboring Arab nations resented their military defeat. Like the Palestinians, these nations violently objected to the existence of Israel. But they also found the Palestinian refugee populations that lived in their countries to be a constant source of trouble.

For most of the 1950s and early 1960s, Israel and its neighbors managed to live together in relative peace (despite a crisis over the Suez Canal in Egypt in 1956, in which Israeli and

The Results of the Six-Day War

As a result of the Six-Day War, fought between June 5 and June 10, 1967, Israel occupied territories formerly held by its neighbors. From Egypt, Israel seized the Sinai Peninsula and the Gaza Strip; from Syria it took the Golan Heights; and from Jordan it seized a region known as the West Bank. From that time on, these territories have been the source of nearly continual dispute between Israel and those neighbors. Arab governments and the Palestine Liberation Organization (PLO) released official statements demanding the return of these lands, but the Israeli government generally refused to make direct statements about its plans for the land.

Israel did not take a consistent official position primarily because the country was deeply divided over what to do with these territories. Some believed in the idea of a "Greater Israel." They wanted to make these territories a permanent part of Israel. They began to build settlements, or small communities, in these territories, in the hopes that if these settlements became large enough Israel would be unable to give back the land. Others did not want Israel to claim these territories, especially the Gaza Strip and the West Bank, because they contained huge Palestinian populations. If these Palestinians became citizens of Israel, they would be a majority and could affect Israel's politics. These Israelis believed that the territories should be used as bargaining chips that Israel could use to gain permanent peace settlements with its Arab neighbors.

In truth, both visions of how to use the Occupied Territories have continued, reflecting the ongoing divisions within Israel. The Sinai was returned to Egypt in the 1970s as part of the peace process with that nation, and the Gaza Strip and West Bank remain a source of negotiations with Palestinians. But settlements have been created nearly continuously since 1967, and removing Israeli citizens from those settlements has created huge problems for politicians who seek to give back these territories. In Israel, the argument over what to do with these territories continues.

money, recognized that they must become better organized if they were to make any advances in their pursuit of an independent state. To this end, they formed the Palestine Liberation Organization in 1964 and issued a National Charter in 1968. The Israelis faced important decisions about what to do with lands gained in the Six-Day War. In the following documents, groups such as the United Nations, the Arab nations, and the Palestinians react to the events of the Six-Day War and make plans to deal with future conflicts in the region.

United Nations Resolution 242

United Nations Security Council Resolution 242
(November 22, 1967)
Reprinted in *Palestine and the Arab-Israeli Conflict*
Edited by Charles D. Smith
Published in 2001

E ver since its founding in 1945, the United Nations has had a special relationship with Palestine and the problems the country faced. Among its first actions as an organization was the creation of the United Nations Special Committee on Palestine (UNSCOP), which in 1947 recommended the division of Palestine into two independent states, one Jewish and one Arab. On November 29, 1947, the United Nations General Assembly adopted Resolution 181, which set in place a plan to partition, or divide, Palestine into two states. That partition did not take place. Arabs denied that partition was a valid solution to the problem, and Arabs and Jews fought a war to control Palestine. The Jews won, and succeeded in creating the state of Israel and, in May 1949, Israel was admitted as a member of the United Nations.

Over time, the United Nations sought to play a mediating role in the conflict that existed between Israel and its Arab neighbors. It passed Resolution 194 in 1948, which called on Israel to allow Palestinian refugees to return to homes they had abandoned during the war, or to compensate those who did not wish to return. In the 1950s and 1960s the United Nations

"The Security Council, expressing its continuing concern with the grave situation in the Middle East . . . and the need to work for a just and lasting peace in which every state in the area can live in security. . . ."

to the war and for the reasonable treatment of civilians in war zones.

- In the aftermath of the Six-Day War, the political status of the captured territories was unclear. Most of the land was considered classified as occupied territory, meaning it was controlled by the Israeli military forces but not officially part of the state of Israel. Only East Jerusalem was annexed, or claimed as part of the state of Israel.

United Nations Security Council Resolution 242 (November 22, 1967)

The Security Council,

Expressing *its continuing concern with the grave situation in the Middle East,*

Emphasizing *the **inadmissibility** of the acquisition of territory by war and the need to work for a just and lasting peace in which every state in the area can live in security,*

Emphasizing further *that all Member States in their acceptance of the Charter of the United Nations have undertaken a commitment to act in accordance with Article 2 of the Charter,*

1. Affirms *that the fulfillment of Charter principles requires the establishment of a just and lasting peace in the Middle East which should include the application of both the following principles:*

(i) Withdrawal of Israel[i] armed forces from territories occupied in the recent conflict;

*(ii) Termination of all claims or states of **belligerency** and respect for and acknowledgement of the sovereignty, territorial integrity and political independence of every State in the area and their right to live in peace within secure and recognized boundaries free from threats or acts of force.*

2. Affirms further *the necessity*

(a) For guaranteeing freedom of navigation through international waterways in the area;

Inadmissibility: Unacceptable situation.

Belligerency: Being at war.

(b) For achieving a just settlement of the refugee problem;

*(c) For guaranteeing the territorial **inviolability** and political independence of every State in the area, through measures including the establishment of demilitarized zones;*

3. Requests *the Secretary-General to designate a Special Representative to proceed to the Middle East to establish and maintain contact with the States concerned in order to promote agreement and assist efforts to achieve a peaceful and accepted settlement in accordance with the provisions and principles in this resolution;*

4. Requests *the Secretary-General to report to the Security Council on the progress of the efforts of the Special Representative as soon as possible.*

Inviolability: Security from attack.

What happened next ...

United Nations Security Council Resolution 242 did not bring immediate peace to the Middle East. Egypt and Jordan interpreted the resolution as a call for Israel to withdraw to pre-1967 borders before any peace negotiations could take place. Israel interpreted the resolution as calling for Arab states to enter into direct negotiations with Israel. Syria rejected the resolution altogether, according to *The Question of Palestine and the United Nations,* "maintaining that the resolution had linked the central issue of Israeli withdrawal to concessions demanded from Arab countries." And the Palestine Liberation Organization (PLO), the political body of Palestinians, rejected the resolution for simplifying and downgrading the question of Palestine to the single issue of the refugee problem. In short, every country directly impacted by the resolution found fault with parts of it.

In the short term, the Arab-Israeli conflict continued. Arab states refused to recognize or negotiate with Israel until the mid-1970s. Periodic clashes along borders occurred through the late 1960s and early 1970s, and open warfare broke out again in 1973, when Israel was attacked by Egypt

Security Council Resolution 338

On October 22, 1973, as a means of concluding the sixteen-day conflict between Israel and Egypt and Syria known as the Yom Kippur War, the United Nations Security Council issued resolution number 338. Resolution 338's call for a ceasefire was accompanied by the demand that all parties begin peace negotiations aimed at realizing the goals of Security Council Resolution 242. Those negotiations remained an ongoing feature of Middle Eastern politics into the 2000s.

Security Council Resolution 338

The Security Council,

1. Calls upon all parties to the present fighting to cease all firing and terminate all military activity immediately, not later than 12 hours after the moment of the adoption of this decision, in the positions after the moment of the adoption of this decision, in the positions they now occupy;

2. Calls upon all parties concerned to start immediately after the ceasefire the implementation of Security Council Resolution 242 (1967) in all of its parts;

3. Decides that, immediately and concurrently with the ceasefire, negotiations start between the parties concerned under appropriate auspices aimed at establishing a just and durable peace in the Middle East.

and Syria. As in the past, the United Nations brokered a ceasefire, this time with Security Council Resolution 338, and established a second United Nations Emergency Force to resolve land claims resulting from the war. Because neither Israel nor the Arab countries had gained or lost any significant land in the 1973 war, the Emergency Force continued to focus on the territories taken by Israel in the Six-Day War of 1967.

Resolution 242 did have important long-term effects, however. It helped initiate peace talks between Egypt and Israel that led to a peace agreement between those nations in 1979, and it was the basis for a peace agreement with Jordan that was signed in 1994. According to Charles Smith, author of *Palestine and the Arab-Israeli Conflict,* 242 "has remained the official basis of negotiating efforts to the present." Certain phrases from Resolution 242—"the need to work for a just and lasting peace," and "live in peace within secure and recognized boundaries free from threats or acts of force"—have been consistently referred to by all sides in the conflict during peace negotiations in the 1990s and early 2000s. With the election of Mahmoud Abbas (1935–) as president of the Palestinian National Authority in 2005 and the historic talks between Abbas and Israeli prime minister Ariel Sharon (1928–), there is renewed hope that a lasting peace may be secured.

Did you know . . .

- United Nations Security Council resolutions are numbered in the order that they are created. The first resolution was issued on January 25, 1946; Security Council Resolution 1584—concerning the weapons embargo, or prohibition of trade, in the African nation of Cote d'Ivoire in the hopes of stopping their civil war—was issued early in 2005. To find the latest resolution, check the Security Council Web site— http://www.un.org/Docs/sc/.

- The Six-Day War between Israel and its Arab neighbors occurred at a time of world crisis. Not only were the United States and the Soviet Union engaged in the Cold War (the conflict between the United States and the Soviet Union from 1945 to 1991 over the ideological differences between democracy and communism), but the United States had also committed its military to fighting the Vietnam War (1954–75; a war between the forces of North Vietnam supported by China and the Soviet Union and the forces of South Vietnam supported by the United States). Both the United States and the Soviet Union did not want to get drawn into further violent conflicts in the Middle East, so they worked through the United Nations to try to bring about peace.

Consider the following. . .

- Critics sometimes complain that United Nations Security Council resolutions are ineffective in influencing a conflict or a nation's policies. Is this true in relation to Israel? What would motivate the countries involved in this conflict to pay attention to these resolutions?

- Historians sometimes try to understand the past by posing counterhistorical questions—questions that ask what would have happened if conditions were different. For example, what would have happened if the Security Council had not pressured Israel and the Arab states to end the Six-Day War? Or, would peace have come more quickly to the Middle East without the involvement of the United Nations? Explore these questions, or invent counterhistorical questions that explore other aspects of this conflict.

For More Information

Books

Brand, Laurie A. *Palestinians in the Arab World: Institution Building and the Search for State.* New York: Columbia University Press, 1988.

Farsoun, Samih K., with Christina E. Zacharia. *Palestine and the Palestinians.* Boulder, CO: Westview Press, 1997.

Smith, Charles D., ed. *Palestine and the Arab-Israeli Conflict: A History with Documents.* 4th ed. Boston and New York: Bedford/St. Martin's, 2001.

Wagner, Heather Lehr. *Israel and the Arab World.* Philadelphia: Chelsea House, 2002.

Worth, Richard. *Israel and the Arab States.* New York: F. Watts, 1983.

Web Sites

The Question of Palestine & the United Nations. http://www.un.org/Depts/dpi/palestine/ (accessed on June 24, 2005).

United Nations Security Council. http://www.un.org/Docs/sc/ (accessed on June 24, 2005).

The Palestinian National Charter

The Palestinian National Charter: Resolutions of the Palestine National Council (July 1–17, 1968)
Issued by the Palestine Liberation Organization
Reprinted in *Palestine and the Arab-Israeli Conflict*
Edited by Charles D. Smith
Published in 2001

For almost twenty years after the creation of the state of Israel in 1948, most of the world saw the conflict in the Middle East as an Arab-Israeli conflict. This was because the major battles—from the war for Israeli independence in 1948–49 to the Six-Day War of 1967—were between Israel and the Arab nations that surrounded it. During this period, the Palestinian people—Arabs who had lived in the area historically known as Palestine before it was claimed by Israel—played a secondary role in the conflict. Though their rights were always mentioned by the leading Arab nations as part of their justification for fighting against Israel, the Palestinians generally lacked political organizations that could give voice to their hopes and desires to reclaim their country. All that began to change after Israel's surprising defeat of the Arab nations in the Six-Day War, where Israeli forces conquered the West Bank, Golan Heights, and the Sinai Peninsula.

"In the immediate wake of their dispossession and expulsion from Palestine in 1948, the Palestinian refugees were so traumatized and consumed with mere physical survival ... that they were politically paralyzed," wrote Samih K. Farzoun in

> "The Palestinians will have three mottoes: national unity, national mobilization, and liberation."

The Khartoum Arab Summit Resolutions

The Israeli victory in the Six-Day War of 1967 was a setback for the members of the Arab League. Even when the Arab nations combined their forces, and even though they had more soldiers, they could not defeat the armies of Israel on the field of battle. But that did not mean that the Arab League was ready to give up its efforts to restore Arab control over Palestine. At a meeting of the League in Khartoum, Sudan, in August 1967, the Arab nations—except Syria, which boycotted the meeting—signed resolutions asserting Arab unity and military cooperation. The third resolution established Arab policy toward Israel. It read:

The Arab Heads of State have agreed to unite their political efforts at the international and diplomatic level to eliminate the effects of the aggression and to ensure the withdrawal of the aggressive Israeli forces from the Arab lands which have been occupied since the aggression of June 5 [1967]. This will be done within the framework of the main principles by which the Arab States abide, namely, no peace with Israel, no recognition of Israel, no negotiations with it, and insistence on the rights of the Palestinian people in their own country.

This statement quickly became known as the "Three NOs," for the Arabs had declared that they would have no peace with Israel, no recognition of Israel, and no negotiations with Israel. In effect, the Arab nations wanted to deny Israel a right to participate in the regional issues facing the Middle East. Eventually, this policy would fall apart, as first Egypt (1978–79) and then Jordan (1994) signed peace agreements with Israel. Today the Palestinians recognize the right of Israel to exist and Israel recognizes the right of the Palestinians to have their own country, but a final peace had yet to be reached between the two groups by early 2005.

Palestine and the Palestinians. But by the early 1960s Palestinians were beginning to function again as an organized people. In the communities that they formed in the nations of Jordan, Lebanon, and Syria, Palestinians began to come together in women's groups, labor unions, charitable societies, and other organizing groups. One of the most important forms of Palestinian organizing came in student groups, which formed at colleges and universities throughout the Arab world. Soon, a sense began to grow among the Palestinian people that they must work together to regain the land of Palestine which they considered to be lost property.

Since most Palestinians lived in Arab nations, their actions against Israel could cause trouble for the nations they lived in if

Yasser Arafat, the leader of the PLO, explains the goals of Palestinians to the United Nations in the hopes of securing aid for the Palestinian people. *(© Bettmann/Corbis.)*

they were not controlled. Therefore, the leaders of Arab nations wanted to direct the way that Palestinians expressed their political goals. In 1964 the member nations of the League of Arab States created the Palestine Liberation Organization (PLO) to represent the interests of the Palestinians. They allowed for the creation of a legislative body, the Palestine National Council (PNC), and a military branch, the Palestine Liberation Army (PLA). But the Arab states kept close control over the PLO and made sure that it adopted policies that did not threaten the policies of Arab League nations through most of the early 1960s.

Israel's defeat of the Arab nations in 1967 and its capture of the Gaza Strip and West Bank—home to millions of

Palestinians—forced the Arab nations to back off their attempts to win back territory from Israel and create an independent Palestinian state. But it did not kill the Palestinians' desire for independence. Instead, it encouraged the more radical Palestinians to become even stronger and more vocal. Such groups as Fatah, under the leadership of a young man named Yasser Arafat (1929–2004), and the Popular Front for the Liberation of Palestine (PFLP), under the leadership of Dr. George Habash (1926?–), called on the Palestinians to take a new approach to combating Israel. They supported the idea that Palestinians should not rely on Arab nations to win their independence, but that they should join in a peoples' struggle for victory. By 1968 these more radicals groups, especially Fatah, had succeeded in taking control of the PLO, and in July of that year they rewrote the Palestinian National Charter, the document that states the goals of the Palestinian people.

Things to remember while reading the "Palestinian National Charter"

- The Charter refers to the diaspora, which means the scattering of a people by a disastrous event. The Palestinian diaspora began with Israel's declaration of independence in 1948, when Palestinians dispersed to countries throughout the Middle East and beyond.

- The authors of the Charter were deeply influenced by other revolutionary movements of the 1960s, including those in Algeria, Cuba, China, and Vietnam. They believed that the only way to gain back Palestine was through armed struggle, not through negotiation.

- The authors of the Charter did not wish to deny the larger popular movement to unite people in all the Arab states. There are frequent references to Arab unity in the Charter, which is a way of referring to the Pan-Arab movement that had infused Middle Eastern politics since the end of World War II (1939–45; war in which Great Britain, France, the Soviet Union, the United States, and their allies defeated Germany, Italy, and Japan).

- Zionism—referenced throughout the Charter—was a movement, begun in the nineteenth century, to create a

Jewish homeland in Palestine. Once Israel was established as that homeland, Zionism changed to a movement in support of maintaining (and sometimes expanding) that Jewish homeland.

The Palestinian National Charter: Resolutions of the Palestine National Council (July 1–17, 1968)

Article 1:

Palestine is the homeland of the Arab Palestinian people; it is an indivisible part of the Arab homeland, and the Palestinian people are an integral part of the Arab nation.

Article 2:

*Palestine, with the boundaries it had during the **British mandate**, is an indivisible territorial unit.*

Article 3:

*The Arab Palestinian people possess the legal right to their homeland and have the right to determine their destiny after achieving the **liberation** of their country in accordance with their wishes and entirely of their own accord and will.*

Article 4:

*The Palestinian identity is a genuine, essential, and inherent characteristic; it is transmitted from parents to children. The **Zionist** occupation and the dispersal of the Arab Palestinian people, through the disasters which befell them, do not make them lose their Palestinian identity and their membership in the Palestinian community, nor do they negate them.*

Article 5:

The Palestinians are those Arab nationals who, until 1947, normally resided in Palestine regardless of whether they were evicted from it or have stayed there. Anyone born, after that date, of a Palestinian father—whether inside Palestine or outside it—is also a Palestinian.

British mandate: Form of rule over a conquered territory, granted by the League of Nations following World War I, that gave Great Britain control over Palestine (1920–47).

Liberation: Freedom from control.

Zionist: Any person working to create an independent Jewish State.

Article 6:

The Jews who had normally resided in Palestine until the beginning of the Zionist invasion will be considered Palestinians.

Article 7:

There is a Palestinian community and that it has material, spiritual, and historical connection with Palestine are indisputable facts. It is a national duty to bring up individual Palestinians in an Arab revolutionary manner. All means of information and education must be adopted in order to acquaint the Palestinian with his country in the most profound manner, both spiritual and material, that is possible. He must be prepared for the armed struggle and ready to sacrifice his wealth and his life in order to win back his homeland and bring about its liberation.

Article 8:

*The phase in their history, through which the Palestinian people are now living, is that of national struggle for the liberation of Palestine. Thus the conflicts among the Palestinian national forces are secondary, and should be ended for the sake of the basic conflict that exists between the forces of Zionism and of **imperialism** on the one hand, and the Arab Palestinian people on the other. On this basis the Palestinian masses, regardless of whether they are residing in the national homeland or in **diaspora** constitute—both their organizations and the individuals—one national front working for the retrieval of Palestine and its liberation through armed struggle.*

Article 9:

*Armed struggle is the only way to liberate Palestine. Thus it is the overall strategy, not merely a tactical phase. The Arab Palestinian people assert their absolute determination and firm resolution to continue their armed struggle and to work for an armed popular revolution for the liberation of their country and their return to it. They also assert their right to normal life in Palestine and to exercise their right to **self-determination** and sovereignty over it.*

Article 10:

***Commando action** constitutes the nucleus of the Palestinian popular liberation war. This requires its escalation, comprehensiveness, and the mobilization of all the Palestinian popular and educational efforts and their organization and involvement in the armed Palestinian revolution. It also requires the*

Imperialism: The practice of expanding power by taking control of other nations or creating colonies.

Diaspora: The scattering of a people by a disastrous event.

Self-determination: Determine their own political status.

Commando action: Military action characterized by surprise and sudden strikes.

achieving of unity for the national struggle among the different groupings of the Palestinian people, and between the Palestinian people and the Arab masses, so as to secure the continuation of the revolution, its escalation, and victory.

Article 11:

The Palestinians will have three mottoes: national unity, national mobilization, and liberation.

Article 12:

The Palestinian people believe in Arab unity. In order to contribute their share toward the attainment of that objective, however, they must, at the present stage of their struggle, safeguard their Palestinian identity and develop their consciousness of that identity, and oppose any plan that may dissolve or impair it.

Article 13:

Arab unity and the liberation of Palestine are two complementary goals, the attainment of either of which facilitates the attainment of the other. Thus, Arab unity leads to the liberation of Palestine, the liberation of Palestine leads to Arab unity; and work toward the realization of one objective proceeds side by side with work toward the realization of the other.

Article 14:

*The destiny of the Arab nation, and indeed Arab existence itself, depend upon the destiny of the Palestine cause. From this interdependence springs the Arab nation's pursuit of, and striving for, the liberation of Palestine. The people of Palestine play the role of the **vanguard** in the realization of this sacred national goal.*

Article 15:

*The liberation of Palestine, from an Arab viewpoint, is a national duty and it attempts to repel the Zionist and **imperialist** aggression against the Arab homeland, and aims at the elimination of Zionism in Palestine. Absolute responsibility for this falls upon the Arab nation— peoples and governments—with the Arab people of Palestine in the vanguard. Accordingly, the Arab nation must mobilize all its military, human, moral, and spiritual capabilities to participate actively with the Palestinian people in the liberation of Palestine. It must, particularly in the phase of the armed Palestinian revolution, offer and furnish the Palestinian people with all possible help, and*

Vanguard: Leading position.

Imperialist: Group that believes in increasing a nation's authority by taking over territory or by dominating another nation's politics and economy.

material and human support, and make available to them the means and opportunities that will enable them to continue to carry out their leading role in the armed revolution, until they liberate their homeland.

Article 16:

The liberation of Palestine, from a spiritual point of view, will provide the Holy Land with an atmosphere of safety and tranquility, which in turn will safeguard the country's religious sanctuaries and guarantee freedom of worship and of visit to all, without discrimination of race, color, language, or religion. Accordingly, the people of Palestine look to all spiritual forces in the world for support.

Article 17:

The liberation of Palestine, from a human point of view, will restore to the Palestinian individual his dignity, pride, and freedom. Accordingly the Arab Palestinian people look forward to the support of all those who believe in the dignity of man and his freedom in the world.

Article 18:

The liberation of Palestine, from an international point of view, is a defensive action necessitated by the demands of self-defense. Accordingly the Palestinian people, desirous as they are of the friendship of all people, look to freedom-loving, and peace-loving states for support in order to restore their legitimate rights in Palestine, to re-establish peace and security in the country, and to enable its people to exercise national sovereignty and freedom.

Article 19:

The partition of Palestine in 1947 and the establishment of the state of Israel are entirely illegal, regardless of the passage of time, because they were contrary to the will of the Palestinian people and to their natural right in their homeland, and inconsistent with the principles embodied in the Charter of the United Nations; particularly the right to self-determination.

Article 20:

*The Balfour Declaration, the mandate for Palestine, and everything that has been based upon them, are deemed null and void. Claims of historical or religious ties of Jews with Palestine are incompatible with the facts of history and the true conception of what constitutes statehood. **Judaism**, being a religion, is not an independent*

Judaism: The religion of the Jewish people.

nationality. Nor do Jews constitute a single nation with an identity of its own; they are citizens of the states to which they belong.

Article 21:

The Arab Palestinian people, expressing themselves by the armed Palestinian revolution, reject all solutions which are substitutes for the total liberation of Palestine and reject all proposals aiming at the liquidation of the Palestinian problem, or its internationalization.

Article 22:

*Zionism is a political movement organically associated with international imperialism and **antagonistic** to all action for liberation and to progressive movements in the world. It is racist and fanatic in its nature, aggressive, expansionist, and colonial in its aims, and **fascist** in its methods. Israel is the instrument of the Zionist movement, and a geographical base for world imperialism placed strategically in the midst of the Arab homeland to combat the hopes of the Arab nation for liberation, unity, and progress. Israel is a constant source of threat **vis-á-vis** peace in the Middle East and the whole world. Since the liberation of Palestine will destroy the Zionist and imperialist presence and will contribute to the establishment of peace in the Middle East, the Palestinian people look for the support of all the progressive and peaceful forces and urge them all, irrespective of their affiliations and beliefs, to offer the Palestinian people all aid and support in their just struggle for the liberation of their homeland.*

Article 23:

*The demand of security and peace, as well as the demand of right and justice, require all states to consider Zionism an **illegitimate** movement, to outlaw its existence, and to ban its operations, in order that friendly relations among peoples may be preserved, and the loyalty of citizens to their respective homelands safeguarded.*

Article 24:

The Palestinian people believe in the principles of justice, freedom, sovereignty, self-determination, human dignity, and in the right of all peoples to exercise them.

Article 25:

For the realization of the goals of this Charter and its principles, the Palestine Liberation Organization will perform its role in the liberation of Palestine in accordance with the Constitution of this Organization.

Antagonistic: Opposed.

Fascist: Group that believes in a system of government ruled by a single leader who controls all economic and political issues and suppresses all opposition.

Vis-á-vis: Opposed to.

Illegitimate: Illogical or illegal.

Article 26:

The Palestine Liberation Organization, representative of the Palestinian revolutionary forces, is responsible for the Arab Palestinian peoples' movement in its struggle—to retrieve its homeland, liberate and return to it and exercise the right to self-determination in it—in all military, political, and financial fields and also for whatever may be required by the Palestine case on the inter-Arab and international levels.

Article 27:

The Palestine Liberation Organization shall cooperate with all Arab states, each according to its potentialities; and will adopt a neutral policy among them in the light of the requirements of the battle of liberation; and on this basis does not interfere in the internal affairs of any Arab state.

Article 28:

The Arab Palestinian people assert the genuineness and independence of their national revolution and reject all forms of intervention, trusteeship, and subordination.

Article 29:

The Palestinian people possess the fundamental and genuine legal right to liberate and retrieve their homeland. The Palestinian people determine their attitude toward all states and forces on the basis of the stands they adopt vis-á-vis to the Palestinian revolution to fulfill the aims of the Palestinian people.

Article 30:

Fighters and carriers of arms in the war of liberation are the nucleus of the popular army which will be the protective force for the gains of the Arab Palestinian people.

Article 31:

The Organization shall have a flag, an oath of allegiance, and an anthem. All this shall be decided upon in accordance with a special regulation.

Article 32:

*A law, known as the Basic Statute of the Palestine Liberation Organization, shall be **annexed** to this Covenant. It will lay down the manner in which the Organization, and its organs and institutions, shall be constituted; the respective competence of each; and the requirements of its obligation under the Charter.*

Annexed: Added or attached.

Article 33:

This Charter shall not be amended save by [vote of] a majority of two-thirds of the total membership of the National Congress of the Palestine Liberation Organization [taken] at a special session convened for that purpose.

What happened next . . .

The emergence in 1968 of the Palestine Liberation Organization as an aggressive and vocal representative of the Palestinian people forever changed the politics of the Middle East. No longer did Palestinians have to look to Arab nations to protect their interests; in the PLO they created an organization dedicated to reclaiming Palestine for Palestinians. The PLO was officially recognized by the Arab League in 1974. Shortly thereafter it was recognized by the United Nations and, eventually, by more than one hundred countries around the world.

The goals the Palestinians set for themselves in the 1968 charter have been difficult to achieve, however, for a variety of reasons. By setting themselves up as a movement committed to waging armed struggle against Israel, the PLO became a problem for any Arab nation that hosted the PLO. Jordan forcibly evicted the PLO in 1970 because the group was the source of many political and social problems between Jordanians who supported the PLOs violent attacks against Israel and others who did not. The PLO moved to Lebanon, where its frequent attacks on Israel from Lebanon drove that country into civil war and eventually led to the PLO leadership being exiled to Tunisia in 1982. The PLO's encouragement of violence against Israel led to it being branded as a terrorist organization by the United States for many years, until its reform in the 1990s during which the PLO and Israel sought peaceful ways to end the long-standing conflict.

Over time, the PLO has had to drop some of its most radical positions. It no longer calls for the utter destruction of Israel, for example, nor does it anticipate that an independent Palestine will exist within the borders that existed during the years of British control (1920–47). In fact, in the late 1990s and early 2000s, the political activities of the Palestinians are increasingly being represented by the Palestinian National Authority, which edges ever closer to negotiations that would create a small but independent Palestine in the West Bank and the Gaza Strip.

Did you know . . .

- Though the end of the Six-Day War of 1967 brought a decrease in battles between Israel and the Arab nations, conflicts with Palestinians in Jordan increased dramatically, from 97 incidents in 1967 to 916 incidents in 1968, 2,432 in 1969, and 1,887 in 1970.

- Many of the elements of the Palestinian National Charter, such as those calling for the destruction of Israel, were abandoned in 1993 during peace talks that led to the signing of the Oslo Accords (also known as the Declaration of Principles), an agreement between Israel and the PLO to accept the rights of both Israelis and Palestinians to exist and to create an independent Palestinian country in the West Bank territory that Israel had taken over during the Six-Day War in 1967. However, a new text of the charter has never been prepared.

Consider the following . . .

- Compare and contrast the Palestinian National Charter with the Declaration of Independence of the State of Israel. What are the essential facts about which they disagree? How do these documents depict the claims made by the other? Is there a basis for common ground to be found in these two documents?

- In 1974 PLO leader Yasser Arafat appeared before the United Nations and said: "Today I have come bearing an olive branch and a freedom-fighter's gun." In what ways does the Palestinian National Charter offer both the olive branch of peace and the prospect of further war?

- The Palestinian National Charter is a very aggressive and strongly worded document. Was this confrontational stance an effective way to organize opposition to Israeli rule? Was there a different path for the Palestinians to take in trying to reach their goals?

For More Information

Books

Carew-Miller, Anna. *The Palestinians*. Philadelphia: Mason Crest, 2004.

Farsoun, Samih K., with Christina E. Zacharia. *Palestine and the Palestinians*. Boulder, CO: Westview Press, 1997.

Sharp, Anne Wallace. *The Palestinians*. Detroit: Lucent Books, 2005.

Web Sites

Permanent Observer Mission of Palestine to the United Nations. http://www.palestine-un.org/ (accessed on June 24, 2005).

The Question of Palestine & the United Nations. http://www.un.org/Depts/dpi/palestine/ (accessed on June 24, 2005).

4

The Road to Peace

E ver since Israel declared its independence from Palestine in 1948, and furthered by its capture of large amounts of land once ruled by Arab states in the Six-Day War of 1967, peace has been difficult to achieve in the Middle East. Israel has insisted on its right to pursue the Zionist mission of creating a national homeland for Jews in Palestine. Arab states such as Egypt, Jordan, Lebanon, and Syria have all denied the right of Israel to exist and engaged in armed conflict against Israel. Palestinians—Arabs who claim ties to the former territory of Palestine—have consistently claimed that they were wrongfully evicted from their land and have tried to reclaim their territory. With this history of conflict and disagreement, learning to live in peace with each other has been difficult for Israelis and Arabs.

The larger disagreements between Israelis and Arabs, and the more particular disputes between Israel and individual Arab countries or peoples, are complicated and often hard to resolve. They involve control of disputed territory, the rights of people driven from their land by armed conflict, and complex matters of religion and ethnicity. In the documents contained in this section, a variety of resolutions are presented by Middle Eastern leaders and activist groups in the hopes of creating permanent peace. One example is Egyptian president Anwar Sadat's (1918–1981) historic address to the Israeli Knesset, or legislature, as well as the response given by Israeli prime minister Menachem Begin (1913–1992). Also examined is a communiqué, or bulletin, issued by Palestinians rising up against Israeli occupation, as well as the historic Israeli-PLO Declaration of Principles, in which Israel and the Palestine Liberation Organization recognize each other and open negotiations. Finally, excerpts from the Disengagement Plan offered by Israel in 2004 to kick-start a peace process that had once again been delayed will be presented.

This selection of documents is a tiny sampling of the various steps toward peace in the Middle East. Each document selected for inclusion in this chapter offers insight into the complexities of negotiating a lasting peace in the Middle East. Peace has not yet been achieved; however, both Israelis and Arabic people continue to work toward and remain committed to pursuing a solution that works.

Speeches to the Knesset

Excerpt from Anwar Sadat's Speech to the Israeli Knesset
(November 20, 1977)
Reprinted in *Palestine and the Arab-Israeli Conflict*
Edited by Charles D. Smith
Published in 2001

Excerpt from Menachem Begin's Reply to President Sadat
(November 20, 1977)
Reprinted in *Palestine and the Arab-Israeli Conflict*
Edited by Charles D. Smith
Published in 2001

Relations between Israel and its Arab neighbors were strained after the Six-Day War of 1967. At the end of the war, Israel controlled huge tracts of land once ruled by Arabs, including the Sinai Peninsula from Egypt, the Golan Heights from Syria, and the West Bank from Jordan. As the emerging dominant power after the war, Israel dictated new areas of negotiation between Israel and Arab nations. In addition to the location of Israel's permanent borders and the question of how to deal with Palestinian refugees (those who fled their homes in response to fighting), negotiations would now include whether or not captured Arab lands would be returned. In response, the Arab states held a summit in Khartoum, Egypt, in 1967, and officially declared that Arab states would condone "no peace with Israel, no recognition of Israel, no negotiations with it, and insistence on the rights of the Palestinian people in their own country."

"What is peace to Israel? To live in the region, together with her Arab neighbors, in security and safety—this is a logic to which I say: 'Yes.'"

These circumstances influenced the next decade of Arab-Israeli relations. Egypt launched a War of Attrition against Israel in 1969, and gained valuable aid from the Soviet Union. Although the United States negotiated a ceasefire in 1970, the negotiations were difficult and incomplete. When Anwar Sadat (1918–1981) became the president of Egypt in 1970, he was eager to finalize a peace agreement with Israel, and he agreed to a solution proposed by United Nations' ambassador Gunnar Jarring (1907–2002) in 1971. But Israel rejected it, not wanting to give up the land it had taken during the Six-Day War, and tensions continued.

Sadat soon became convinced that diplomacy would not help Egypt regain the Sinai region, nor other Arab nations their lost land. On October 6, 1973, Sadat, with the cooperation of Syria, launched the Yom Kippur War. Despite early Arab victories, the war ended in late October 1973 with neither side having achieved definite success. Because the Israelis and Arabs were unwilling to negotiate directly with each other, U.S. secretary of state Henry Kissinger (1923–) became instrumental in negotiating a plan to stop the fighting between Israel and the Arab states by traveling back and forth between Israel and various Arab capitals. By 1975 he had successfully concluded a plan for Egypt to gain some land, but the question of what to do with the Palestinian refugees became a roadblock (Palestinians wanted to be reimbursed for or return to their land, while Israelis believed the land belonged to them now).

Frustrated with the stalemate and wanting peace to progress, Sadat announced on November 9, 1977, to the surprise of most of the world, that he would be willing to travel to Israel to pursue peace. At the time, Israel's prime minister was Menachem Begin (1913–1992), a man who had rejected the idea that Israel should return any land to the Arabs, and who refused to acknowledge the Palestine Liberation Organization. Although hostile toward Arabs, Begin accepted Sadat's proposal and invited him to visit a session of the Knesset, Israel's legislative body. The following are excerpts from the speeches Sadat and Begin gave to the Israeli Knesset on November 20, 1977.

Things to remember while reading Anwar Sadat's "Speech to the Israeli Knesset" and Menachem Begin's "Reply to President Sadat":

- Before Sadat proposed his willingness to visit Israel for peace, few would have expected Begin to be a man who would offer compromises for peace. Begin was known as one of Israel's most aggressive and stubborn leaders. Look for evidence that points to his unwillingness to make agreements that would compromise Israel's safety.

- Notice the difference between Sadat and Begin's comments about the Palestinians.

- Sadat's trip to Israel cost him diplomatic ties with other Arab states. While reading the speech, look for the reasons why he felt his trip was worth the price he would pay.

Excerpt from Anwar Sadat's Speech to the Israeli Knesset (November 20, 1977)

In the Name of God, Mr. Speaker of the Knesset, ladies and gentlemen....

God's peace and mercy be with you. God willing, peace for us all. Peace for us in the Arab land and in Israel and in every part of the land of this wide world, this world which is made complex by its bloody conflicts and which is made tense by its sharp contradictions and which is threatened every now and then by destructive wars—wars made by man to kill his brother man and, in the end, amid the debris and mutilated bodies of men, there is neither victor nor ***vanquished*** *....*

All of us in this land, the land of God, Moslems, Christians and Jews, worship God and no other god. God's decrees and commandments are: love, honesty, chastity and peace ....

Ladies and gentlemen: There are moments in the life of nations and peoples when those who are known for their wisdom and foresight are

Vanquished: Defeated.

Egyptian president Anwar Sadat addresses the Israeli Knesset on peace between Egypt and Israel. (© William Karel/Sygma/Corbis.)

required to look beyond the past, with all its complications and remnants, for the sake of a courageous **upsurge** towards new horizons . . . .

We must rise above all forms of **fanaticism** and self-deception and obsolete theories of superiority. It is important that we should never forget that virtue is God's alone. If I say that I want to protect the Arab people from the terrors of new, terrifying wars, I declare before you with all sincerity that I have the same feelings and I carry the same responsibility for every human being in the world and, most certainly, for the Israeli people.

A life which is taken away in war is the life of a human being, whether it is an Arab or an Israeli life. The wife who becomes a widow is a human being and has the right to live in a happy family environment whether she is an Arab or an Israeli. The innocent children who lose the care and love

Upsurge: Rapid rise.

Fanaticism: Excessive devotion to a cause.

of their parents are all our children; they are all our children, whether in the land of the Arabs or in Israel; we have a great responsibility to provide them with a prosperous present and a better future . . . .

Ladies and gentlemen, let us be frank with each other, using straightforward words and clear thoughts which cannot be twisted . . . . How can we achieve a just and lasting peace? . . .

Firstly, I did not come to you with a view to concluding a separate agreement between Egypt and Israel, this is not provided for in Egypt's policy. The problem does not lie just between Egypt and Israel; moreover, no separate peace between Egypt and Israel—or between any **confrontation state** and Israel—could secure a lasting and just peace in the region as a whole. Even if a peace agreement was achieved between all the confrontation states and Israel, without a just solution to the Palestinian problem it would never ensure the establishment of the durable, lasting peace the entire world is now trying to achieve . . . .

I have come to you so that together we can build a lasting and just peace, so that not one more drop of the blood of either side may be shed . . . .

This in itself forms a giant turning-point, a decisive landmark of an historic transformation. We used to reject you, and we had our reasons and **grievances**. Yes, we used to reject meeting you anywhere. Yes, we used to describe you as "so-called Israel." Yes, conferences and international organizations used to bring us together. Our representatives have never and still do not exchange greetings and **salaams**. Yes, this is what happened, and it still goes on . . . . But I say to you today and I say to the whole world that we accept that we should live with you in a lasting and just peace. We do not want to surround you or to be surrounded ourselves with missiles which are ready to destroy, with the missiles of hatred and bitterness.

More than once, I have said that Israel has become a living reality. The world recognized it and the **two superpowers** shouldered the responsibility of its security and the defense of its existence. And when we want peace both in theory and in practice we welcome you to live amongst us in security and peace, in theory and practice . . . .

Ladies and gentlemen, the truth is—and it is the truth that I am telling you—that there can be no peace in the true sense of the word, unless this peace is based on justice and not on the occupation of the territory of others. It is not right that you seek for yourselves what you deny to others. In all frankness and in the spirit which prompted me to come to you, I say to you: You have finally to abandon the dreams of

Confrontation state: Country at war with Israel.

Grievances: Valid complaints.

Salaams: Arabic greetings.

Two superpowers: The United States and the Soviet Union.

tomorrow and you have also to abandon the belief that force is the best means of dealing with the Arabs. You have to absorb very well the lessons of confrontation between ourselves and you; expansion will be of no avail to you . . . .

To put it clearly, our territory is not a subject of bargaining; it is not a topic for wrangling . . . .

What is peace to Israel? To live in the region, together with her Arab neighbours, in security and safety—this is a logic to which I say: "Yes." For Israel to live within her borders secure from any aggression—this is a logic to which I say: "Yes." For Israel to get all kinds of assurances that ensure for her these two facts—this is a demand to which I say "YES." . . .

But how can this be achieved? How can we arrive at this result so that it can take us to a permanent and just peace? There are facts that must be confronted with all courage and clarity. There is Arab land which Israel has occupied and still occupies by armed force. And we insist that complete withdrawal from this land be undertaken and this includes Arab Jerusalem, Jerusalem to which I have come, as it is considered the city of peace and which has been and will always be the living embodiment of coexistence between believers of the **three religions**. *It is inadmissible for anyone to think of Jerusalem's special position within the context of* **annexation** *and expansion. It must be made a free city, open to all the faithful. What is more important is that the city must not be closed to those who have chosen it as a place of residence for several centuries . . . .*

Let me tell you without hesitation that I have not come to you, under this dome, to beg you to withdraw your forces from the occupied territory. This is because complete withdrawal from the Arab territories occupied after 1967 is a matter that goes without saying, over which we accept no controversy and in respect of which there is no begging to anyone or from anyone. There will be no meaning to talk about a lasting, just peace and there will be no meaning to any step to guarantee our lives together in this part of the world in peace and security while you occupy an Arab land by armed forces. There can never be peace established or built with the occupation of others' land . . . .

As regards the Palestine question, nobody denies that it is the essence of the entire problem. Nobody throughout the entire world accepts today slogans raised here in Israel which disregard the existence of the people of Palestine and even ask where the people of Palestine are. The problem of the Palestinian people, and the legitimate rights of the Palestinian people are now no longer ignored or rejected by anybody; no thinking mind supposes that they could be ignored or

Three religions: Islam, Judaism, and Christianity, all of which claim holy sites within the city of Jerusalem.

Annexation: Adding or attaching.

rejected; they are facts that meet with the support and recognition of the international community both in the West and the East and in international documents and official declarations . . . .

Even the USA—your first ally, which is the most committed to the protection of the existence and security of Israel . . . has opted for facing up to the reality and to facts, to recognize that the Palestinian people have legitimate rights, and that the Palestine question is the **crux** and essence of the conflict . . . .

In all sincerity, I tell you that peace cannot be achieved without the Palestinians, and that it would be a great mistake, the effect of which no one knows, to turn a blind eye to this question or to set it aside . . . .

When the bells of peace ring, there will be no hand to beat the drums of war; should such a hand exist, it will not be heard. Imagine with me the peace agreement in Geneva, the good news of which we herald to a world thirsty for peace: (Firstly) a peace agreement based on ending the Israeli occupation of the Arab territory occupied in 1967; (secondly) the realization of basic rights of the Palestinian people and this people's right to self-determination, including their right to setting up their own state; thirdly, the right of all the countries of the region to live in peace within their secure and guaranteed borders, through agreed measures for the appropriate security of international borders, in addition to the appropriate international guarantees; fourthly, all the States in the region will undertake to administer relations among themselves in accordance with the principles and aims of the UN Charter, in particular **eschewing** the use of force and settling differences among them by peaceful means; and fifthly, ending the state of war that exists in the region . . . .

The experiences of past and contemporary history teach us all that missiles, warships and nuclear weapons, perhaps, cannot establish security. On the contrary, they destroy all that was built by security. For the sake of our peoples, for the sake of a civilization made by man, we must protect man in every place from the rule of the force of arms. We must raise high the rule of humanity with the full force of principles and values which hold man high . . . .

Excerpt from Menachem Begin's Reply to President Sadat (November 20, 1977)

Mr. Speaker, Mr. President of the State of Israel, Mr. President of the Arab Republic of Egypt, Ladies and Gentlemen, members of the **Knesset**, we send our greetings to the President and to all the people of the Islamic

Crux: Basic or essential point.

Eschewing: Avoiding.

Knesset: Legislative body of the Israeli government.

*religion in our country, and wherever they may be, on the occasion of the Feast, the Festival of the Sacrifice, Id al-Adha. This feast reminds us of the binding of **Isaac**. This was the way in which the Creator of the World tested our forefather, Abraham—our common forefather—to test his faith, and Abraham passed this test.... Thus we contributed, the people of Israel and the Arab people, to the progress of mankind, and thus we are continuing to contribute to human civilization to this day.*

I greet and welcome the President of Egypt for coming to our country and on his participating in the Knesset session. The flight time between Cairo and Jerusalem is short, but the distance between Cairo and Jerusalem was until last night almost endless. President Sadat crossed the distance courageously. We, the Jews, know how to appreciate such courage, and we know how to appreciate it in our guest, because it is with courage that we are here and this is how we continue to exist, and we shall continue to exist.

*Mr. Speaker, this small nation, the remaining refuge of the Jewish People which returned to its historic homeland—has always wanted peace and, since the dawn of our independence, on 14 May 1948..., in the Declaration of Independence in the founding scroll of our national freedom, **David Ben-Gurion** said: We extend a hand of peace and good-neighbourliness to all neighbouring countries and their peoples. We call upon them to cooperate, to help each other, with the Hebrew people independent in its own country. One year earlier, even from the underground, when we were in the midst of the fateful struggle for the liberation of the country and the redemption of the people, we called on our neighbours in these terms: In this country we shall live together and we shall advance together and we shall live a life of freedom and happiness. Our Arab neighbours: Do not reject the hand stretched out to you in peace.*

*But it is my **bounden** duty, Mr. Speaker, and not only my right, not to pass over the truth, that our hand outstretched for peace was not grasped and, one day after we had renewed our independence—as was our right, eternal right, which cannot be disputed—we were attacked on three fronts and we stood almost without arms, the few against many, the weak against the strong, while an attempt was made, one day after the Declaration of Independence, to strangle it at birth, to put an end to the last hope of the Jewish People, the yearning renewed after the years of destruction and **holocaust**.*

No, we do not believe in might and we have never based our attitude to the Arab people on might; quite the contrary, force was used against us. Over all the years of this generation we have never stopped being attacked by might, the might of the strong arm stretched

Isaac: The son of Abraham, one of the founders of Judaism, whom God asked Abraham to sacrifce.

David Ben-Gurion: First prime minister of Israel (1886–1973; served 1948–53 and 1955–63).

Bounden: Required.

Holocaust: Great destruction resulting in the deaths of many people; a direct reference to the slaughter of millions of European civilians, especially Jews, by the Nazis during World War II.

Menachem Begin, prime minister of Israel, surprised many people when he accepted Anwar Sadat's proposal for peace talks. *(© Bettmann/Corbis.)*

out to exterminate our people, to destroy our independence, to deny our rights. We defended ourselves, it is true.... With the help of Almighty God, we overcame the forces of aggression, and we have guaranteed the existence of our nation, not only for this generation, but for the coming generations too. We do not believe in might; we believe in right, only in right and therefore our aspiration, from the depth of our hearts, has always been, to this very day, for peace....

Therefore, permit me, today, to set out the peace programme as we understand it. We want full, real peace, with absolute reconciliation between the Jewish and the Arab peoples....

The first clause of a peace treaty is **cessation** of the state of war, for ever. We want to establish normal relations between us, as they exist between all nations, even after wars....

Let us sign a peace treaty and let us establish this situation forever, both in Jerusalem and in Cairo....

Cessation: Stopping.

Mr. Speaker, it is my duty today to tell our guest and all the peoples watching us and listening to our words about the link between our people and this land. The President [of Egypt] recalled the **Balfour Declaration**. *No, sir, we did not take over any strange land; we returned to our homeland. The link between our people and this land is eternal. It arose in the earliest days of humanity and was never altered. In this country we developed our civilization . . . . And when we were expelled from our land, when force was used against us, no matter how far we went from our land, we never forgot it for even one day. We prayed for it; we longed for it; we have believed in our return to it . . . .*

This, our right, was recognized. The Balfour Declaration was included in the **mandate** *laid down by the nations of the world, including the United States of America, and the preface to this recognized international document says: Whereas recognition has the bible given to the historical connection of the Jewish people with Palestine and to the grounds for reconstituting their national home in that country, the historic connection between the Jewish people and Palestine or, in Hebrew Eretz Yisra'el, was given reconfirmation—reconfirmation—as the national homeland in that country, that is in Eretz Yisra'el . . . .*

President Sadat knows and he knew from us before he came to Jerusalem that we have a different position from his with regard to the permanent borders between us and our neighbours. However, I say to the President of Egypt and to all our neighbours: Do not say there is not, there will not be negotiations about any particular issue. I propose, with the agreement of the decisive majority of this parliament, that everything will be open to negotiation. Anyone who says, with reference to relations between the Arab people, or the Arab peoples around us, and the State of Israel, that there are things which should be omitted from negotiations is taking upon himself a grave responsibility, everything can be negotiated. No side will say the contrary. No side will present prior conditions. We will conduct the negotiations honourably. If there are differences of opinion between us, this is not unusual. Anyone who has studied the history of wars and the signing of peace treaties knows that all negotiations over a peace treaty began with differences of opinion between the sides. And in the course of the negotiations they came to an agreement which permitted the signing of peace treaties and agreements. And this is the road we propose to take.

Balfour Declaration: A 1917 declaration by Britain which supported the creation of a Jewish homeland in Palestine.

Mandate: Form of rule over a conquered territory, granted by the League of Nations following World War I (1914–18), that gave Great Britain and France control over much of the Middle East.

What happened next ...

After unsuccessful attempts to conduct peace negotiations, Anwar Sadat and Menachem Begin met with U.S. president Jimmy Carter (1924–; served 1977–81) at Camp David, the presidential retreat in Maryland, from September 5 to September 17, 1978. The meeting concluded with the signing of two agreements, known as the Camp David Accords, at the White House. The first agreement outlined a compromise over the Sinai Peninsula, which had been captured from Egypt by Israel in the Six-Day War of 1967. The second established a framework in which negotiations about the future of the West Bank and the Gaza Strip would be conducted. The Camp David Accords generated further negotiations which culminated in the Israel-Egypt peace treaty, which was signed in Washington on March 26, 1979.

Did you know ...

- Although Anwar Sadat had noted that the Palestinians were central to peace in the Middle East, the Israel-Egypt peace treaty signed in 1979 did not include a plan for lasting peace with the Palestinians.

- The Arab League, a group of Arab Nations that worked together to keep Arab power strong in the Middle East, expelled Egypt from its membership and issued political and economic sanctions against Egypt as punishment for signing the peace agreement with Israel. Arab League members, except for Oman and Sudan, refused to conduct diplomatic relations with Egypt after it signed the peace agreement.

- The Israeli-Egyptian peace agreement did not include guarantees for the Arab Palestinian refugees. After Egypt signed the agreement the PLO broke off relations with it.

- Anwar Sadat was assassinated in 1981 by activists opposed to Egypt's peace with Israel.

Consider the following ...

- Why might a peace agreement with Israel be more important to Egypt than maintaining its place as a leader among Arab nations?

- Sadat and Begin had very different opinions about how to achieve lasting peace in the Middle East. What is the biggest difference of opinion between the two speeches?

- In the two speeches are there clues that predict why a solution regarding the Arab Palestinians was ultimately left out of the final peace agreement?

For More Information

Books

Amdur, Richard. *Menachem Begin,* New York: Chelsea House, 1988.

Brackett, Virginia. *Menachem Begin,* Philadelphia: Chelsea House, 2003.

Israeli, Raphael, with Carol Bardenstein. *Man of Defiance: A Political Biography of Anwar Sadat.* Totowa, NJ: Barnes and Noble Books, 1985.

Kras, Sara Louise. *Anwar Sadat.* Philadelphia: Chelsea House, 2003.

Smith, Charles D., ed. *Palestine and the Arab-Israeli Conflict: A History with Documents.* 4th ed. Boston and New York: Bedford/St. Martin's, 2001.

Web Sites

"Guide to the Middle East Peace Process." *Israeli Ministry of Foreign Affairs.* http://www.mfa.gov.il/mfa/peace%20process/guide%20to%20the%20peace%20process/ (accessed on June 24, 2005).

Comminiqué No. 1
of the Intifada

Excerpt from Comminiqué No. 1 of the Intifada (January 8, 1988)
Issued by Unified National Leadership (UNL)
Reprinted in *Palestine and the Arab-Israeli Conflict*
Edited by Charles D. Smith
Published in 2001

The West Bank and the Gaza Strip were captured by Israel during the Six-Day War in 1967 and then occupied by Israeli military forces. These Occupied Territories, as they came to be known, were already home to hundreds of thousands of Palestinians, and many more Palestinians moved there to live in refugee camps as a result of the war.

After taking over the territories, the Israeli government maintained strict control over the Palestinians living there. Israel determined who had access to land, water, and electricity. It set curfews, monitored movement within and between the territories, and severely punished any anti-Israeli activities. Israel also outlawed certain organizations and political groups in the territories. Over the years, the restrictions and limitations placed on Palestinians living within the Occupied Territories became increasingly difficult for them to tolerate.

Adding to the difficulties for Palestinians was the problem of Jewish settlements. Jewish settlers built houses, then small villages, in lands once thought of as Palestinian. By the 1980s the number of Jewish settlements had more than doubled in the territories. These settlements were built close to Arab towns

"We continue to be loyal to the pure blood martyrs and to our detained brothers. We also reiterate our rejection of the occupation and its policy of repression. . . ."

Many Palestinians took part in the First Intifada, sparking riots, violence, and damage to many cities under Israeli control. *(© Patrick Robert/Sygma/Corbis.)*

and villages, sometimes annexing, or taking away, part of the Arab land. The Jewish settlers were allowed greater access to limited resources, such as water. Any Palestinian resistance to Israeli activities was met with what came to be called "iron fist" policies, including beatings, arrests, detentions (holding a person without trial for a period of up to six months), confiscation of Arab land, and destruction of Arab homes. Over time, these sources of friction led to nearly constant conflict between Jews and Palestinians in the Occupied Territories.

Despite nearly two decades of ongoing, isolated conflicts and riots, Palestinians for the most part had hoped that neighboring Arab countries would come to their aid. Arab nations had been working through diplomatic channels to solve the Palestinian problem since Israel declared its independence in 1948. By the 1980s, however, many Palestinians were growing tired of waiting. They had no self-government and little land to call their own.

On December 8, 1987, an Israeli driver lost control of his vehicle and struck and killed four Palestinians in the Gaza Strip. The people of the Occupied Territories rioted in response, accusing the Israeli driver of killing the Palestinians on purpose. A generation of Arabs who had lived their entire lives under Israeli rule revolted. Children grabbed rocks from the ground and hurled them at armed Israeli soldiers, and adults rose up in anger in what became known as the First Intifada, or uprising. For nearly a month the uprising continued through the Occupied Territories.

By January 1988 a group calling itself the Unified National Leadership for the Uprising emerged as a coordinator of the attacks. The group was made up of members of Palestinian political groups—all of which were illegal according to Israeli law—including Communists, the Democratic Front for the Liberation of Palestine, Fatah (a group within the Palestine Liberation Organization), Islamic Jihad, and the Popular Front for the Liberation of Palestine. The Unified National Leadership circulated thousands of flyers and broadcast announcements on Palestinian radio to coordinate general strikes and waves of violent protest. The following Communiqué of the Intifada No. 1 expresses a sense of the frustration felt by the Palestinians at the time, and also provides a good outline for Palestinian demands for independence.

Things to remember while reading "Comminiqué No. 1 of the Intifada"

- Notice that the Unified Leadership of the Uprising names the Palestine Liberation Organization (PLO; a Palestinian group that used military force to gain Palestinian goals) as the legitimate representative of the Palestinian people.

- At the time of the Comminiqué, the PLO headquarters were in Tunis, Tunisia.

- Israelis considered the First Intifada to be a form of terrorism.

- Those directing protests of the First Intifada tried to limit the use of weapons, believing that Palestinian use of sticks and stones against Israeli military weapons would garner international support for their cause.

Excerpt from Comminiqué No. 1 of the Intifada (January 8, 1988)

In the name of God, the merciful, the compassionate.

*Our people's glorious uprising continues. We affirm the need to express solidarity with our people wherever they are. We continue to be loyal to the pure blood of our **martyrs** and to our detained brothers. We also reiterate our rejection of the occupation and its policy of repression,*

Martyrs: People who give their life for a cause.

represented in the policy of deportation, mass arrests, curfews, and the demolition of houses.

We reaffirm the need to achieve further **cohesion** with our revolution and our heroic masses. We also stress our **abidance** by the call of the PLO, the Palestinian people's legitimate and sole representative, and the need to pursue the bountiful offerings and the heroic uprising. For all these reasons, we address the following call:

All sectors of our heroic people in every location should abide by the call for a general and comprehensive strike until Wednesday evening, 13 January, 1988. The strike covers all public and private trade utilities, the Palestinian workers and public transportation. Abidance by the comprehensive strike must be complete. The slogan of the strike will be: Down with occupation; long live Palestine as a free and Arab country.

Brother workers, your abidance by the strike by not going to work and to plants is real support for the glorious uprising, a sanctioning of the pure blood of our martyrs, a support for the call to liberate our prisoners, and an act that will help keep our brother deportees in their homeland.

Brother businessmen and grocers, you must fully abide by the call for a comprehensive strike during the period of the strike. Your abidance by previous strikes is one of the most splendid images of solidarity and sacrifice for the sake of rendering our heroic people's stand a success.

We will do our best to protect the interests of our honest businessmen against measures the **Zionist occupation force** may resort to against you. We warn against the consequences of becoming involved with some of the occupation authorities' henchmen who will seek to make you open your businesses. We promise you that we will punish such traitor businessmen in the not too distant future. Let us proceed united to forge victory.

Brother owners of taxi companies, we will not forget your honorable and splendid stand of supporting and implementing the comprehensive strike on the day of Palestinian **steadfastness**. We pin our hopes on you to support and make the comprehensive strike a success. We warn some bus companies against the consequences of not abiding by the call for the strike, as this will make them liable to revolutionary punishment.

Brother doctors and pharmacists, you must be on emergency status to offer assistance to those of our **kinfolk** who are ill. The brother pharmacists must carry out their duties normally. The brother doctors must place the doctor badge in a way that can be clearly identified.

Cohesion: Unity.

Abidance: Following a set of accepted rules.

Zionist occupation force: Zionism was the movement to create a Jewish homeland in Palestine; its occupation force is the Israeli army.

Steadfastness: Steadiness by working together.

Kinfolk: Relatives.

*General warning: We would like to warn people that walking in the streets will not be safe in view of the measures that will be taken to make the comprehensive strike a success. We warn that **viscous** material will be poured on main and secondary streets and everywhere, in addition to the roadblocks and the strike groups that will be deployed throughout the occupied homeland.*

Circular: The struggler and brother members of the popular committees and the men of the uprising who are deployed in all the working locations should work to support and assist our people within the available means, particularly the needy families of our people. The strike groups and the popular uprising groups must completely abide by the working program, which is in their possession. Let us proceed united and loudly chant: Down with occupation; long live Palestine as a free and Arab country.

Viscous: Liquid resistant to flowing when pressure is applied.

What happened next . . .

Israel had a difficult time containing the First Intifada, and the violence continued for nearly six years. Far more Palestinians died in the riots than Israelis, and tens of thousands of Palestinians were detained or arrested for their actions. Despite the costs, the Palestinians had found a voice of their own in the First Intifada.

The First Intifada did not bring peace, but it did change the nature of the Arab-Israeli conflict and helped lead to further diplomatic actions. In November 1988 the Palestine National Council, an elected body of Palestinian representatives, issued a declaration of Palestinian independence. The council also recognized the land-for-peace and mutual recognition guidelines of the 1967 **UN Security Council Resolution 242** (see entry). Furthermore, PLO chairman Yasser Arafat (1929–2004) denounced terrorism, acknowledged that the future Palestinian state would co-exist with—not replace—the Jewish state of Israel, and sought opportunities to begin peace negotiations with the United States acting as mediator. By 1991, Palestinian leaders had entered into their first direct negotiations with Israel.

Did you know . . .

- The international peace conference held in Madrid, Spain, in 1991, was held in part to help address the Palestinian-Israeli conflict.

- The Israeli government and the PLO formally recognized each other with the signing of the **Oslo Accords (see entry)** in September of 1993.

- The First Intifada came to adopt political principles, called the Fourteen Points, which called for Israeli withdrawal from the Occupied Territories and an independent state for Palestinians, among other things.

- Israeli military personnel subdued the First Intifada with strong counter measures, including shooting at unarmed demonstrators, using tear gas in enclosed areas (against international law), and random vandalism of Arab homes.

Consider the following . . .

- The Israeli military had been controlling inhabitants of the Occupied Territories with strict rules. Why was it so difficult to contain the First Intifada?

- Why would the violence of the First Intifada lead to diplomatic relations between Israel and the Palestinians?

- What other means could the Palestinians living in the Occupied Territories have used instead of mass strikes and demonstrations to bring their plight to the attention of the world?

For More Information

Books

Long, Cathryn J. *The Middle East in Search of Peace.* Brookfield, CT: Millbrook Press, 1996.

Sharp, Anne Wallace. *The Palestinians.* Detroit: Lucent Books, 2005.

Smith, Charles D., ed. *Palestine and the Arab-Israeli Conflict: A History with Documents.* 4th ed. Boston and New York: Bedford/St. Martin's, 2001.

Periodicals

"Revealed: The Groups Plotting against Israel." *Sunday Times* (London, England) (January 31, 1988).

Web Sites

"Intifada: Then and Now." *BBC News.* http://news.bbc.co.uk/1/hi/world/middle_east/1061537.stm (accessed June 24, 2005).

The Oslo Accords

Excerpt from the Israeli-PLO Declaration of Principles (September 13, 1993)

Reprinted in *Palestine and the Arab-Israeli Conflict*
Edited by Charles D. Smith
Published in 2001

"The Government of the State of Israel and the PLO team ... agree that it is time to put an end to decades of confrontation and conflict ... to achieve a just, lasting and comprehensive peace...."

During rounds of negotiations, or discussions aimed at settling disputes, between Israel and its Arab neighbors in the early 1990s, the role of Palestine Liberation Organization (PLO) became more and more important. Previously, Israel had considered the PLO to be a terrorist group and refused diplomatic relations with it. But as Israel conducted negotiations with Syria, Jordan, and Lebanon, the authority of the PLO as a representative of Palestinians became a reality when delegates from Arab countries refused to make decisions regarding Palestinians without first consulting with the PLO.

During the eleventh round of seemingly unsuccessful peace talks between Arab and Israeli delegates held in Washington, D.C., in 1993, the world was shocked by the announcement of an agreement between Israel and the PLO that had been negotiated in secret discussions in Oslo, Norway. On September 13, 1993, Israel and the PLO agreed on the principles that would assist the two political entities in an effort to set up an interim, or temporary, self-government for Palestinians that would be recognized by Israel. PLO chairman Yasser Arafat (1929–2004) and Israeli prime minister Yitzhak Rabin (1922–1995) agreed to the

The Palestine Liberation Organization

The Palestine Liberation Organization (PLO) emerged as the representative of the Palestinian people in 1968, under the leadership of the dynamic chairman Yasser Arafat (1929–2004). The charter, or stated set of laws and beliefs, of the organization committed the PLO to waging armed struggle against Israel in order to reclaim Palestine from the Israelis for Palestinians. These policies caused many conflicts in the Middle East for many years.

The PLO originally organized its military forces in Jordan, but the attacks the PLO launched on Israel and the internal problems it caused in Jordan prompted the Jordanian government to remove the organization from the country in 1970. By the 1980s similar PLO activities in Lebanon had driven the country into civil war and prompted an invasion by Israel, which eventually led to the PLO leadership being exiled, or forcibly removed, to Tunisia in 1982. For its violent attacks on Israel, the PLO was branded as a terrorist organization by many countries. However, by the 1990s, the power of the PLO among Palestinians was such that neither the Arab nations nor Israel nor its allies could deny the legitimate role of the PLO as representative of the Palestinian people.

Oslo Accords, as the declaration came to be called, which established the Palestinian National Authority, an elected self-governing body for Palestinians; outlined the terms of Israeli withdrawal from some of the Occupied Territories, land that had been taken over by Israel during the Six-Day War in 1967; and detailed the terms of the transition of power from Israel to the Palestinians.

Things to remember while reading the "Israeli-PLO Declaration of Principles, September 13, 1993"

- The Oslo Accords marked a historic moment in the Arab-Israeli conflict because it was a formal document in which Israel recognized the authority of the PLO to speak for the Palestinian people and the PLO accepted Israel as an independent country.

- For their efforts in the Oslo Accords, Israeli prime minister Yitzhak Rabin, Israeli foreign minister Shimon Peres (1923–), and PLO chairman Yasser Arafat shared the Nobel Peace Prize in 1994.

- Notice that the Oslo Accords left several issues for future negotiations, including Israel's permanent borders, the

Israeli prime minister Yitzhak Rabin and PLO leader Yasser Arafat shake hands as a symbol of peace between Israel and the Palestinians after the signing of the Oslo Peace Accords. *(Reuters/Gary Hershorn/Archive Photos.)*

accepted areas for Jewish settlements, the permanent home of Palestinian refugees, and the political authority over Jerusalem.

Excerpt from the Israeli-PLO Declaration of Principles (September 13, 1993)

Declaration of Principles on Interim Self-Government Arrangements:

The Government of the State of Israel and the PLO team (in the Jordanian-Palestinian delegation to the Middle East Peace

Conference) (the "Palestinian Delegation"), representing the Palestinian people, agree that it is time to put an end to decades of confrontation and conflict, recognise their mutual legitimate and political rights, and strive to live in peaceful coexistence and mutual dignity and security and achieve a just, lasting and comprehensive peace settlement and historic reconciliation through the agreed political process. Accordingly, the two sides agree to the following principles:

Article I

Aim of Negotiations

The aim of the Israeli-Palestinian negotiations within the current Middle East peace process is, among other things, to establish a Palestinian **Interim** Self-Government Authority, the elected Council (the "Council"), for the Palestinian people in the West Bank and the Gaza Strip, for a transitional period not exceeding five years, leading to a permanent settlement based on **Security Council resolutions 242 (1967) and 338 (1973).**

It is understood that the interim arrangements are an integral part of the whole peace process and that the negotiations on the permanent status will lead to the implementation of Security Council resolutions 242 (1967) and 338 (1973). . . .

Article IV

Jurisdiction

Jurisdiction of the Council will cover West Bank and Gaza Strip territory, except for issues that will be negotiated in the permanent status negotiations. The two sides view the West Bank and the Gaza Strip as a single territorial unit, whose integrity will be preserved during the interim period.

Article V

Transitional period and permanent status negotiations. . .

2. Permanent status negotiations will commence as soon as possible, but not later than the beginning of the third year of the interim period, between the Government of Israel and the Palestinian people's representatives.

3. It is understood that these negotiations shall cover remaining issues, including: Jerusalem, refugees, settlements, security arrangements, borders, relations and co-operation with other neighbours, and other issues of common interest.

Interim: Temporary.

Security Council resolutions 242 and 338: Two recommendations made by the United Nations Security Council on how to resolve matters between Israel and the Palestinians and bring peace to the region.

Jurisdiction: The territorial range of authority or control.

Yitzhak Rabin signs the Oslo Peace Accords, a step toward what many hoped would be a lasting peace between Israelis and Palestinians.
(© Peter Turnley/Corbis.)

4. The two parties agree that the outcome of the permanent status negotiations should not be prejudiced or pre-empted by agreements reached for the interim period.

Article VI

Preparatory transfer of powers and responsibilities. . .

2. Immediately after the entry into force of this Declaration of Principles and the withdrawal from the Gaza Strip and Jericho area, with the view to promoting economic development in the West Bank and Gaza Strip, authority will be transferred to the Palestinians in the following spheres: education and culture, health, social welfare, direct taxation and tourism. The Palestinian side will commence in building the Palestinian police force, as agreed upon. Pending the inauguration of the Council, the two parties may negotiate the transfer of additional powers and responsibilities, as agreed upon.

Article VII

Interim agreement

1. The Israeli and Palestinian delegations will negotiate an agreement on the interim period (the "Interim Agreement").

2. The Interim Agreement shall specify, among other things, the structure of the Council, the number of its members, and the transfer of powers and responsibilities from the Israeli military government and its Civil Administration to the Council. The Interim Agreement shall also specify the Council's executive authority, legislative authority in accordance with Article IX below, and the independent Palestinian judicial organs.

3. The Interim Agreement shall include arrangements, to be implemented upon the inauguration of the Council, for the assumption by the Council of all of the powers and responsibilities transferred previously in accordance with Article VI above.

4. In order to enable the Council to promote economic growth, upon its inauguration, the Council will establish, among other things, a Palestinian Electricity Authority, a Gaza Sea Port Authority, a Palestinian Development Bank, a Palestinian Export Promotion Board, a Palestinian Environmental Authority, a Palestinian Land Authority and a Palestinian Water Administration Authority and any other Authorities agreed upon, in accordance with the Interim Agreement, that will specify their powers and responsibilities.

5. After the inauguration of the Council, the Civil Administration will be dissolved, and the Israeli military government will be withdrawn.

Article VIII

Public Order and Security

In order to guarantee public order and internal security for the Palestinians of the West Bank and the Gaza Strip, the Council will establish a strong police force, while Israel will continue to carry the responsibility for defending against external threats, as well as the responsibility for overall security of Israelis for the purpose of safeguarding their internal security and public order. . . .

Article XIII

Redeployment of Israeli Forces

1. After the entry into force of this Declaration of Principles, and not later than the eve of elections for the Council, a **redeployment** of Israeli military forces in the West Bank and the Gaza Strip will take place, in addition to withdrawal of Israeli forces carried out in accordance with Article XIV.

2. In redeploying its military forces, Israel will be guided by the principle that its military forces should be redeployed outside populated areas.

3. Further redeployments to specified locations will be gradually implemented **commensurate** with the assumption of responsibility for public order and internal security by the Palestinian police force pursuant to Article VIII above.

Article XIV

Israeli Withdrawal from the Gaza Strip and Jericho Area

Israel will withdraw from the Gaza Strip and Jericho area, as detailed in the protocol attached as Annex II.

Article XV

Resolution of Disputes

[...]

3. The parties may agree to submit to arbitration disputes relating to the interim period, which cannot be settled through **conciliation**. To this end, upon the agreement of both parties, the parties will establish an Arbitration Committee....

Annex I

Protocol on the Mode and Conditions of Elections

1. Palestinians of Jerusalem who live there will have the right to participate in the election process, according to an agreement between the two sides.

2. In addition, the election agreement should cover, among other things, the following issues:

(a) The system of elections;

(b) The mode of the agreed supervision and international observation and their personal composition;

Redeployment: To move military forces from one combat zone to another.

Commensurate: Corresponding in size, extent, or degree.

Conciliation: Overcoming anger or distrust.

(c) Rules and regulations regarding election campaigns, including agreed arrangements for the organizing of mass media, and the possibility of licensing a broadcasting and television station.

3. The future status of displaced Palestinians who were registered on 4 June 1967 will not be prejudiced because they are unable to participate in the election process owing to practical reasons.

Annex II

Protocol on Withdrawal of Israeli Forces from the Gaza Strip and Jericho Area

*1. The two sides will conclude and sign within two months from the date of entry into force of this Declaration of Principles an agreement on the withdrawal of Israeli military forces from the Gaza Strip and Jericho area. This agreement will include comprehensive arrangements to apply in the Gaza Strip and the Jericho area **subsequent to** the Israeli withdrawal.*

2. Israel will implement an accelerated and scheduled withdrawal of Israeli military forces from the Gaza Strip and Jericho area, beginning immediately with the signing of the agreement on the Gaza Strip and Jericho area and to be completed within a period not exceeding four months after the signing of this agreement.

3. The above agreement will include, among other things:

(a) Arrangements for a smooth and peaceful transfer of authority from the Israeli military government and its Civil Administration to the Palestinian representatives.

(b) Structure, powers and responsibilities of the Palestinian authority in these areas, except: external security, settlements, Israelis, foreign relations and other mutually agreed matters.

(c) Arrangements for the assumption of internal security and public order by the Palestinian police force consisting of police officers recruited locally and from abroad (holding Jordanian passports and Palestinian documents issued by Egypt). Those who will participate in the Palestinian police force coming from abroad should be trained as police and police officers.

(d) A temporary international or foreign presence, as agreed upon.

(e) Establishment of a joint Palestinian-Israeli Co-ordination and Co-operation Committee for mutual security purposes.

(f) An economic development and stabilization program, including the establishment of an Emergency Fund, to encourage

Subsequent to: Following.

foreign investment and financial and economic support. Both sides will co-ordinate and co-operate jointly and unilaterally with regional and international parties to support these aims.

(g) Arrangements for a safe passage for persons and transportation between the Gaza Strip and Jericho area. . . .

Article IV

It is understood that:

1. Jurisdiction of the Council will cover West Bank and Gaza Strip territory, except for issues that will be negotiated in the permanent status negotiations: Jerusalem, settlements, military locations and Israelis.

2. The Council's jurisdiction will apply with regard to the agreed powers, responsibilities, spheres and authorities transferred to it. . . .

Article VII (5):

The withdrawal of the military government will not prevent Israel from exercising the powers and responsibilities not transferred to the Council. . . .

Annex II:

It is understood that, subsequent to the Israeli withdrawal, Israel will continue to be responsible for external security, and for internal security and public order of settlements and Israelis. Israeli military forces and civilians may continue to use roads freely within the Gaza Strip and the Jericho area.

What happened next . . .

Although many of the provisions, or requirements, detailed in the Declaration of Principles were fulfilled, a lasting peace had yet to be agreed upon by 2005. The successes of the Oslo Accords were the establishment of the Palestinian National Authority (the recognized government of the Palestinian people), Palestinian control over portions of the Occupied Territories, and the organization of a Palestinian police force.

Despite these gains, Palestinians and Israelis remained unable to agree on how Jerusalem should be controlled, the nature of permanent borders, or what to do about the more than one million Palestinian refugees. By 2000, frustration among Palestinians culminated in the Second Intifada, or rebellion against Israeli occupation. Over the next several years, violence would alternate with negotiations, but there was still no peace in the region when Yasser Arafat died in 2004.

Did you know...

- The five-year transitional period called for in the Oslo Accords was to begin upon Israeli withdrawal from the Gaza Strip and Jericho area. As of early 2005, this withdrawal had still not yet occurred, but plans were put in place in 2004 to complete this before the end of 2005.

- The Declaration of Principles called for a Palestinian civil administration to take over governing authority from the Israeli military government upon Israeli withdrawal from the Gaza Strip and the Jericho area, after which time a Palestinian Council would be elected.

- It was hoped that the Declaration of Principles would provide an opening for negotiations about economic cooperation with Egypt and Jordan, as well as an opportunity for all sides to negotiate regional development programs.

Consider the following ...

- Why were the Oslo Accords inadequate as a final solution to the Israeli-Arab conflict?

- Describe the features of the Oslo Accords that were most important in continuing the peace process.

- Identify the parts of the Oslo Accords that were the most difficult for Israeli citizens to accept, as well as those most difficult for Arab Palestinians. Explain why these were the most difficult parts for each side.

For More Information

Books

Freedman, Robert O., ed. *The Middle East and the Peace Process: The Impact of the Oslo Accords.* Gainesville: University Press of Florida, 1998.

Smith, Charles D., ed. *Palestine and the Arab-Israeli Conflict: A History with Documents.* 4th ed. Boston and New York: Bedford/St. Martin's, 2001.

Watson, Geoffrey R. *The Oslo Accords: International Law and the Israeli-Palestinian Peace Agreements.* New York: Oxford University Press, 2000.

Web Sites

"Shattered Dreams of Peace: The Road from Oslo." *Frontline.* http://www.pbs.org/wgbh/pages/frontline/shows/oslo/ (accessed on June 24, 2005).

Israel's Revised
Disengagement Plan

Excerpt from Israel's Revised Disengagement Plan—Main Principles
(June 6, 2004)

Published by the Israeli Prime Minister's Office

B y the early 2000s, relations between the state of Israel and Palestinians living in territories occupied by Israel had once again deteriorated. Despite several peace conferences and numerous rounds of negotiations, despite signed resolutions and accords (formal agreements), Israelis and Palestinians could not establish and maintain peace between them. In 2000, Palestinians once again erupted in sustained popular violence against both Israel and the ineffective Palestinian administration in the Occupied Territories (areas in the West Bank and Gaza Strip taken over by Israel during the Six-Day War in 1967). The Second Intifada, or uprising, led Israel to cut off diplomatic relations with the Palestinians.

Unable and unwilling to work together, Israelis and Palestinians appealed to the international community. United Nations Secretary-General Kofi Annan, U.S. secretary of state Colin Powell, Russian foreign minister Igor Ivanov, Danish foreign minister Per Stig Moeller, High Representative for European Common Foreign and Security Policy Javier Solana, and European Commissioner for External Affairs Chris Patten met to establish a workable Israeli-Palestinian

"The purpose of the plan is to lead to a better security, political, economic and demographic situation."

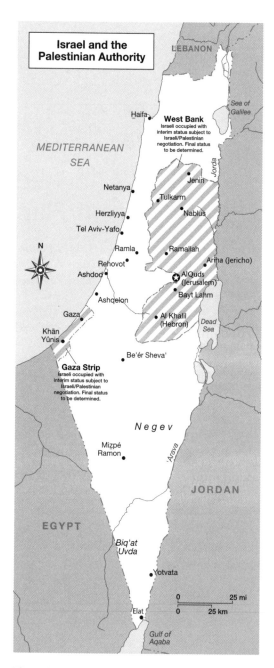

Israel and the Palestinian Authority

LEBANON

Sea of Galilee

Haifa

West Bank
Israeli occupied with
interim status subject to
Israeli/Palestinian
negotiation. Final status
to be determined.

MEDITERRANEAN
SEA

Jordan

Jenin

Netanya

Tulkarm

Herzliyya

Nablus

Tel Aviv-Yafo

N

Ramla

Ramallah

Rehovot

Ariha (Jericho)

Ashdod

AlQuds
(Jerusalem)

Bayt Lahm

Ashqelon

Gaza

Al Khalil
(Hebron)

Dead
Sea

Khān
Yūnis

Be'ér Sheva'

Gaza Strip
Israeli occupied with
interim status subject to
Israeli/Palestinian
negotiation. Final status
to be determined.

N e g e v

Mizpé
Ramon

'Arava

JORDAN

EGYPT

Biq'at
Uvda

Yotvata

0   25 mi
0   25 km

Elat

Gulf of
Aqaba

The striped portions of this map show the areas
that the Palestinian Authority will control once
Israeli forces have withdrawn. *(The Gale Group.)*

peace plan in 2002. On September 17, 2002, the group, called the Quartet because it included representatives from the European Union, Russia, the United States, and the United Nations (an international organization founded in 1945 and made up of most of the countries of the world), issued a document named "the roadmap to peace." The roadmap was designed as a political plan that would implement a lasting peace in the Middle East after a three-year transition. The transitional stages included a Palestinian ceasefire and an Israeli army withdrawal from the Occupied Territories, followed by the establishment of a provisional, or temporary, Palestinian state in 2005, and then negotiations to resolve the future of Jerusalem, Palestinian refugees, and permanent borders for Israel and the Palestinian state—all long-standing issues in the conflict. The plan was greeted by the Israelis and Palestinians with varying degrees of acceptance, yet it remained, as of 2005, the most complete plan for peace in the region. However, continued violence in the region prevented any progress toward peace.

Israeli prime minister Ariel Sharon (1928–) knew that either Israel or Palestine had to take action if peace was ever to be a reality in the region. Unable to negotiate a satisfactory peace with the Palestinians, Sharon decided to have Israel take the first step toward peace on its own. In 2004 he announced that Israel would withdraw military personnel and remove selected settlements from the Gaza Strip and portions of the West Bank, without the need for the Palestinian Authority, the government of the Palestinian people, to yield any land or resources. The following document is a portion of the Israeli disengagement plan to remove their army and people from parts of the Occupied Territories.

Things to remember while reading "Israel's Revised Disengagement Plan—Main Principles, June 6, 2004"

- The disengagement plan does not replace the roadmap to peace proposed by the Quartet.

- Think about the Israeli strategy behind its disengagement plan. What benefits to the Israelis are there in the plan?

- The Palestinians have argued for Israeli withdrawal from the Occupied Territories for many years. Why might Israel agree that this is a good policy?

Excerpt from Israel's Revised Disengagement Plan—Main Principles (June 6, 2004)

1. Background—Political and Security Implications

The State of Israel is committed to the peace process.... The State of Israel has come to the conclusion that there is currently no reliable Palestinian partner with which it can make progress in a two-sided peace process. Accordingly, it has developed a plan of revised disengagement (hereinafter—the plan), based on the following considerations:

*One. The **stalemate** dictated by the current situation is harmful. In order to break out of this stalemate, the State of Israel is required to initiate moves not dependent on Palestinian cooperation.*

Two. The purpose of the plan is to lead to a better security, political, economic and demographic situation.

Three. In any future permanent status arrangement, there will be no Israeli towns and villages in the Gaza Strip. On the other hand, it is clear that in the West Bank, there are areas which will be part of the State of Israel, including major Israeli population centers, cities, towns and villages, security areas and other places of special interest to Israel.

Four. The State of Israel supports the efforts of the United States, operating alongside the international community, to promote the

Stalemate: Situation in which further action is blocked.

reform process, the construction of institutions and the improvement of the economy and welfare of the Palestinian residents, in order that a new Palestinian leadership will emerge and prove itself capable of fulfilling its commitments under the Roadmap.

*Five. Relocation from the Gaza Strip and from an area in **Northern Samaria** should reduce friction with the Palestinian population.*

Six. The completion of the plan will serve to dispel the claims regarding Israel's responsibility for the Palestinians in the Gaza Strip.

Seven. The process set forth in the plan is without prejudice to the relevant agreements between the State of Israel and the Palestinians. Relevant arrangements shall continue to apply.

Eight. International support for this plan is widespread and important. This support is essential in order to bring the Palestinians to implement in practice their obligations to combat terrorism and effect reforms as required by the Roadmap, thus enabling the parties to return to the path of negotiation. . . .

3.1 The Gaza Strip

1) The State of Israel will evacuate the Gaza Strip, including all existing Israeli towns and villages, and will redeploy outside the Strip. This will not include military deployment in the area of the border between the Gaza Strip and Egypt ("the Philadelphi Route") as detailed below.

2) Upon completion of this process, there shall no longer be any permanent presence of Israeli security forces in the areas of Gaza Strip territory which have been evacuated.

3.2 The West Bank

3) The State of Israel will evacuate an area in Northern Samaria (Ganim, Kadim, Sa-Nur and Homesh), and all military installations in this area, and will redeploy outside the vacated area.

4) Upon completion of this process, there shall no longer be any permanent presence of Israeli security forces in this area.

Northern Samaria: An area in the northern half of the West Bank.

Territorial contiguity: A continuous stretch of land.

Infrastructure: The basic structure of a system; in this case roads and canals.

*5) The move will enable **territorial contiguity** for Palestinians in the Northern Samaria area.*

*6) The State of Israel will assist, together with the international community, in improving the transportation **infrastructure** in the West Bank in order to facilitate the contiguity of Palestinian transportation.*

7) The process will facilitate normal life and Palestinian economic and commercial activity in the West Bank.

3.3 The intention is to complete the planned relocation process by the end of 2005. . . .

10. Economic Arrangements

. . . In the longer term, and in line with Israel's interest in encouraging greater Palestinian economic independence, the State of Israel expects to reduce the number of Palestinian workers entering Israel, to the point that it ceases completely. The State of Israel supports the development of sources of employment in the Gaza Strip and in Palestinian areas of the West Bank, by international elements. . . .

13. Conclusion

The goal is that implementation of the plan will lead to improving the situation and breaking the current deadlock. If and when there is evidence from the Palestinian side of its willingness, capability and implementation in practice of the fight against terrorism, full cessation of terrorism and violence and the institution of reform as required by the Roadmap, it will be possible to return to the track of negotiation and dialogue.

What happened next . . .

On February 8, 2005, at the Sharm el-Sheik summit in Egypt, Palestinian and Israeli leaders met for the first time in four years. Newly elected Palestinian Authority president Mahmoud Abbas (1935–) met with Israeli prime minister Ariel Sharon to formalize a truce, or temporary peace, between Israelis and Palestinians. Although both Israeli and Palestinian leaders acknowledged that the violence and division between their peoples may continue for a time, both were hopeful of eventual peace as neighbors.

Israel's Cabinet approved the plan for the removal of the Israeli army and settlements in the Occupied Territories on February 20, 2005. The very next day, 500 Palestinian prisoners were released. The Israeli government planned to send 8,500 eviction notices to Jewish settlers, which would remove all Jewish settlers from the Gaza Strip and evacuate four settlements in the northern portion of the West Bank. The same day the Israeli Cabinet voted on the plan, it also announced its intention to build a wall, or barrier, to guard Jewish settlements left in the West Bank. It has yet to be seen whether or not the disengagement plan will result in further peace negotiations. However, it does raise the question of how Israel will use the disengagement plan to its advantage during future discussions about permanent borders between Israel and the proposed state of Palestine.

Did you know . . .

- The disengagement plan is the first Israeli proposal to evacuate settlements in the Occupied Territories since occupation started in 1967.

- 130,000 Israelis protested the disengagement plan in a demonstration in Jerusalem on January 30, 2005.

- Observers note that Ariel Sharon's plan removes settlers from areas of the Occupied Territories that are the most difficult to defend.

- The disengagement plan leaves Jewish settlements of nearly 85,000 settlers in the West Bank.

Consider the following . . .

- What advantages did Israel gained by making this decision to withdraw from certain of the Occupied Territories without requiring anything in return from the Palestinians? Explain.

- Describe the disadvantages of the Disengagement Plan for both Israelis and the Arab Palestinians.

- Could the Palestinians have made a decision that would have made as big an impact on peace as the Israeli Disengagement Plan? Explain.

For More Information

Books

Gunderson, Cory Gideon. *The Israeli-Palestinian Conflict*. Edina, MN: Abdo Publishing, 2004.

Sharp, Anne Wallace. *The Palestinians*. Detroit: Lucent Books, 2005.

Smith, Charles D., ed. *Palestine and the Arab-Israeli Conflict: A History with Documents*. 4th ed. Boston and New York: Bedford/St. Martin's, 2001.

Periodicals

"Israeli Cabinet OKs Gaza Withdrawal." *Los Angeles Times,* February 21, 2005.

Web Sites

"Address to the Fourth Herzliya Conference." *Israeli Ministry of Foreign Affairs.* http://www.mfa.gov.il/MFA/Peace+Process/Guide+to+the+Peace+Process/Israeli+Disengagement+Plan+20-Jan-2005.htm#doc1 (accessed on June 24, 2005).

"The Cabinet Resolution Regarding the Disengagement Plan," *Israeli Ministry of Foreign Affairs.* http://www.mfa.gov.il/MFA/Peace+Process/Reference+Documents/Revised+Disengagement+Plan+6-June-2004.htm? DisplayMode=print (accessed on June 24, 2005).

"Q&A: The Middle East Summit and Its Aftermath." *NPR.* http://www.npr.org/templates/story/story.php?storyId=4502428 (accessed on June 24, 2005).

"The Renewed Road to Peace." *Foreign Policy Association.* http://www.fpa. org/newsletter_info2583/newsletter_info_sub_list.htm?section=The%20Renewed%20Road%20to%20Peace (accessed on June 24, 2005).

5

Competing Visions of the Middle East

T oday, the Middle East is a region of the world characterized by nations with a wide variety of political systems. There are monarchies (governments ruled by a single person), as in Saudi Arabia and Jordan; republics (governments ruled by representatives of the people), as in Egypt and Lebanon; Islamic republics (governments ruled by representatives of the Islamic faith), as in Iran; republics under military rule (governments ruled by representatives of the military), as in Syria; and democracies (governments ruled directly by the people), as in Israel. There are also militant organizations within many states pushing for change, even revolution. Some nations are ruled primarily by Islamic religious law, or Sharia, as in Saudi Arabia and Iran, and most of the Arab nations show the influence of Islamic law. However, some nations' governments are primarily secular, or nonreligious, such as Egypt, Syria, Lebanon, and Israel. Only Israel has a multiparty democracy, similar to the form of government in the United States and most European nations. Most Middle Eastern nations have a single leader who severely limits the expression of political groups that do not support the current government. (Egypt, for example, which is often considered one of the more progressive of the Middle Eastern countries, authorized its first multiparty elections in 2005.)

Differing beliefs in the Middle East have caused many groups to protest and commit acts of violence. (© *Maher Attar/Corbis Sygma.*)

Not only do the political systems in the Middle Eastern nations show real variety, but so do their cultures. Some of the Arab countries—Iraq and Lebanon, for example—allow women full access to employment, education, and other civil rights. Others, such as Saudi Arabia, insist that women be strictly separated from men in most circumstances, and restrict women's right to drive or show their faces in public. Most Middle Eastern countries experience friction between their Muslim and non-Muslim populations, and also—as in Iraq and Lebanon—between the Sunni and Shiite branches of Islam.

These great variations in political and cultural life indicate that the Middle East is a region where important questions about religion, government, and philosophy come up on a daily basis. In this chapter of the book, some of the fundamental guiding visions for the nature of social and political life in the Middle East that have emerged since the late nineteenth century will be presented. One of the most controversial issues in all of Middle Eastern history has been the influence of Zionism, a political movement that sought to create a Jewish homeland in Palestine—and succeeded when it created the state of Israel in 1948. Included in this chapter are excerpts from Theodor Herzl's book *The Jewish State* (1896), which gave birth to the international Zionist movement.

Zionism was a nationalist movement. Like all nationalist movements, it sought to create a nation that reflected the interests and culture of a particular social group, in this case followers of the Jewish faith. Arab nations that came into being after the collapse of the Ottoman Empire (a vast empire of southwest Asia, northeast Africa, and southeast Europe that reigned from the thirteenth century to the early twentieth century. It was ruled mainly from Turkey and was heavily influenced by the Islamic religion) during World War I (1914–18; war in which Great Britain, France, the United States, and their allies defeated Germany, Austria-Hungary, and their allies) also embraced nationalism as they formed states and gained political independence. For many Arab leaders, however, nationalism wasn't enough. They wanted independent Arab nations to join together to increase their strength and promote their Arab identity. Their vision was called Pan-Arabism, and one of its greatest spokesmen was Gamal Abdel Nasser (1918–1970), the president of Egypt from 1958 to 1970 and one of the founders of the United Arab Republic, a short-lived effort to unite Arab nations. In 1959 he laid out his vision in a speech to military officers; excerpts from that important speech are included in this chapter.

The most extreme visions for transforming the Middle East come from supporters of Islam who want to see a more radical transformation of Muslim societies, both in the Middle East and in any country with a large Muslim population. These people, often called Islamic fundamentalists, or Islamists, want to make religion the basis of their entire political and social system. They also want to eliminate all traces of Western influence in the Middle East. Some of them resort to acts of terrorism to try to achieve their goals. Osama bin Laden (1957–), best known as the orchestrator of the terrorist attacks on the World Trade Center in New York City and the Pentagon in Washington, D.C., on September 11, 2001, proposed his violent vision for the triumph of Islamic fundamentalism in a statement attributed to the World Islamic Front.

All of the documents in this chapter present ideas on how the Middle East region should be structured both politically and religiously. Many of these documents continue to influence the politics and social organization of Middle Eastern countries today.

The Jewish State

Excerpts from **The Jewish State**
Written by Theodor Herzl
Originally published as *Das Judenstaat* in 1896
Reprinted in *The Jewish State: An Attempt at a Modern Solution*
of the Jewish Question
Published in 1946

One cannot hope to understand the historic and ongoing conflict in the Middle East without understanding the role that Israel plays in the region, and one cannot understand Israel without first understanding Zionism. Zionism was, and still is, a political movement aimed at creating a national homeland for the Jewish people. Today, that homeland exists in the nation of Israel. Yet many feel that Jews are still not secure from the persecution they had faced in other countries, even in Israel, for many Arabs in the Middle East, who feel some of their own land was taken from them, have devoted themselves to the destruction of Israel. Moreover, anti-Semitism, or acts of hostility directed against Jews, continues to exist in many countries in the twenty-first century. To this day, Zionists continue to argue that an independent Jewish nation is the key to the eventual end of Jewish persecution.

Zionism itself was the product of the anti-Semitic social conditions existing in Europe and Russia during the nineteenth century. Though anti-Semitism among Christians traces its roots back to the time of the Roman Empire, it flourished again in the nineteenth century due to racial theories that

> "The Jews who wish for a State shall have it, and they will deserve to have it."

held that the Jews, or Semites, were a distinct and inferior race. A series of events across Europe and Russia—including pogroms (massacres of Jews) in Russia and Poland, anti-Jewish publications in France and Britain, and attacks and riots against Jews in Germany—forced many Jews to acknowledge that despite their best efforts to assimilate, or fit, into European society, they were not truly welcomed as citizens of any major country. One Hungarian-born Jew who came to this conclusion was Theodor Herzl (1860–1904).

Herzl began to look for a solution to the problems facing Jews in Europe when he experienced anti-Semitic riots in France in the mid-1890s. He soon learned of a small movement to relocate Russian Jews to a place the Jews called Zion, an ancient name for holy sites near the city of Jerusalem, in the territory known as Palestine, then part of the Ottoman Empire (a vast empire of southwest Asia, northeast Africa, and southeast Europe that reigned from the thirteenth century to the early twentieth century). Inspired by the promise of religious freedom that these small Jewish settlements seemed to offer, Herzl became an immediate convert to the cause. He expanded the ideas of Zionism by suggesting actual plans that Jewish people could take to create a true nation of their own and creating organizations to further this cause. These ideas were so integral in convincing the worldwide Jewish population that Zionism could be a reality that he is often heralded as the father of Zionism. In 1896 Herzl published a pamphlet, or small book, called *The Jewish State*, which outlined his ideas for how Jews and other supporters of Zionism could work to create a national homeland for Jews.

Things to remember while reading excerpts from *The Jewish State*:

- Herzl's book was predated by a work called *Auto-Emancipation* (1881), in which Polish Jew Leo Pinsker (1821–1891) suggested that all Jews relocate to Palestine. This book was not read by a large Jewish audience and only a few copies of it were published. Herzl claimed not to have read the work prior to writing *The Jewish State*.

- *The Jewish State* was both an immediate and lasting publishing success. First published in England, it was later published in eighty editions and in eighteen different languages. The version consulted for this publication was published in 1946, on the fiftieth anniversary of the original publication.

Excerpts from The Jewish State

Preface

The idea which I have developed in this pamphlet is a very old one: it is the restoration of the Jewish State.

The world resounds with outcries against the Jews, and these outcries have awakened the slumbering idea.

*I wish it to be clearly understood from the outset that no portion of my argument is based on a new discovery. I have discovered neither the historic condition of the Jews nor the means to improve it. In fact, every man will see for himself that the materials of the structure I am designing are not only in existence, but actually already in hand. If, therefore, this attempt to solve the **Jewish Question** is to be designed by a single world, let it be said to be the result of an inescapable conclusion rather than that of a flighty imagination.*

*I must, in the first place, guard my scheme from being treated as **Utopian** by superficial critics who might commit this error of judgment if I did not warn them. I should obviously have done nothing to be ashamed of if I had described a Utopia on philanthropic lines; and I should also, in all probability, have obtained literary success more easily if I had set forth my plan in the irresponsible guise of a romantic tale. But this Utopia is far less attractive than any one of those portrayed by **Sir Thomas More** and his numerous forerunners and successors. . . .*

Everything depends on our propelling force. And what is that force? The misery of the Jews.

Who would venture to deny its existence? We shall discuss it fully in the chapter on the causes of Anti-Semitism.

Everybody is familiar with the phenomenon of steam-power, generated by boiling water, which lifts the kettle-lid. Such tea-kettle

Jewish Question: Question of what to do with the millions of Jews in Poland, Germany, and elsewhere.

Utopian: Impossibly ideal.

Sir Thomas More (1779–1852): British writer who penned the first Utopian novel.

Theodor Herzl, a famous figure in the creation of Zionism.

phenomena are the attempts of Zionist and kindred associations to check Anti-Semitism.

I believe that this power, if rightly employed, is powerful enough to propel a large engine and to move passengers and goods: the engine having whatever form men may choose to give it. . . .

I shall therefore clearly and emphatically state that I believe in the practical outcome of my scheme, though without professing to have discovered the shape it may ultimately take. The Jewish State is essential to the world; it will therefore be created.

The plan would, of course, seem absurd if a single individual attempted to do it; but if worked by a number of Jews in co-operation it would appear perfectly rational, and its accomplishment would present no difficulties worth mentioning. The idea depends only on the number of its supporters. Perhaps our ambitious young men, to whom every road of progress is now closed, seeing in this Jewish State a bright prospect of freedom, happiness and honors opening to them, will ensure the **propagation** of the idea. . . .

It depends on the Jews themselves whether this political pamphlet remains for the present a political romance. If the present generation is too dull to understand it rightly, a future, finer and a better generation will arise to understand it. The Jews who wish for a State shall have it, and they will deserve to have it.

I.—Introduction . . .

The Jewish Question still exists. It would be foolish to deny it. It is a remnant of the Middle Ages, which civilized nations do not even yet seem able to shake off, try as they will. They certainly showed a generous desire to do so when they emancipated us. The Jewish question exists wherever Jews live in perceptible numbers. Where it does not exist, it is carried by Jews in the course of their **migrations**. We naturally move to those places where we are not persecuted, and there our presence produces persecution. This is the case in every country, and will remain so, even in those highly civilized—for instance, France—until the Jewish

Propagation: Spread.

Migrations: Moves from one country to another.

question finds a solution on a political basis. The unfortunate Jews are now carrying the seeds of Anti-Semitism into England; they have already introduced it into America.

I believe that I understand Anti-Semitism, which is really a highly complex movement. I consider it from a Jewish standpoint, yet without fear or hatred. I believe that I can see what elements there are in it of vulgar sport, of common trade jealousy, of inherited prejudice, of religious intolerance, and also of pretended self-defence. I think the Jewish question is no more a social than a religious one, notwithstanding that it sometimes takes these and other forms. It is a national question, which can only be solved by making it a political world-question to be discussed and settled by the civilized nations of the world in council.

We are a people—one people.

We have honestly endeavored everywhere to merge ourselves in the social life of surrounding communities and to preserve the faith of our fathers. We are not permitted to do so. In vain are we loyal patriots, our loyalty in some places running to extremes; in vain do we make the same sacrifices of life and property as our fellow-citizens; in vain do we strive to increase the fame of our native land in science and art, or her wealth by trade and commerce. . . .

Oppression and persecution cannot exterminate us. No nation on earth has survived such struggles and sufferings as we have gone through. **Jew-baiting** has merely stripped off our weaklings; the strong among us were invariably true to their race when persecution broke out against them.[. . .]

No human being is wealthy or powerful enough to transplant a nation from one habitation to another. An idea alone can achieve that and this idea of a State may have the requisite power to do so. The Jews have dreamt this kingly dream all through the long nights of their history. "Next year in **Jerusalem**" is our old phrase. It is now a question of showing that the dream can be converted into a living reality.

For this, many old, outgrown, confused and limited notions must first be entirely erased from the minds of men. Dull brains might, for instance, imagine that this **exodus** would be from civilized regions into the desert. That is not the case. It will be carried out in the midst of civilization. We shall not revert to a lower stage, we shall rise to a higher one. We shall not dwell in mud huts; we shall build new more beautiful and more modern houses, and possess them in safety. We shall not lose our acquired possessions; we shall realize them. We shall surrender our

Jew-baiting: The denial of the Jewish faith in the face of persecution.

Jerusalem: The capital city of Palestine, home to numerous holy sites.

Exodus: Mass departure.

well earned rights only for better ones. We shall not sacrifice our beloved customs; we shall find them again. We shall not leave our old home before the new one is prepared for us. Those only will depart who are sure thereby to improve their position; those who are now desperate will go first, after them the poor; next the prosperous, and, last of all, the wealthy. Those who go in advance will raise themselves to a higher grade, equal to those whose representatives will shortly follow. Thus the exodus will be at the same time an ascent of the class.

The departure of the Jews will involve no economic disturbances, no crises, no persecutions; in fact, the countries they abandon will revive to a new period of prosperity. There will be an inner migration of Christian citizens into the positions evacuated by Jews. The outgoing current will be gradual, without any disturbance, and its initial movement will put an end to Anti-Semitism. The Jews will leave as honored friends, and if some of them return, they will receive the same favorable welcome and treatment at the hands of civilized nations as is accorded to all foreign visitors. Their exodus will have no resemblance to a flight, for it will be a well-regulated movement under control of public opinion. The movement will not only be **inaugurated** with absolute conformity to law, but it cannot even be carried out without the friendly cooperation of interested governments, who would derive considerable benefits from it.

Security for the integrity of the idea and the vigor of its execution will be found in the creation of a body corporate, or corporation. This corporation will be called "The Society of Jews." In addition to it there will be a Jewish company, an economically productive body.

An individual who attempted even to undertake this huge task alone would be either an impostor or a madman. The personal character of the members of the corporation will guarantee its integrity, and the adequate capital of the Company will prove its stability.

These **prefatory** remarks are merely intended as a hasty reply to the mass of objections which the very words "Jewish State" are certain to arouse. Henceforth we shall proceed more slowly to meet further objections and to explain in detail what has been as yet only indicated; and we shall try in the interests of this pamphlet to avoid making it a dull exposition. Short **aphoristic** chapters will therefore best answer the purpose.

If I wish to substitute a new building for an old one, I must demolish before I construct. I shall therefore keep to this natural sequence. In the first and general part I shall explain my ideas, remove all prejudices, determine essential political and economic conditions, and develop the plan.

Inaugurated: Started offcially.

Prefatory: Introductory.

Aphoristic: Stated clearly, concisely, and understandably.

In the special part, which is divided into three principal sections, I shall describe its execution. These three sections are: The Jewish Company, Local Groups, and the Society of Jews. The Society is to be created first, the Company last; but in this exposition the reverse order is preferable, because it is the financial soundness of the enterprise which will chiefly be called into question, and doubts on this score must be removed first.

In the conclusion, I shall try to meet every further objection that could possibly be made. My Jewish readers will, I hope, follow me patiently to the end. Some will naturally make their objections in an order of succession other than that chosen for their **refutation**. But whoever finds his doubts dispelled should give allegiance to the cause.

Although I speak of reason, I am fully aware that reason alone will not suffice. Old prisoners do not willingly leave their cells. We shall see whether the youth whom we need are at our command—the youth, who irresistibly draw on the old, carry them forward on strong arms, and transform rational motives into enthusiasm.

II.—The Jewish Question . . .

THE PLAN: The whole plan is in its essence perfectly simple, as it must necessarily be if it is to come within the comprehension of all.

Let the **sovereignty** be granted us over a portion of the globe large enough to satisfy the rightful requirements of a nation; the rest we shall manage for ourselves.

The creation of a new State is neither ridiculous nor impossible. We have in our day witnessed the process in connection with nations which were not largely members of the middle class, but poorer, less educated, and consequently weaker than ourselves. The Governments of all countries scourged by Anti-Semitism will be keenly interested in assisting us to obtain the sovereignty we want.

The plan, simple in design, but complicated in execution, will be carried out by two agencies: The Society of Jews and the Jewish Company.

The Society of Jews will do the preparatory work in the domains of science and politics, which the Jewish Company will afterwards apply practically.

The Jewish Company will be the liquidating agent of the business interests of departing Jews, and will organize commerce and trade in the new country.

Refutation: Denial.

Sovereignty: Political control.

PALESTINE OR ARGENTINE?: *Shall we choose Palestine or Argentine? We shall take what is given us, and what is selected by Jewish public opinion. The Society will determine both these points.*

*Argentine is one of the most fertile countries in the world, extends over a vast area, has a sparse population and a mild climate. The Argentine Republic would derive considerable profit from the **cession** of a portion of its territory to us. The present infiltration of Jews has certainly produced some discontent, and it would be necessary to enlighten the Republic on the intrinsic difference of our new movement.*

*Palestine is our ever-memorable historic home. The very name of Palestine would attract our people with a force of marvelous potency. If **His Majesty the Sultan** were to give us Palestine, we could in return undertake to regulate the whole finances of Turkey. We should there form a portion of a **rampart** of Europe against Asia, an outpost of civilization as opposed to barbarism. We should as a neutral State remain in contact with all Europe, which would have to guarantee our existence. The **sanctuaries of Christendom** would be safeguarded by assigning to them an extra-territorial status such as is well-known to the law of nations. We should form a guard of honor about these sanctuaries, answering for the fulfillment of this duty with our existence. This guard of honor would be the great symbol of the solution of the Jewish question after eighteen centuries of Jewish suffering. . . .*

VI. Conclusion

*How much has been left unexplained, how many defects, how many harmful **superficialities**, and how many useless repetitions in this pamphlet, which I have thought over so long and so often revised!*

But a fair-minded reader, who has sufficient understanding to grasp the spirit of my words, will not be repelled by these defects. He will rather be roused thereby to cooperate with his intelligence and energy in a work which is not one man's task alone, and to improve it.

Have I not explained obvious things and overlooked important objections?

I have tried to meet certain objections; but I know that many more will be made, based on high grounds and low.

To the first class of objections belongs the remark that the Jews are not the only people in the world who are in a condition of distress. Here I would reply that we may as well begin by removing a little of this misery, even if it should at first be no more than our own.

Cession: Yielding control or rights to another.

His Majesty the Sultan: The ruler of the Ottoman Empire.

Rampart: Protective barrier.

Sanctuaries of Christendom: Religious sites revered by Christians.

Superficialities: Thoughts and actions concerned only with what is apparent on the surface.

It might further be said that we ought not to create new distinctions between people; we ought not to raise fresh barriers, we should rather make the old disappear. But men who think in this way are amiable visionaries; and the idea of a native land will still flourish when the dust of their bones will have vanished tracelessly in the winds. Universal brotherhood is not even a beautiful dream. **Antagonism** *is essential to man's greatest efforts.*

But the Jews, once settled in their own State, would probably have no more enemies. As for those who remain behind, since prosperity **enfeebles** *and causes them to diminish, they would soon disappear altogether. I think the Jews will always have sufficient enemies, such as every nation has. But once fixed in their own land, it will no longer be possible for them to scatter all over the world. The* **diaspora** *cannot be reborn, unless the civilization of the whole earth should collapse; and such a consummation could be feared by none but foolish men. Our present civilization possesses weapons powerful enough for its self-defence.*

Innumerable objections will be based on low grounds, for there are more low men than noble in this world. I have tried to remove some of these narrow-minded notions; and whoever is willing to fall in behind our white flag with its seven stars, must assist in this campaign of enlightenment. Perhaps we shall have to fight first of all against many an evil-disposed, narrow-hearted, short-sighted member of our own race.

Again, people will say that I am furnishing the Anti-Semites with weapons. Why so? Because I admit the truth? Because I do not maintain that there are none but excellent men amongst us?

Will not people say that I am showing our enemies the way to injure us? This I absolutely dispute. My proposal could only be carried out with the free consent of a majority of Jews. Action may be taken against individuals or even against groups of the most powerful Jews, but Governments will never take action against all Jews. The equal rights of the Jew before the law cannot be withdrawn where they have once been conceded; for the first attempt at withdrawal would immediately drive all Jews, rich and poor alike, into the ranks of revolutionary parties. The beginning of any official acts of injustice against the Jews invariably brings about economic crises. Therefore, no weapons can be effectually used against us, because these injure the hands that wield them. Meantime hatred grows apace. The rich do not feel it much, but our poor do. Let us ask our poor, who have been more severely **proletarized** *since the last removal of Anti-Semitism than ever before.*

Antagonism: Hostility.

Enfeebles: Weakens.

Diaspora: Scattering of Jews from Palestine in about 600 BCE.

Proletarized: Made into the proletariat, or laboring class.

Some of our prosperous men may say that the pressure is not yet severe enough to justify emigration, and that every forcible expulsion shows how unwilling our people are to depart. True, because they do not know where to go; because they only pass from one trouble into another. But we are showing them the way to the Promised Land; and the splendid force of enthusiasm must fight against the terrible force of habit.

*Persecutions are no longer so **malignant** as they were in the Middle Ages? True, but our sensitiveness has increased, so that we feel no **diminution** in our sufferings; prolonged persecution has overstrained our nerves.*

Will people say, again, that our enterprise is hopeless, because even if we obtained the land with supremacy over it, the poor only would go with us? It is precisely the poorest whom we need at first. Only the desperate make good conquerors.

Will some one say: Were it feasible it would have been done long ago?

It has never yet been possible; now it is possible. A hundred—or even fifty—years ago it would have been nothing more than a dream. Today it may become a reality. Our rich, who have a pleasurable acquaintance with all our technical achievements, know full well how much money can do. And thus it will be: just the poor and simple, who do not know what power man already exercises over the forces of Nature, just these will have the firmest faith in the new message. For these have never lost their hope of the Promised Land.

Here it is, fellow Jews! Neither fable nor deception! Every man may test its reality for himself, for every man will carry over with him a portion of the Promised Land—one in his head, another in his arms, another in his acquired possessions.

Now, all this may appear to be an interminably long affair. Even in the most favorable circumstances, many years might elapse before the commencement of the foundation of the State. In the meantime, Jews in a thousand different places would suffer insults, mortifications, abuse, blows, depredation, and death. No; if we only begin to carry out the plans, Anti-Semitism would stop at once and for ever. For it is the conclusion of peace.

The news of the formation of our Jewish Company will be carried in a single day to the remotest ends of the earth by the lightning speed of our telegraph wires.

And immediate relief will ensue. The intellects which we produce so superabundantly in our middle classes will find an outlet in our first

Malignant: Mean or evil.

Diminution: Reduction.

organizations, as our first technicians, officers, professors, officials, lawyers, and doctors; and thus the movement will continue in swift but smooth progression.

Prayers will be offered up for the success of our work in temples and in churches also; for it will bring relief from an old burden, which all have suffered.

But we must first bring enlightenment to men's minds. The idea must make its way into the most distant, miserable holes where our people dwell. They will awaken from gloomy brooding, for into their lives will come a new significance. Every man need think only of himself, and the movement will assume vast proportions.

And what glory awaits those who fight unselfishly for the cause!

Therefore I believe that a wondrous generation of Jews will spring into existence. The **Maccabeans** *will rise again.*

Let me repeat once more my opening words: The Jews who wish for a State will have it.

We shall live at last as free men on our own soil, and die peacefully in our own homes.

The world will be freed by our liberty, enriched by our wealth, magnified by our greatness.

And whatever we attempt there to accomplish for our own welfare, will react powerfully and beneficially for the good of humanity.

Maccabeans: Family of Jewish patriots who revolted against Syrian rule in Judea in the first century BCE.

What happened next . . .

Rarely has the publication of a single book had such a large impact on the history of a people and a nation. *The Jewish State* ignited interest in the question of Jewish immigration from countries experiencing anti-Semitism. Almost immediately Herzl became the figurehead of a growing movement to promote the ideas of Zionism. He published a newspaper, *Die Welt* (*The World*), which helped to spread his ideas. He also organized the First Zionist Congress in Basle, Switzerland, in 1897, which attracted two hundred delegates from around the world. From that very first Congress, delegates stated their preference for Palestine as the destination for Jewish immigration. From that point on, Zionism's major efforts were directed toward creating a Jewish homeland in Palestine. In the years that followed the Zionist Organization formed in Basle grew in wealth and influence and Jewish immigration to Palestine increased.

The Zionist goal of creating a Jewish homeland in Palestine did not progress as easily as Herzl had predicted, however. From the beginning, Arabs living in the area resented the Zionists' claim that Palestine was a land awaiting proper management. Arab peasants were evicted from their homes and farms when wealthy Zionists bought up the land. From the early 1900s, Arabs resisted the Jewish presence in Palestine. To this day, many Arabs in the region feel that Palestine was stolen from its rightful inhabitants by ruthless Zionists willing to use their wealth and power to build a state.

Summing up the events of the First Zionist Congress in 1897, Herzl declared: "In Basle I created the Jewish State. Were I to say this aloud I would be greeted by universal laughter. But perhaps five years hence, in any case, certainly fifty years hence, everyone will perceive it. The state exists as essence in the will-to-the-state of a people...," as quoted by Naomi Pasachoff in *Links in the Chain: Shapers of the Jewish Tradition*. In fact, he was correct, almost to the year. In 1948 the nation of Israel declared its independence as a Jewish state. Herzl's vision had been realized, but not without consequences. Jews fought with Arabs in the region from the beginning of the Jewish immigration to Palestine, and since its establishment in 1948 Israel has engaged in several costly wars with its Arab neighbors. Even today, Israel is under constant threat from attacks conducted by Palestinians, Arabs who claim ties to the region once known as Palestine. Certainly, Herzl did not anticipate that the realization of the Zionist dream would cause such lasting conflict.

Did you know ...

- Among Jews, a period of substantial immigration to Israel is known by the Hebrew word "aliyah." The first aliyah occurred in the early 1880s, when some thirty-five thousand Russian Jews immigrated to Palestine. The second aliyah—encouraged by Herzl's Zionist organizing—drew about forty thousand Jews to Palestine between 1904 and 1914.

- One of the most common objections to early Jewish immigration to Palestine was that the arid region would not be able to support the increased population. Jewish settlers disproved this argument by developing successful dry-farming methods and building irrigation networks using a complicated system of canals.

- The nation of Israel offers Jews around the world the right to immigrate to Israel. This right is referred to as the "right of return."

- Theodor Herzl died in 1904, well before Zionists had secured their goal of creating a homeland for Jews.

Consider the following . . .

- Herzl imagined that Jewish migration to a national homeland would benefit the countries that these Jews were leaving, because it would bring an end to the social unrest caused by anti-Semitism. Was this part of his dream realized?

- Herzl speaks of steam power with enough force to propel an engine. What is this a metaphor for? Does this metaphor work to explain the conditions Herzl describes?

- There are a number of statements in Herzl's book that appear very prophetic. Identify these statements and the ways in which they have come to be fulfilled.

- Herzl proposes that Argentina might have been a reasonable place to create a Jewish state. How would history have been different if the Jewish national homeland had been created in Argentina? Some factors to consider are the stability of that part of the world, the availability of natural resources, and the role played by race and religion.

- Compare and contrast *The Jewish State* to one or more of the other documents in this section of the book. How do these visions for the Middle East differ? Are they compatible or contrary to each other? To what extent do these visions still shape politics in the region?

For More Information

Books

Elon, Amos. *Herzl*. New York: Holt, Rinehart, and Winston, 1975.

Finkelstein, Norman H. *Theodor Herzl: Architect of a Nation*. Minneapolis, MN: Lerner Publications, 1991.

Herzl, Theodor. *Das Judenstaat*. 1896; translated as *The Jewish State: An Attempt at a Modern Solution of the Jewish Question*. New York: American Zionist Emergency Council, 1946.

Pasachoff, Naomi. *Links in the Chain: Shapers of the Jewish Tradition*. New York: Oxford University Press, 1997.

Vital, David. *The Origins of Zionism*. Oxford U.K.: Clarendon Press, 1975.

Web Sites

"Immigration." *Jewish Virtual Library*. http://www.jewishvirtuallibrary.org/jsource/Immigration/immigtoc.html (accessed on June 24, 2005).

Israel, Steve. "The Story of Zionism." *Jewish Agency for Israel*. http://www.jafi.org.il/education/100/zionism/ (accessed on June 24, 2005).

"Theodor (Binyamin Ze'ev) Herzl." *Jewish Virtual Library*. http://www.jewishvirtuallibrary.org/jsource/biography/Herzl.html (accessed on June 24, 2005).

Speech to the Officers' Club

Excerpts from Gamal Abdel Nasser's Speech to the Officers' Club
(April 25, 1959)
Speech given in Cairo, Egypt
Reprinted in *The Arab States and the Arab League: A Documentary Record*
Published in 1962

W ell before the collapse of the Ottoman Empire, a vast empire of southwest Asia, northeast Africa, and southeast Europe that reigned from the thirteenth century to the early twentieth century, in 1918, Arabs in the Middle East had dreamed that they would attain political independence, perhaps in a single state encompassing the entire Arabian peninsula. Husayn Ibn Ali (1852–1931)—who held the title of Sherif of Mecca, making him the leading Muslim religious figure on the Arabian peninsula—led an Arab revolt against Ottoman rule in 1916, at the height of World War I (1914–18; war in which Great Britain, France, the United States, and their allies defeated Germany, Austria-Hungary, and their allies). But at the end of the war, Britain and France divided the Middle East into territories under their control. Arab dreams of independence were thus temporarily thwarted.

By the 1950s the Arab world had developed into a multinational region. European control of the region had carved the Middle East—an area that had once been loosely defined by small emirates, or kingdoms—into numerous nations, including the newly created Jewish state of Israel in the former territory of

"The obliteration of Arab nationalism from any Arab country means that our turn will come to defend nationalism in our country."

Palestine. Though these nations went about creating their own unique national identities upon gaining their independence, there remained a desire among many to unite all Arabs within a single Arab state. This desire was known as Pan-Arabism.

Pan-Arabism was a vision for the Middle East that enjoyed popularity in the 1950s and 1960s. Pan-Arabism held that all Arabs would unite in a single state. That state would obey the following principles: it would be secular, with the government not tied to any particular religion; it would be socialist, following a system by which the major means of production and distribution are owned, managed, and controlled by the government; and it would be anti-imperialist, meaning it would not ally itself with either of the major powers trying to exert political influence in the world—the United States and its allies, or the Soviet Union. Pan-Arabists believed that the only way for Arabs to realize their potential was to follow these principles.

The greatest proponent of Pan-Arabism was Egyptian president Gamal Abdel Nasser (1918–1970). Nasser had come to power in the early 1950s as part of a movement that removed the country's monarch, or king, and promoted Egyptian nationalism (devotion to the interests and culture of Egypt). In 1956 he became the country's first president and soon emerged as a champion of Arab political causes. Nasser believed that the Arab world could only escape the domination of foreign powers if governments directed the actions of people toward improving agriculture and industry. In 1958 he joined with Syrian president Shukri al-Quwatli to form the United Arab Republic, a political union intended as a first step toward further Arab unification. In 1959 Nasser spoke of his goals for the Pan-Arabist movement to a group of military and political leaders in Cairo, Egypt.

Things to remember while reading excerpts from Gamal Abdel Nasser's "Speech to the Officers' Club"

- The key components of Nasser's ideology are Pan-Arabism, anti-imperialism (being against large countries taking over smaller countries), and anti-Zionism (being against the creation of a Jewish state in Palestine). Watch for the different ways that he refers to each of these key issues.

- Some of Nasser's longtime rivals for power in the Middle East were Jordan and Iraq. Look for the subtle ways that he criticizes his political enemies.

- Nasser's speech contains both a short version of recent Middle Eastern history and proposals for future action.

Excerpts from Gamal Abdel Nasser's Speech to the Officers' Club (April 25, 1959)

Brethren:

I extend my congratulations to you all and wish you success in the great work you undertake for the glory of our nation.

*Circumstances and occasions often change, but whatever changes may occur, the men of the Armed Forces always bear the same eternal duty of protecting the **Fatherland** and the people's objectives. Moreover, they must always be ready at any time to protect the gains we make. . . .*

When we look at the position we occupy in the world, this world in which we live and from which we cannot separate ourselves, we find that our zone is one of great strategic importance, that its history reflects all sorts of differences, particularly the struggles of the great powers for domination over the area on account of its vital and strategic importance.

We men of the Armed Forces therefore have a great responsibility, as our country has always been the target of the ambitions of the big powers, those big powers that always seek power and think they can have it through dominating our land.

*However, we have resolved to follow an independent policy and to maintain the independence of our country. We made that known when we declared that our policy is based on positive neutrality and **non-alignment**, for this means that we shall not submit to power politics, and shall not, under any circumstances, accept the role of a **satellite** or allow our fate to be decided in a foreign country or our policy to be planned in a foreign capital. . . .*

*As soon as **Cairo** achieved its independence through freeing the country from British occupation and domination . . . the banner of Arab*

Fatherland: Egypt.

Non-alignment: The refusal to create a political alliance with any of the "big powers," i.e. the United States, Britain, France, or the Soviet Union.

Satellite: Country that is dependent on another country in terms of government or economic stability.

Cairo: The capital of Egypt.

Gamal Abdel Nasser, a firm supporter of Pan-Arabism, often prompted the military in his country for support. *(© Bettmann/Corbis.)*

nationalism and Arab solidarity was raised in Cairo and we felt that we could not really feel free or enjoy our independence until each and every Arab country became independent. The independence of all Arab countries is a closely knit entity and we consider that there is a serious threat to our independence if any Arab country remains under foreign domination. When both Egypt and Syria achieved their freedom and the two countries raised the banner of Arab nationalism, we find that the Arab people in Egypt and Syria united in defending and upholding the independence of the Arab world and Arab nationalism.

We felt that the armed forces were imperative in defending and safeguarding this freedom and this great call for Arab nationalism which now came to prove its existence. The call for Arab nationalism is not a *racial call, it is not the call of any one person, neither is it a new call; the call of Arab nationalism rang throughout the centuries and showed its strength whenever the Arab countries were independent or whenever they felt the threat of danger. The banner of Arab nationalism was raised in the 10th Century—when the Arab countries were threatened with invasion and outside pressures they realized that their very existence depended on their strong belief in and adherence to Arab nationalism, to protect the Arab world and its civilization. The united Arab army was then able to defeat the* **Crusaders** *who occupied the Arab world for over 80 years. The Arab armies achieved this victory only when they felt that their unity brought them strength and that Arab nationalism was their shield of protection. The union between the armies of Egypt and Syria brought them success and they saved Syria and Egypt and Palestine and all the other Arab countries from the occupation of the Crusaders. In truth the call of Arab nationalism is not a new call, nor is it a newly discovered mission—indeed it is a deeply-rooted factor in the heart and mind of the Arab nation; the Arab nation was sometimes distracted from it but rallied round it and clung to it whenever it was faced with danger.*

When the **Tartars** *invaded this part of the world, occupying Baghdad and crossing the Euphrates into Syria and threatened Egypt, it became clear that the only way to repel this invasion was by rallying under the flag of Arab nationalism. Eventually the Syrian and Egyptian armies united and successfully pushed the Tartar forces back of the Euphrates. The Tartars had not met such a setback in their invasion until they reached Syria. Once again were the Arab armies by means of their united strength able to defeat the enemy and save the Arab nation and its civilization. This was by no means a racial mission, it was a mission of sacrifice for and defence of the Arab world.*

During the First World War, when the Arabs wanted to rid themselves of the Ottoman occupation which lasted for over 500 years they resorted again to Arab nationalism and unity. The Arab revolution rallied round the banner of Arab nationalism but committed the error of allying itself with Britain instead of depending only on the Arab people to reach its goal of independence and freedom. It is inconceivable that any major power would desire us to achieve independence and unity. Britain exploited Arab nationalism and used it to defeat the Ottoman Empire. After the First World War Britain did not fulfill its promises to the Arab people—instead the Arab world was divided under British and French rule. But the people of the Arab nations

Crusaders: Christian soldiers who traveled to the Middle East to fight Muslims in the Middle Ages (c. 500–c. 1500).

Tartars: Muslims from Turkey and northward.

rebelled against this foreign rule and fought for their independence until the **Palestine War** broke out. The Arab countries entered the Palestine War, not under the unified flag of Arab nationalism, but torn by internal feuds, jealousies and **rancour**. We were seven armies fighting in Palestine under 6 or 7 different and separate commands. The great tragedy which befell the Arab nation was a direct result of the jealous ambitions between the different commands. We all know how these battles were carried out and how Israel, exploiting our division upon ourselves and our jealous feuds, struck at one Arab army after another; we know the tragic end of the Palestine War. We know that the Arabs, the Palestinians, were kicked out of Palestine and became refugees after the victory of international **Zionism**. International Zionism constitutes a threat to all the Arab countries for Israel is not the outcome of Zionism's efforts in 1948 only—these efforts started a long time ago and stretched over the years until they achieved their first material victory, the **Balfour Declaration** of 1917. From 1917 until 1948 Zionism and **Imperialism** continued their efforts and intrigues to put this declaration into effect. We can say that 1948 is not the year in which the Palestine story started and ended—it started long before that and Zionist aims were not restricted to that part of Palestine which their forces occupied. The Zionists always claimed that their holy state extends from the Nile to the Euphrates. As they seized opportunities in the past, they will try to do the same in the future. We all know that when they **annexed** part of the Egyptian territory in the Sinai peninsula after their aggression against us, they did so in the hope of keeping it under their rule.

This does not suit in any way the interests of International Zionism, because it knows, together with Israel, that Arab Union, or Arab solidarity and military strength spells a quick end to their expansionist schemes in the Arab world. What it actually means for them is that with the springing up of a strong Arab community on their borders, it will be utterly impossible for them to realize their ambitions, or to go on violating the rights of the Palestinians Arabs who have been thrown out of their homeland in 1948, and who still are determined to regain their rights in their own country, their rights to their own land and their own properties which have long been **usurped** from them.

International Zionism, then, spared no efforts in its fight against Arab Nationalism, and its attempts at preventing the Arab countries from coming together in a military agreement. They used every possible means to achieve this end, through the influence they have in the

Palestine War: War between Israel and surrounding Arab nations that began when Israel declared its independence in 1948.

Rancour: Bitterness, resentment.

Zionism: An international political movement that called for the creation of an independent Jewish state in Palestine.

Balfour Declaration: Declaration by Britain which supported the creation of a Jewish homeland in Palestine.

Imperialism: Increasing a nation's strength by acquiring territories or political dominance over other nations.

Annexed: Took possession of.

Usurped: Taken.

imperialist countries, through money, inducement and even through using traitors inside the Arab world, who were known to have betrayed their countries in the past.

Imperialism, on its part too, which long aspired to place this part of the world in its spheres of influence, in order to dominate it and usurp its wealth at the cheapest of prices, establish military and air bases on its soil so as to achieve military superiority, this same Western imperialism also felt it could never reach its goals as long as there was a strong Arab nation facing it; it also realised that it would not have a chance as long as it was encountered with the kind of solidarity that the Arabs now had, the solidarity that enabled them to have one strong unified army working for the sole purpose of protecting the Arab nation.

Imperialism therefore strove in every way it could to divide the Arab countries, and to sow the seeds of dissension and hatred among them, using the traitors and agents of imperialism who have always collaborated with it, and who already accepted to become stooges selling their countries at a cheap price.

Those are the treacherous statesmen who accepted to work as agents and stooges for imperialism, and for a fifth column against their own countries and against the freedom of their own peoples.

*Western imperialism went along this road using every possible means; money, influence, propaganda, economic warfare and economic blockade. Relying on these agents, it attempted to spread **discord** between the Arab countries, fabricate crises so as to **disseminate** hatred among the Arabs.*

These were the bases of this alliance between Western imperialism and Zionism, the spreading of disunity and hatred among the Arab people. But the Arab awakening which made the people aware of all such methods, the Arab determination to achieve complete freedom and independence for their countries and their knowledge of the road that leads to the realization of their aspirations, defeated all these attempts of the Imperialist-Zionist alliance. . . .

But, to their misfortune, this hatred the imperialists hoped to disseminate among the Arab countries or among the sons of the Arab nation, was doomed to failure because the Arab people firmly believe in Arab nationalism and knew that in adhering to this nationalism lay their only salvation and their future security. They knew that the unity of the Arab countries and their solidarity were the only means to achieve Arab strength, dignity, freedom and independence. . . .

Discord: Conflict.

Disseminate: Spread.

Gamal Abdel Nasser often invited foreign leaders to Egypt, such as Sudanese prime minister al-Azhari, to keep ties strong between Arab countries. *(© Bettmann/Corbis.)*

*In all their struggles, the Arab people firmly believe in their armed forces, in the Arab army which had determined to protect this mission and to sacrifice everything for the cause of Arab nationalism. We all believe that our survival depends on the defence of every Arab country. The **obliteration** of Arab nationalism from any Arab country means that our turn will come to defend nationalism in our country. The obliteration of Arab nationalism in Palestine is a sign of danger to us. Should we slacken or weaken, our turn will come; we shall suffer the same fate as Palestine. . . .*

Obliteration: Destruction.

But our victory over the attempts of imperialism would not bring us to the end of our road, for imperialism will never despair, and will continue its endeavours to bring this area into spheres of influence by all possible means, depending on the use of its agents.

In the meantime, new factors appeared, for at this stage, after we had gained our great victory over the forces of imperialism, the **Communists** *in the Arab countries felt that the time had come for them to strike at the Arab nationalist movement and destroy it, because they saw in it an obstacle to their domination of the Arab countries.*

And with this started a new phase in our Arab Nationalism battle.

The first phase was the struggle of Arab Nationalism with Zionism…coupled with the struggle against the imperialist powers and their efforts to bring the Arab countries into spheres of influence.

The new phase in the battle was the struggle against the activities of Communist parties in the area. This phase started after the outbreak of the revolution in Iraq.

This revolution broke out in order to do away with the agents of imperialism in the country. It adopted the call for Arab Nationalism. Then the Communist party in Iraq started to launch attacks against the United Arab Republic and its policy, one month after the Iraqi Revolution. . . .

Attacks were launched against the United Arab Republic, and the policy of Arab solidarity, in which the Arab people had put their faith. The Communists did not consider Zionism as the danger threatening the Arab states, but preferred to attack Arab Nationalism, for they believed that this nationalism and its appeal to the Arab nation constituted the real threat to their domination of the Arab countries. . . .

Brethren, it is not a matter of difference over a doctrine or idea, but of domination, of centres of political power, of the policy of the great powers, and whether we Arab countries are free, or satellites, lying within spheres of influence, and whether we shall follow a policy of positive neutrality or align ourselves with either camp.

It was the policy of Arab Nationalism which prevented the Communist Party in Syria from gaining control of the country, and which threatens the plans of the Communists in Iraq. And it is because of this Arab nationalism that world Zionism and Israel are violently

Communists: Believers in a system of government in which the state plans and controls the economy and a single party holds power.

fighting the United Arab Republic. World imperialism also is fighting the United Arab Republic, depending on agents, stooges and opportunists, as in Iraq, for imperialism sees in the success of the United Arab Republic and its policy a consolidation of the strength of the Arabs in the area, and the potentiality of creating an independent strong zone, which would render the return of Western Imperialism to the area, in an attempt to bring it within spheres of influence, a practical impossibility. Imperialism has been defeated in several rounds, but it has not despaired and continues its attempts to bring the area within spheres of influence, by all possible means, in order to affect the international situation accordingly.

And then comes Communism . . . the aims of which were proclaimed by the Communist parties in our land. At the same time, the Eastern camp, or the Soviet Union, which had supported us in our struggle against Western imperialism, and when we declared that our policy would be built on positive neutrality and non-alignment, changed its policy. . . .

If the East intends to align the United Arab Republic to its side it will have no alternative but to fight us because the United Arab Republic is adamant in its refusal to be included in any sphere of influence. Likewise if the West desires to include this area in its sphere of influence, it will have to fight and subjugate us. The West has already waged all sorts of war against us; armed, economic, psychological and **propaganda** wars. Thus we find that there is perfect accord between these powers in their efforts to influence the people of the United Arab Republic. . . .

We have a long struggle ahead of us before we can complete our independence. The road to independence is strewn with sacrifices and requires firmness and constant protection. The price we are paying for the safeguarding of our freedom, independence and dignity does not compare in any way to the price being paid by those countries which accept the role of attendant countries to other bigger countries or which allow themselves to be **goaded** into spheres of influence. We are determined, rulers and people, to pursue a policy aiming at complete independence, non-alignment to either East or West and non-subjection to any foreign nation.

Anything we might sacrifice in pursuit of this policy is nothing compared to what the people would have to suffer if they fell under the **yoke** of a foreign power and had to live under its rule. We can see how the dominated nations cannot in any way have a will or character of their own.

Propaganda: Material distributed for the purpose of convincing people that a certain viewpoint is true, regardless of the truth or fairness of the viewpoint.

Goaded: Provoked, pushed.

Yoke: Control.

You men of the armed forces are the guardians of this country as you carry a great responsibility for a noble cause on which depends the destiny of every individual in the Arab nation, as well as the destiny of the Arab nation at large. It is the mission of Arab nationalism.

This is why the nation and the people feel confident in their struggle as they feel that they are backed by a strong national army ready to sacrifice everything.

The people feel confident. We who have drawn this policy and determined to make it independent, must do our utmost and sacrifice everything to fulfil this mission, from the President of the Republic to the last soldier. We all work for the establishment of these principles and the achievement of these goals. All the people are one army working for this cause.

May God guide our steps.

What happened next . . .

Nasser's speech, and his larger Pan-Arabist political philosophy, caused quite a stir, both in the Middle East and around the world. Within the Arab community, it excited those who supported the prospects for a unified Arab world. They saw in Pan-Arabism a way to regain Arab dignity and improve the Arab economy. They also believed that the only way to defeat Israel and regain Palestine was through united action. But others within the Arab community did not embrace Nasser's vision. Saudi Arabia preferred its monarchy and its strict religious legal system. Jordan preferred to ally itself with Britain and the United States. And political factions within every Arab nation resisted Nasser's attempts to consolidate power in his hands.

Despite the fervor of Nasser's vision, Pan-Arab unity proved very difficult to achieve. The alliance between Syria and Egypt was strained from the beginning, with Syrians feeling that they had given up too much power to Egypt. By September 1961 the Syrian military led Syria in leaving the United Arab Republic. Nasser did not wish to use the Egyptian military to fight against fellow Arabs, and the union dissolved. Egypt also formed a short-lived union with Yemen which lasted from 1958 to 1961. Pan-Arabism lost most of its supporters in 1967, when Israel defeated the combined but poorly organized troops of Egypt, Jordan, and Syria in the Six-Day War. After that time, few seriously supported the idea of Arab unification, and Arab nations each pursued their own independent course into the future. It would take the passion of Islamic fundamentalism to revive dreams of a unified Arab world in the coming years.

Did you know . . .

- From the 1940s through the early 1970s, Egypt was the wealthiest and most powerful nation in the Middle East. However, the oil-producing capacity of nations like Saudi Arabia and Iraq has since shifted the balance of economic power in the region.

- Though Syria withdrew from the United Arab Republic in 1961, Egypt continued to use the name until Nasser's death in 1970, when it was renamed the Arab Republic of Egypt.

Consider the following . . .

- Nasser offers a short version of Middle Eastern history. Is his history accurate? How has he shaped what he said to suit his political goals?

- What are the ways in which Nasser draws attention to the failings of other Arab nations? Point to those places in which he attacks his enemies, and identify those he attacks. (Hint: He doesn't refer to them directly.)

- Policy makers in the United States and Britain have often tried to depict Pan-Arabism as a radical, dangerous political philosophy. Is the tone of Nasser's speech one of a radical nature? Why might Nasser appear as a threat to those in the West?

- Compare and contrast Nasser's speech to one or more of the other documents in this section of the book. How do these visions for the Middle East differ? Are they compatible or contrary to each other? To what extent do these visions still shape politics in the region?

For More Information

Books

Farah, Tawfic E., ed. *Pan-Arabism and Arab Nationalism: The Continuing Debate.* Boulder, CO: Westview Press, 1987.

Khalil, Muhammad, ed. *The Arab States and the Arab League: A Documentary Record.* Vol. II. Rue Bliss, Beirut, Lebanon: Khayats, 1962.

Luciani, Giacomo, and Ghassan Salamé, eds. *The Politics of Arab Integration.* New York: Croom Helm, 1988.

Paparchontis, Kathleen. *100 Leaders Who Changed the World.* Milwaukee, WI: World Almanac, 2003.

Web Sites

"Nasserist Rule." *Arab Net.* http://www.arab.net/egypt/et_nasser.htm (accessed on June 24, 2005).

Jihad Against Jews and Crusaders

"Jihad Against Jews and Crusaders"
Written by the World Islamic Front
Published in *Al-Quds al-Arabi*, February 23, 1998

"All these crimes and sins committed by the Americans are clear declaration of war on Allah, his messenger, and Muslims."

For hundreds of years, Arabs in the Middle East did not hold full control over their own countries and governments. Under the Ottoman Empire (1288–1918; a vast empire of southwest Asia through northeast Africa that was ruled mainly from Turkey and was heavily influenced by the Islamic religion), they had been forced to report to governors in the capital city of Constantinople. When the Ottoman Empire collapsed during World War I (1914–18; war in which Great Britain, France, the United States, and their allies defeated Germany, Austria-Hungary, and their allies), Arabs hoped they would achieve political independence. Instead, Great Britain and France divided the region into separate states and ruled them as if they were colonies. As the twentieth century progressed, these states all gained political independence. Still, many Arabs felt that their countries were unduly influenced by the demands of other countries, either in the West (the United States, Great Britain, and France, for example) or in the East (the Soviet Union). Whether they admired Pan-Arabism (a belief that Arab countries in the Middle East would be economically and politically stronger if they combined resources and functioned as a single country) promoted by Egyptian leader Gamal Abdel Nasser (1918–1970) or took part in the Islamic Revolution achieved by Iran in 1979, Arabs throughout the Middle East sought ways to limit outside influences and establish local control of their government and society.

Religion has always played an enormous role in shaping Arabs' visions of their society. Unlike the West, where institutions of religion and government are set up to have unconnected roles in society, many countries in the Middle East are occupied by groups and individuals who want religion to directly influence governmental policy and law. Saudi Arabia, for example, has used Islamic religious law, or Sharia, as its legal system ever since its founding in 1932, and Iran adopted Sharia after its revolution in 1979 where the Iranian people overthrew the secular, or non-religious, government and installed religious leaders as lawmakers. But many of the governments established in Middle Eastern countries did not fully incorporate Islamic holy law into their governments, preferring to remain secular. Beginning in the 1960s, but gathering momentum especially after the 1980s, many Muslims in these countries began to call for Islam to play a greater role in society. No one has been more vocal in those calls than the Saudi Arabian Osama bin Laden (1957–).

In the West, Osama bin Laden has been labeled as an Islamic fundamentalist (someone who believes in a strict or literal interpretation of religious teachings) and also as a terrorist (someone who uses violence against civilian targets to accomplish a goal, often for political reason). He is known for the numerous attacks that his organization, Al Qaeda, has made, especially on American targets, such as the September 11, 2001, attacks on the World Trade Center and the Pentagon. Yet to his followers, bin Laden is a hero. By expressing his hatred of Western influences, his desire to destroy the Jewish nation of Israel, and his goal of establishing Sharia as law in every predominantly Muslim nation, bin Laden has become a figurehead for those who would like to permanently rid the Middle East of non-Islamic influences.

Osama bin Laden, one of the leaders of the World Islamic Front, is known for his attacks on Western ideas and his promotion of Islam. *(AP/Wide World Photos.)*

In 1998 bin Laden joined with several other Muslim clerics to issue a statement declaring their principles. This group called itself the World Islamic Front, though it is widely believed that this was merely a front for bin Laden's organization Al Qaeda. In the statement, reproduced below, the World Islamic Front tells Muslims that they have a duty to kill Americans. The statement was issued as a *fatwa,* a statement of religious law issued by an Islamic cleric and intended to instruct devout Muslims.

Things to remember while reading the "Jihad Against Jews and Crusaders"

- Though Osama bin Laden, one of the heads of the World Islamic Front, is a member of a wealthy Saudi Arabian family, he has been banned from his native country since 1991. He lived for a time in Sudan, and went into hiding after the bombings of the World Trade Center and Pentagon in 2001.

- Al Qaeda has conducted attacks against U.S. targets since 1992, when it bombed hotels holding U.S. soldiers in Yemen. It attacked U.S. embassies in Kenya and Tanzania in 1998. Since the United States occupied Iraq in 2003, many U.S. government officials suspect that attacks on U.S. troops stationed in Iraq have been linked to Al Qaeda, although no solid proof of this had surfaced by early 2005.

- U.S. troops have had a presence in the Middle East ever since 1990, when they were stationed in Saudi Arabia just before the start of the first Gulf War, a war where the

United States stopped Iraq from overtaking Kuwait, another Middle Eastern country.

- The other clerics who signed the statement are leaders of Islamic groups within their country.

"Jihad Against Jews and Crusaders"

23 February 1998

Shaykh Usamah Bin-Muhammad Bin-Ladin, Ayman al-Zawahiri, **amir** of the Jihad Group in Egypt, Abu-Yasir Rifa'i Ahmad Taha, Egyptian Islamic Group, Shaykh Mir Hamzah, secretary of the Jamiat-ul-Ulema-e-Pakistan, Fazlur Rahman, amir of the Jihad Movement in Bangladesh.

Praise be to **Allah**, who revealed the **Book**, controls the clouds, defeats **factionalism**, and says in His Book: "But when the forbidden months are past, then fight and slay the **pagans** wherever ye find them, seize them, **beleaguer** them, and lie in wait for them in every stratagem (of war)"; and peace be upon our Prophet, **Muhammad Bin-'Abdallah**, who said: I have been sent with the sword between my hands to ensure that no one but Allah is worshipped, Allah who put my livelihood under the shadow of my spear and who inflicts humiliation and scorn on those who disobey my orders.

The Arabian Peninsula has never—since Allah made it flat, created its desert, and encircled it with seas—been stormed by any forces like the **crusader armies** spreading in it like locusts, eating its riches and wiping out its plantations. All this is happening at a time in which nations are attacking Muslims like people fighting over a plate of food. In the light of the grave situation and the lack of support, we and you are obliged to discuss current events, and we should all agree on how to settle the matter.

No one argues today about three facts that are known to everyone; we will list them, in order to remind everyone:

First, for over seven years the United States has been occupying the lands of Islam in the holiest of places, the Arabian Peninsula, plundering its riches, dictating to its rulers, humiliating its people, terrorizing

Shaykh: An Arab chief (also spelled sheik).

Amir: A ruler or commander in Islamic countries (also spelled emir).

Allah: The supreme being of Islam.

Book: Koran, the key Islamic holy book.

Factionalism: Infighting among groups.

Pagans: People with little or no religion.

Beleaguer: Harass or persecute.

Muhammad Bin-'Abdallah: The prophet of Islam, through whom it is said Allah spoke.

Crusader armies: American soldiers directly, but also the Christian soldiers, called crusaders, who fought against Muslims in the Middle Ages.

its neighbors, and turning its bases in the Peninsula into a spearhead through which to fight the neighboring Muslim peoples.

If some people have in the past argued about the fact of the occupation, all the people of the Peninsula have now acknowledged it. The best proof of this is the Americans' continuing aggression against the Iraqi people using the Peninsula as a staging post, even though all its rulers are against their territories being used to that end, but they are helpless.

Second, despite the great devastation inflicted on the Iraqi people by the **crusader-Zionist** alliance, and despite the huge number of those killed, which has exceeded 1 million ... despite all this, the Americans are once against trying to repeat the horrific massacres, as though they are not content with the protracted blockade imposed after the ferocious war or the fragmentation and devastation.

So here they come to annihilate what is left of this people and to humiliate their Muslim neighbors.

Third, if the Americans' aims behind these wars are religious and economic, the aim is also to serve the Jews' petty state Israel and divert attention from its occupation of Jerusalem and murder of Muslims there. The best proof of this is their eagerness to destroy Iraq, the strongest neighboring Arab state, and their endeavor to fragment all the states of the region such as Iraq, Saudi Arabia, Egypt, and Sudan into paper statelets and through their disunion and weakness to guarantee Israel's survival and the continuation of the brutal crusade occupation of the Peninsula.

All these crimes and sins committed by the Americans are a clear declaration of war on Allah, his messenger, and Muslims. And **ulema** have throughout Islamic history unanimously agreed that the **jihad** is an individual duty if the enemy destroys the Muslim countries. This was revealed by Imam Bin-Qadamah in "Al-Mughni," Imam al-Kisa'i in "Al-Bada'i," al-Qurtubi in his interpretation, and the shaykh of al-Islam in his books, where he said: "As for the fighting to repulse an enemy, it is aimed at defending **sanctity** and religion, and it is a duty as agreed by the ulema. Nothing is more sacred than belief except repulsing an enemy who is attacking religion and life."

On that basis, and in compliance with Allah's order, we issue the following **fatwa** to all Muslims:

The ruling to kill the Americans and their allies—civilians and military—is an individual duty for every Muslim who can do it in any country in which it is possible to do it, in order to liberate the al-Aqsa Mosque and the holy mosque in **Mecca** from their grip, and in order for

Crusader-Zionist: A reference to Israel, which was formed by Zionists, who wanted to create a Jewish national homeland in Palestine.

Ulema: The community of Islamic scholars.

Jihad: Holy war waged on behalf of Islamic religious duty.

Sanctity: Holiness.

Fatwa: Islamic religious decree.

Mecca: The holiest site in Islam, found in Saudi Arabia.

their armies to move out of all the lands of Islam, defeated and unable to threaten any Muslim. This is in accordance with the words of Almighty Allah, "and fight the pagans all together as they fight you all together," and "fight them until there is no more tumult or oppression, and there prevail justice and faith in Allah."

This is in addition to the words of Almighty Allah: "And why should ye not fight in the cause of Allah and of those who, being weak, are ill-treated (and oppressed)?—women and children, whose cry is: 'Our Lord, rescue us from this town, whose people are oppressors; and raise for us from thee one who will help!'"

We—with Allah's help—call on every Muslim who believes in Allah and wishes to be rewarded to comply with Allah's order to kill the Americans and plunder their money wherever and whenever they find it. We also call on Muslim ulema, leaders, youths, and soldiers to launch the raid on Satan's U.S. troops and the devil's supporters allying with them, and to displace those who are behind them so that they may learn a lesson.

Almighty Allah said: "O ye who believe, give your response to Allah and His Apostle, when He calleth you to that which will give you life. And know that Allah cometh between a man and his heart, and that it is He to whom ye shall all be gathered."

Almighty Allah also says: "O ye who believe, what is the matter with you, that when ye are asked to go forth in the cause of Allah, ye cling so heavily to the earth! Do ye prefer the life of this world to the hereafter? But little is the comfort of this life, as compared with the hereafter. Unless ye go forth, He will punish you with a grievous penalty, and put others in your place; but Him ye would not harm in the least. For Allah hath power over all things."

Almighty Allah also says: "So lose no heart, nor fall into despair. For ye must gain mastery if ye are true in faith."

What happened next . . .

Osama bin Laden and Al Qaeda followed through on their threats to use violence against the United States wherever they could. Al Qaeda militants bombed a U.S. Navy destroyer, the

USS *Cole,* in Yemen on October 12, 2000, killing seventeen American soldiers. The most dramatic attack occurred on September 11, 2001, when Al Qaeda operatives hijacked four American jets and piloted them into targets that included the World Trade Center in New York City and the Pentagon in Washington, D.C. These attacks claimed more than three thousand American lives. The attacks, however, only increased the U.S. presence in the Muslim world. President George W. Bush (1946–) sent American troops to remove from power the Islamic government of Afghanistan, which had been harboring Osama bin Laden and thus supported the terrorist attacks. President Bush also ordered U.S. troops into a war against Iraq, based on that country's alleged possession of weapons of mass destruction.

In this and various other pronouncements and fatwas, bin Laden tried to inspire Muslims to rise up against all Western influences, including Israel, in order to create an Islamic world free of outside interference and dedicated to Islamic values. The name for his approach is Islamism, and it became the dominant revolutionary ideology in the Middle East—and in every country with a majority Muslim population—beginning in the 1990s. Islamist groups challenged government power in Algeria, Sudan, and Nigeria in the 1990s, and the Islamist Taliban group took power in Afghanistan in the late 1990s. Many Western observers suspect Saudi Arabia, despite its political ties to the West, of secretly supporting Islamist causes.

By the early 2000s, it was still not clear how powerful the Islamist view would be in shaping events in the Middle East. To some, bin Laden and other Islamists represent an extremist fringe that will disappear once established Middle Eastern governments devoted themselves to removing terrorist groups from within their country. Others believe that these acts of terrorism will help Islamism gain a following, and that the Muslim peoples in the Middle East will eventually rise up in support of Islamist goals. One clear influence that Islamism has had is in providing support for the idea that Muslim terrorists are serving Allah when they participate in suicide attacks. In Palestinian attacks against Israel, in Iraqi rebel attacks against U.S. forces in that country, and in Al Qaeda strikes against Western targets, suicide bombers are considered heroic martyrs, or people who give their lives for a holy cause.

Did you know . . .

- The Taliban, a strict Islamist group, held power in Afghanistan from 1996 to 2001. They banned all television and music in their country, restricted laughing in public, and used strict punishments such as cutting off hands and feet or stoning people to death to enforce government laws. Under Taliban rule, women could not obtain the same education as men, nor could they show their faces in public.

- In Turkey, an Islamist group called the Justice and Development Party has modified its views to try to bring Islamic religious values into a democratic political system.

- Saudi Arabia follows a version of Islam called Wahhabism, which urges its followers to live as the prophet Muhammad lived in the seventh century. Yet as one of the world's leading oil producers, Saudi Arabia has tried to maintain political friendships with the United States and other large, oil-consuming nations.

Consider the following . . .

- Think about bin Laden's call for Muslims to kill Americans. Is there any way to justify such a command from a religious leader? Are there any other instances where religious or political leaders have made such demands?

- Using the arguments put forth in the World Islamic Front statement, explain how the Islamist approach to Middle East politics offers solutions to the problems of the region. Then, consider whether there might be more moderate ways to solve those problems.

- Compare and contrast the World Islamic Front document to one or more of the other documents in this section of the book. How do these visions for the Middle East differ? Are they compatible or contrary to each other? To what extent do these visions still shape politics in the region?

For More Information

Books

Bergen, Peter. *Holy War, Inc.* New York: Touchstone, 2002.

Burke, Jason. *Al-Qaeda: Casting a Shadow of Terror.* New York and London: I.B. Tauris, 2003.

Loehfelm, Bill. *Osama bin Laden.* Farmington Hills, MI: Lucent Books, 2003.

Randal, Jonathan. *Osama: The Making of a Terrorist.* New York: Alfred A. Knopf, 2004.

Periodicals

World Islamic Front. "Jihad against Jews and Crusaders." *Al-Quds al-Arabi,* February 23, 1998.

Web Sites

Burke, Jason. "The Making of Osama bin Laden." *Salon.* http://dir.salon.com/news/feature/2001/11/01/osama_profile/index.html (accessed on June 24, 2005).

"Hunting Bin Laden." *PBS Frontline.* http://www.pbs.org/wgbh/pages/frontline/shows/binladen/ (accessed on June 24, 2005).

"Is Islamism a Threat?: A Debate." *The Middle East Quarterly* (December 1999). http://www.meforum.org/article/447 (accessed on June 24, 2005).

"Patterns of Global Terrorism." *U.S. Department of State.* http://www.state.gov/s/ct/rls/pgtrpt/ (accessed on June 24, 2005).

6

Personal Accounts of the Middle East Conflict

F or most people who do not live in the Middle East, the conflicts that have disrupted life in that region over the last century have been little more than reports in newspapers and magazines and on television. News stories about the dueling claims to land that set Israeli Jews against Palestinians; about the questions over whether nations in the Middle East should be secular or religious; about the tensions that exist between conservative Islamic values and the modernizing trends brought by Western commercialism; and about the lingering hatred many Arabs bear toward the West because of the West's long history of involvement in Middle Eastern affairs are often impersonal and fail to convey the misery and hardships of everyday life in the region. Instead these stories usually detail troop movements in combat zones, distant bombings, and the cautious relief of political figures who have shaken hands with an opponent after signing a peace treaty.

However, to those people who live in the Middle East, have relatives in Middle Eastern countries, or have recently visited the region, these conflicts are not merely

People of all ages and nationalities have been affected by the constant conflicts in the Middle East. *(© Peter Turnley/Corbis.)*

stories in a newspaper or on the evening news. They are daily events that shape and change lives in dramatic ways. To a Palestinian living in a village in Israeli-occupied territory, these conflicts are represented by soldiers in the street or a security checkpoint on the road to a neighbor's house. To an Israeli mother whose son has gone off to serve his required time in the Israeli army, each newscast is a chance to see her son or to hear news of his well-being. To an American reporter taken hostage and held for years, Islamic fundamentalism is not an abstract threat, but a bearded young man bringing food twice a day.

In this chapter, the conflict in the Middle East will be presented in very personal ways by several different people who have experienced it firsthand. Some of these people commit violent acts in response to events in the Middle East. Soha Bechara is a Christian Lebanese woman who was imprisoned for her attempted assassination of a military leader in Lebanon. Era Rapaport is an Israeli settler jailed for helping to plant a bomb under the vehicle of a Palestinian town mayor. Others turned to political means to make a personal impact on the Middle East conflict. Meir Kahane is an American-born Jew whose belief in Zionism, the idea of creating a stable independent Jewish state in Palestine, brought him to Israel. There he became convinced of the necessity for a radical solution to the Arab-Israeli conflict. His solution got him elected to the Israeli Knesset (legislature) and then thrown into an Israeli prison. Sumaya Farhat-Naser is a Palestinian activist whose efforts to bring about peace were frustrated by Israeli occupation. Still others were drawn into the conflict in the Middle East as pawns in the larger issues that have torn the region apart. Terry Anderson is an American journalist who was held hostage in Lebanon for more than six years by an Iranian-supported Islamic terrorist group. It is through these accounts that the true personal impacts of the various conflicts in the Middle East can be seen.

Resistance

Excerpts from **Resistance: My Life for Lebanon**
Written by Soha Bechara
Printed in 2003

"Inevitably, I would be arrested. But what would they do to me? Torture me? Execute me on the spot?"

Born in Lebanon on June 15, 1967, Soha Bechara remembered her childhood as happy and peaceful, filled with playtime with her cousins and village-wide festivals and celebrations. In her memoir, *Resistance: My Life for Lebanon,* Bechara described her village of Deir Mimas as "like paradise to me."

By the time Bechara was a teenager the situation had changed. From the early 1970s, Bechara had grown increasingly aware of the troubles that came to plague her country, as Palestinians living in camps along Lebanon's southern border fought with Jews in the neighboring country of Israel. (Palestinians—Arabs who claimed historic ties to land that now comprised the nation of Israel—had been forced to leave Jordan in 1970 and many of them, including the leadership of the political group called the Palestine Liberation Organization [PLO] settled in southern Lebanon.) Palestinian raids into Israel from southern Lebanon brought counterattacks by Israeli planes dropping bombs near Bechara's hometown.

Bechara also experienced firsthand the political differences between the Lebanese people that led to a civil war in 1975, and forced her family to travel back and forth between their village and shelters in Beirut for a time. "We were refugees in our own city," she recalled in *Resistance: My Life for Lebanon*. And by 1976 "the daily reality was war." She expressed her growing political activism by volunteering at Red Cross clinics and joining the Communist Party. When Israel invaded in 1978 and occupied a portion of Lebanon that included her childhood village, Bechara had already become accustomed to war. Despite the leaflets dropped by Israeli war planes in 1982 advising the Lebanese to leave West Beirut, Bechara wanted to stay.

A sense of devotion to the interest and culture of Lebanon had blossomed in her. "I could not stop thinking about Israel and my duty as a Lebanese," she wrote in *Resistance*, recalling her experiences in the early 1980s. She was humiliated and angered by Israel's occupation of her homeland. Eventually her nationalist beliefs culminated in her desire to do "anything" for her country. The following excerpt from Bechara's memoir, *Resistance: My Life for Lebanon*, will paint a picture of her decision to become an assassin, as well as her terrible experiences in prison.

Many Lebanese women, like Soha Bechara, fought to free portions of Lebanon from Israeli control. *(© Alain DeJean/ Sygma/Corbis.)*

Things to remember while reading Excerpts from Soha Bechara's *Resistance: My Life for Lebanon:*

- The resistance movement to which Bechara refers throughout her memoirs was a group of militant political activists who attempted to oust Israel from Lebanon throughout the late 1970s and 1980s.

- The South Lebanon Army (SLA) was a militia, or loosely organized civilian army, that served as an Israeli ally in Lebanon. Sometimes the SLA would work with the Israeli Defense Forces, Israel's army.

- Rabih was the only name by which Soha Bechara knew her superior in the resistance movement. She met him in 1986, and he was her main contact with the resistance movement as she prepared for and attempted the assassination of the South Lebanon Army leader Antoine Lahad in 1988.

- Bechara had earned the trust of Antoine Lahad by working as his wife Minerva's aerobics instructor. The position enabled her to enter the Lahad household as a guest and offered her the opportunity to spend time alone with the Lahads.

- Issam is the name of Soha Bechara's cousin, with whom she lived in Marjayoun in the area occupied by Israelis in the south of Lebanon. Issam had no idea of his cousin's activities for the resistance movement prior to her imprisonment.

- On November 7, 1988, Bechara was arrested by the South Lebanon Army and, after being interrogated in Israel, was sent to Khiam prison in southern Lebanon without being officially charged or put on trial for her attempted assassination of SLA chief Antoine Lahad.

Excerpts from Resistance: My Life for Lebanon

Chapter 8: The Operation

I met again with my contact at the heart of the resistance.

Rabih listened as I told him about my first interview with Antoine Lahad. Right away, he made it clear that we would have to plan for me to be replaced by someone whose job it would be to eliminate the militia chief. I answered that, considering the circumstances, I myself was in the best position to succeed. Rabih was not very taken with this idea. He admitted its efficiency, but he seriously doubted that I was capable of carrying out the operation. But faced with my stubbornness, he resigned himself to taking the risk. There was still the question of the weapon. . . .

Time was short, so Rabih and I decided to meet in a discreet spot, a café where couples often went on dates. That day, he secretly brought with him a 5.5 mm revolver. In a few words he told me how it worked, pointing out the safety catch. . . .

[. . .]

I took my role of aerobics instructor very seriously. Little by little, I became quite close to Minerva. . . . So I found myself going again and again to her house, either to bring her videocassettes or to work out problems with the classes. When she was busy or indisposed and I had to wait, I would play with her little son, whose affection I easily gained.

Step by step, I fine-tuned my plan. . . .

[. . .]

*Wearing a white shirt, blue pants, and black ballet slippers, I made it once again without difficulty into the couple's beautiful house. I had been dropped off by Issam, who, to kill time, liked to join the nightly **cavalcade** of cars that filled the streets of Marjayoun. Before leaving, I had taken the revolver from its **cache** and hid it among a few other little things in my purse. The SLA chief's bodyguards let me pass without suspicion.*

The usual routine.

*I found Minerva in the garden with a Spanish friend. We moved inside, where we met her friend's husband, César, the director of a television station. Later, Antoine Lahad joined us. The atmosphere was pleasant. We spoke in French. Minerva lamented once again the small-mindedness of people in the occupied zone. We moved into the living room. The militia chief sat down near the telephone, with me to his right, as I had imagined. The conversation **idled** along. I kept myself a bit behind it all.*

I listened.

*After a half-hour, our hostess asked us what we'd like to drink. I murmured my thanks, but said that it was late and I had to go. Her husband insisted, and I made as if I was staying out of politeness. The militia chief turned on the television. It was the nightly news, on the station of the occupied zone. There was a report on the **Intifada**. On the screen, I had time to see a young Palestinian throwing a stone. Antoine Lahad watched distractedly, playing with the remote control. Suddenly, the telephone rang. He picked it up. His face darkened. Whoever he was talking to was obviously bringing up an unpleasant subject.*

Cavalcade: Procession of vehicles.

Cache: Hiding place.

Idle: To go slowly.

Intifada: The armed and violent popular uprising of Palestinians against Israeli occupation in the West Bank and Gaza Strip.

I stole a glance at the living room clock.

It was nearly eight. Sitting to my left, Antoine Lahad continued his conversation. His gaze rested on me for a moment. He examined me, as if curious. I drew towards me the bag lying at my feet. I was extraordinarily calm. I slid my hand into the opening, telling Minerva that I had brought the keys and videotapes she wanted. My hand, hidden from sight, closed on the handle of the gun. Still sitting, I took the weapon from the bag like it was the most natural thing in the world. Instantly, I pointed it towards the militia chief, supporting my fist with my left hand.

*I struggled to aim at the **condemned** man's heart.*

I pulled the trigger once and thought I saw the bullet bury itself in his khaki shirt. Antoine Lahad, taken aback, shot to his feet, as Rabih had predicted. An insult sprang from his lips. . . . I fired a second time, as planned.

He staggered.

For a second, life in the living room froze. Minerva, lying on the ground, let out a scream, shattering the silence. She cried for a gun to settle me and a helicopter to evacuate her husband. I threw a sweeping glance around me. The Spanish woman, her face ashen, looked at me fixedly, like a madwoman. Her husband, paralyzed with terror, was staring at me like he would be next. I took the chance to throw the gun into the bedroom off the living room, trying to gain a little time. The bodyguards would look for the weapon as soon as they burst into the room, which would be soon enough. Six feet away from me, the militiaman's body had rolled to the floor and lay there, motionless.

Chapter 9: The Arrest

It was done. I had completed my mission.

What would happen to me now?

*I had asked myself the question a thousand times since deciding to carry out the operation, and I had never found an answer. We had made no plans for me to escape, or for someone to rescue me. It would have been too dangerous. Antoine Lahad's house was like a fortified camp. I had been able to enter an hour earlier, fooling the guards one last time, then fire on the leader of Israel's **proxy** militia. But now the two shots had sounded the alert.*

Inevitably, I would be arrested. But what would they do with me? Torture me? Execute me on the spot?

[. . .]

Condemned: Doomed.

Proxy: A person authorized to act with the authority of another.

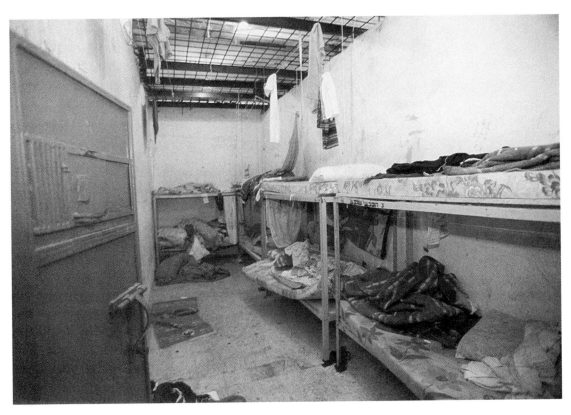

Bechara and other Lebanese resistance fighters were held for interrogation by the Israeli army inside cells at Khiam prison.

(© Thomas Hartwell/Corbis.)

Chapter 10: Khiam

Khiam, or hell with no name, with no existence.

The Khiam prison, set up in an old military installation, was created in 1985.... Khiam sat on a **promontory** *that was strategically important for the* **occupied zone**. *It was far from any fighting, quite close to Israel, and difficult to access. Officially, the SLA was responsible for the prison, although the Israelis had managed it directly when it was created and then gradually shifted the interrogation work to Lebanese* **mercenaries**. *Shin Bet, the Israeli internal security agency, kept files on all the detainees, and now and then its agents would come to inspect the premises. The squat buildings of Khiam looked down upon the village of the same name. They consisted of interrogation rooms and two sets of usually overcrowded collective cells, one set for men and one for women.*

Promontory: A high point of land overlooking a lowland or a body of water.

Occupied zone: The part of Lebanon occupied by Israeli troops.

Mercenaries: Hired soldiers.

A few other buildings housed the guards, and that was all. The prison was encircled by watchtowers and surrounded by a minefield. It would have been extraordinarily difficult, if not impossible, to escape.

When I landed there, its reputation was already well established.

[. . .]

*The prison fed on two kinds of prey. First there were the resistance fighters, myself among them, captured in battle or exposed by the security forces. We all suffered the same fate. Interrogation and torture to start, then seclusion without trial or sentence, the length of detention set by the whims of the jailers. Israel did not want to appear responsible for these **cumbersome** detainees. Probably, a part of the Israeli public would not accept such human rights violations committed under the **auspices** of their country. The proof: when Lebanese were detained on Israeli soil, kept as hostages in exchange for information about soldiers missing in action, or even more **macabre**, in exchange for the bodies of those killed and abandoned to the enemy, Israeli and Palestinian human-rights groups and lawyers would struggle tirelessly for the prisoners. In comparison, Khiam was perfect for Israel. No laws, no judges, no lawyers. Prisoners in Khiam were negated, buried, conveniently wiped from the world of the living.*

*But the security forces were not satisfied with locking up the ones who fought them. The prison was often bursting with people who had no relation to the **guerrillas**. Women, children, and the elderly, from all backgrounds, were also transferred to Khiam for the purposes of intimidation, pressure, and torture. For the SLA, it was a means to get information about people judged to be suspicious, and a way to blackmail or threaten the prisoners into collaborating with the security services in the occupied zone. For these prisoners, too, detention became a kind of lottery. No one knew, on going into Khiam, if he would be released the next week or many years later.*

*And no one could be sure of coming out alive, particularly the women—the daily routine wore down even the most healthy. In part, this was because of the climate. The prison, located to the south of Beirut but at a high altitude, was **stifling** hot in summer and freezing cold in winter. Snow would fall at that height, and the buildings, like all those in hot countries, were designed without the slightest protection against the cold. The cells, which naturally had no running water, were **spartan**. The detainees slept under sheets on old foam mattresses. Blankets were rare. Because of poor construction, the floors of the jail were never clean. Moisture rose from the ground and seeped through the mattresses at*

Cumbersome: Burdensome, awkward.

Auspices: Guidance or authority.

Macabre: Horrific.

Guerrillas: Soldiers who use unconventional fighting methods.

Stifling: Airless, oppressive.

Spartan: Simple, without comforts.

*night, chilling you to the bone. Apart from these pallets and some iron water-tanks, the detainees shared a plastic bucket, often without a lid, as a **latrine**. It was emptied twice a day, in the heat of summer as in winter. The buckets were usually constructed out of kitchen-oil jugs.*

In Khiam, the rhythm never changed.

*The women detainees were woken at dawn and given a **frugal** breakfast. They then had to clean their cell, come out by turns and empty the bucket, quickly wash themselves in the cramped room designated for that purpose, and fill up their water-cans. Time outside the cell was limited to five minutes, measured by stopwatch in a quasi-military fashion. Tardiness was severely punished. At noon, a scanty lunch was brought into the cells. In mid-afternoon, a few pieces of food were also served. These three moments were the only times of day when the prison became somewhat animated. At all other times, silence was the rule, and any raised voices were subject to punishment. Coughing, or clearing one's throat, was also prohibited. The detainees could talk in low voices with other women inside the same cell, but communication between cells was not allowed.*

*The prisoners, shut up in their cells, were cut off from all contact with the outside world. Visits were forbidden, even for families who lived only a few miles from Khiam. Nothing came to lighten the dull **monotony**. Whether they had been captured during an operation or torn unsuspecting from their beds, the women were all in the same boat. . . .*

*The mediocre food and uncomfortable cells encouraged sickness in bodies already tired out by interrogations and intensive torture. In the prison, where the detainees (men and women) sometimes numbered over two hundred, there were supposed to be two medical orderlies, of extremely limited competence and means, but usually there was only one. In Khiam, you were better off not getting sick. It was very difficult to get permission from the camp authorities to be transferred to the nearest hospital in Margayoun. You were also better off not complaining too much or breaking the rules. **Reprisals** were instant. Beatings and time in solitary subdued the more rebellious.*

. . . For the male prisoners, living conditions were even harsher than for the women, partly because of overcrowding and the constant beatings administered by the guards. This was especially true of the solitary cells. A woman confined to solitary was locked up in a sort of box, two and a half feet wide by six and a half feet long and eight feet high, in which she could still move a little. For the men, the solitary was a nightmare; the cell was a cube, measuring less than three feet a side, pierced by a tiny hole. The prisoner, swallowed up, compressed, folded

Latrine: Toilet.

Frugal: Minimal.

Monotony: Sameness.

Reprisals: Retaliatory actions.

over on himself, was of course unable to stand and could barely move except to eat. He was sometimes taken out so that he could hurriedly wash himself. Yet somehow prisoners survived in that half-light for many months, though they often suffered heavy consequences: skeletal disorders and problems of vision. One of them held out for a year and a half of this inhuman treatment.

What happened next . . .

Antoine Lahad survived Soha Bechara's attack, and Bechara spent ten years in the prison at Khiam. The mistreatment of prisoners at Khiam came to international attention, and several groups rallied in their calls for better treatment of Khiam's prisoners and for Bechara's freedom in particular. The horror of her imprisonment continues to haunt Bechara. Freed on September 3, 1998, Bechara confessed in her memoir that "I have not spent a single day since I was freed without thinking of the camp, of those men and women who suffered there." In 2000, when the Israeli forces left southern Lebanon, Khiam closed. Bechara wrote of the time as "a rare moment of unity for the Lebanese," who had been divided for so long.

But that moment was short-lived. Although the enemies had changed since Bechara first took up her fight for freedom, Lebanon remained divided in the 2000s. Religious and political differences continued to cause conflict in the nation. In addition, the neighboring country of Syria, which had become a strong political force in Lebanon since sending troops to support various factions in the civil war in 1976, maintained its troops in Lebanon even after the civil war ended in 1990, and tried to gain control of the Lebanese government.

On March 13, 2005, an estimated one-fourth of the Lebanese population demonstrated for national unity and against Syria. Demonstrators called for the withdrawal of Syrian troops and an investigation into the deaths of Lebanese officials perceived to be at odds with Syria. The rally was considered to be the "biggest anti-government demonstration ever staged in the Arab world," according to the Everett, Washington, *Herald.* In what demonstrators called "an independent revolution," according to the *Herald,* Sunni Muslims, Christians, Shiites, and Druze united to announce, as one Beirut resident put it, "The most important thing is that I'm Lebanese." Bechara's desire for "a free Lebanon, a country at peace," which she wrote about in *Resistance,* continued to be the quest for millions of its citizens.

Did you know . . .

- Of Bechara's ten years in prison, six were spent alone in a cell that measured six feet by two feet. During this time she was allowed only ten minutes to eat the one meal served each day.

- Israeli troops forced the Palestine Liberation Organization (PLO) out of Lebanon in 1982, but Israel remained an occupying force in Lebanon until 2000.

- In 1989 Khiam prisoners revolted against their poor treatment. The uprising resulted in the deaths of two inmates and only a few improvements, such as blankets and sanitary buckets.

- In 1994 the International Committee of the Red Cross (ICRC) won the prisoners of Khiam many rights once denied, including communication with relatives and limited visits, the ability to receive packages of clothing, food, and toiletries, and access to news and books.

- Upon her release from Khiam on September 3, 1998, Soha Bechara found it difficult to adjust to life outside of prison, especially because she was overwhelmed by questions from thousands of journalists and visitors. To adapt to her new life away from the public eye, she moved to France.

Consider the following . . .

- Soha Bechara's personal account of conflict is unusual because most prison memoirs have been written by men. Identify the details in her story that are unique because of her gender.

- Female participants in revolutionary movements are often characterized as acting out plans designed by men without being fully knowledgeable about the consequences or meanings of their activities. Describe Soha Bechara's knowledge of her own activities. Use specific examples from the excerpt to support the description.

- Soha Bechara describes inmates' poor treatment at Khiam. Imagine that the world has just learned of Khiam inmates' miserable conditions during its years of operation. Write a persuasive letter to the United Nations requesting international support for the humane treatment of prisoners. Possibly do extra research on the historical treatment of prisoners to make the letter more convincing.

For More Information

Books

Bechara, Soha. *Resistance: My Life for Lebanon.* Brooklyn, NY: Soft Skull Press, 2003.

Periodicals

"Giant Crowd Rallies in Lebanon." *Herald* (Everett, Washington) (March 15, 2005): p. A3.

Web Sites

"Syria Withdraws Up to 6, 000 Troops from Lebanon." *The New York Times.* http://www.nytimes.com/reuters/international/international-lebanon. html? (accessed on June 24, 2005).

They Must Go

Excerpts from **They Must Go**
Written by Meir Kahane
Published in 1981

American-born Meir Kahane (1932–1990) became an infamous political radical in Israel during the 1970s and 1980s. A fervent Zionist, or person who supports the creation of an independent Jewish state, he moved to Israel with the goal of securing a homeland for Jews. Once there, he became convinced that a Jewish homeland must restrict and limit Arab participation. He noticed a detail in the Israeli constitution that he considered fatal to the survival of the Jewish state, namely that Arabs were allowed to coexist in Israel as full citizens. Kahane was not afraid to voice his opinions about it.

Kahane built a political party around his vision of an Israel created for Jews alone. Labeled a racist by some Israelis, Kahane was embraced by others as the Jewish radical needed to combat Palestinians who threatened Israel. His positions drew support from those in Israeli politics who were very conservative, even as he encouraged violent acts against Arabs. But for those hoping to solve the dilemma of Jews' and Arabs' conflicting claims to the land once called Palestine, Kahane seemed dangerous.

Kahane gained his reputation, for good and for bad, when he was detained by Israeli police and became involved in several

"A time bomb in the Holy Land ticks away relentlessly."

Meir Kahane was known for his extreme views against Arabs living within Israel, which he wrote about in *They Must Go*. (© *Hulton-Deutsch Collection/Corbis.*)

trials throughout the 1970s and 1980s. Along with his political rallying, his most infamous activities included a plan to avenge the Israeli athletes killed by Palestinians at the 1972 Olympic Games, an attempted assassination of the Soviet ambassador, and a plot to explode a bomb at the Iraqi Embassy in Washington, D.C.

On May 13, 1980, Kahane was imprisoned in Israel's maximum security prison at Ramle without being formally charged with a crime. In his prison cell, Kahane wrote *They Must Go,* a book detailing his philosophy against the coexistence of Arabs and Jews in Israel, and his argument about the "flaw," or what he called the "ultimate contradiction," that he noticed in the Israeli constitution. The following excerpts from *They Must Go* illustrate Kahane's powerful voice and his extreme opinions.

Things to remember while reading excerpts from Meir Kahane's *They Must Go:*

- Meir Kahane was born Martin David Kahane on August 1, 1932, in Brooklyn, New York.

- In his teens Kahane joined a militant Zionist youth group called Betar, which trained its members in military tactics in order to fight for a Jewish state.

- Kahane was highly educated; he became a rabbi at the Yeshiva Mirrer seminary and earned a law degree from the New York Law School in the 1950s.

- Kahane wrote several books, all about his views on the creation of a Jewish state free of Arabs in Israel

Excerpts from They Must Go

*Some years ago I was arrested by the Israeli police and charged with "**incitement** to revolution." The grounds? I had reached the conclusion that it was impossible to find a solution for the Arab-Jewish confrontation in the Land of Israel (both the State of Israel and the lands liberated in **1967**;) that the Jewish state was inevitably headed towards a situation like that in Northern Ireland; that the only possible way to avoid or to **mitigate** it was the **emigration** of Arabs. Consequently, I had sent letters to several thousand Arabs offering them an opportunity (funds and visas) to emigrate voluntarily. The fact that many Arabs replied positively and that a major Arab village in the **Galilee**, Gush Halev, offered to move all its inhabitants to Canada in return for a village there did not prevent the worried Israeli government from arresting me.*

Four long years and one important war later, a scandal broke in Israel. It was revealed that Yisrael Koenig, a high official in the Ministry of the Interior who is in charge of the northern region of Israel, had drafted a secret memorandum in which he warned of the increasing danger of Arab growth (which would make Arabs in the Galilee a majority by 1978) as well as of increasing Arab national militancy. His solution included several measures that he hoped would lead to Arab emigration.

*The pity is that vital years have passed since my original proposal, wasted years that saw the **Yom Kippur War** produce a major psychological change in Arab thinking. In the aftermath of that war and its political consequences, vast numbers of Arabs, who in 1972 were depressed and convinced that Israeli **sovereignty** could not be destroyed, are today just as convinced that time is on their side, that it will not be long before the **Zionist** state collapses. Then they—the Arabs—will hold sway over all that will be "Palestine." The necessary **corollary** is, of course, that hundreds of thousands who were potential voluntary **émigrés** nine years ago are now determined to stay and await the day of Arab victory.* But they must go.

It is in order to convince the Jew of this that I have written this book.

Incitement: Encouragement.

1967: The year of the Six-Day War, in which Israel captured portions of land that are now called the occupied territories.

Mitigate: Lessen.

Emigration: To leave one's country or region to live elsewhere.

Galilee: A region in northern Israel.

Yom Kippur War: A 1973 war between Israel and the allied Arab nations of Egypt and Syria.

Sovereignty: Political control.

Zionist: Any person working to create an independent Jewish State.

Corollary: Result.

Émigré: A person who has left his native country for political reasons.

The problem with so many people who proclaim the virtues of coexistence between the Jewish majority of the Jewish state and its Arab minority is that they hold the Arab, as well as his intelligence, and his national pride, in contempt.

There is an ultimately **insoluble** contradiction between a Jewish state of Israel that is the fulfillment of the 2,000-year-old Jewish-Zionist dream and a state in which Arabs and Jews possess equal rights—including the right of the Arabs democratically and peacefully to put an end to the Jewish state. Those who refuse to give the Arab that right but tell him he is equal think he is a fool. He is not.

The reality of the situation is therefore, clear. The Jews and Arabs of the Land of Israel ultimately cannot coexist in a Jewish-Zionist state. A time bomb in the Holy Land ticks away relentlessly.

A Jewish state means Jewish orientation and ties. It means Jewish culture and a Jewish spirit in the Jewish body politic. But above all, a Jewish spirit in the Jewish body politic. But above all, a Jewish state means Jewish sovereignty and control of its destiny. That can be accomplished only by a permanent Jewish majority and a small, insignificant, and **placid** Arab minority. But the Arabs believe that the Jews are thieves who stole their land. The Arabs feel no ties to or emotions for a state that breathes "Jewishness." And they grow, **quantitatively and qualitatively**. They will surely make violent demands for more power, including "autonomy" in various parts of the land. Eventually, the very majorityship of Jews will be threatened by the Arab birthrate. The result will be bloody conflict.

If we hope to avoid this terrible result, there is only one path for us to take: the immediate transfer of Arabs from Eretz Yisrael, the Land of Israel, to their own lands. For Arabs and Jews of Eretz Yisrael there is only one answer: separation, Jews in their land, Arabs in theirs. Separation. Only separation.

[. . .]

Chapter 6: The Ultimate Contradiction

There is an ultimate insoluble contradiction between the State of Israel that is the fulfillment of the 2,000-year-old Jewish-Zionist dream and the modern nation-state that sees all its citizens as possessing equal rights and privileges. There is an ultimately **immutable** clash between that part of Israel's Declaration of Independence that created the Jewish state and the part that promised "complete equality of social and political rights to all its citizens," even though they be Arabs and not

Insoluble: Having no solution.

Placid: Peaceful, mild.

Quantitatively and qualitatively: In number and in strength of belief.

Immutable: Not open to change.

Jews. There is—let it be said once and for all—a potential confrontation between the Jewish-Zionist state that was the millennial dream of the Jewish people and modern concepts of democracy and citizenship.

We are pained, embarrassed, thrown into intellectual agony. We hasten to avoid such talk. It is unnecessary, dangerous, irresponsible, better left unspoken. Nonsense! Far better to meet the issue, deal with it boldly and courageously, explain it to our children and ourselves, than to have it explode in our faces tomorrow.

*There is nothing for which the Jew need apologize. A people that has suffered **ecumenical agony** and that has been deprived of the rights that other nations demand for themselves owes no one an explanation. The Middle East sees Islamic republics in which the Arabic quality and the Muslim character of the state are inscribed in the constitution; who shouts about Arabic "racism"? Africans insist upon the blackness of their state, and exclusiveness of culture and identity are the foundations of scores of nations. Who apologizes? The Zionist state is Judaism, the need for a land of the Jews where the people can escape **Holocaust** and build a distinctive Jewishness that will flourish.*

*The very kernel of Jewish longing for a homeland through nearly 2,000 years of exile was the belief that the Jews were a separate and distinct people. In a world in which we recognize the right of self-determination for **Papua**, who will challenge Jewish rights?*

*Moreover, the Jews constituted a unique people in that they were at one and the same time a religion and a nation, a religio-nation, which had lived as a unique society and culture in its own land—Eretz Yisrael. On the one hand they suffered unparalleled horrors and massacres in their wanderings in foreign lands. They knew no peace in any country in which their numbers grew large and their quality shone through. There was no society, religion, or economic or social system that gave them permanent haven and rest. Jews were burned to death, drowned, cut to pieces, converted to death, **Inquisitioned** to death, **Crusaded** to death, **Islamized** to death, **pogromed** to death, and **Auschwitzed** to death. The Jews learned a bitter lesson in their twenty centuries of being strangers, of existing as a minority. The lesson? It is not good to be a stranger. Never be a minority. Never again!*

As impolite as it may sound, the Jews learned, after rivers of blood, not to trust to the tolerance and mercies and hospitality of others. They no longer wished to rely on the armies and the police and the swords of others to protect them from holocausts. Enough of being strangers.

Ecumenical agony: Religious persecution worldwide.

Holocaust: The slaughter of millions of European civilians, especially Jews, by the Nazis during World War II (1939–45).

Papua: The southeast portion of the island of New Guinea.

Inquisitioned; Inquisition: Former Roman Catholic court system for the discovery and punishment of heresy.

Crusaded; Crusades: Military expeditions undertaken by Christian churches in the eleventh, twelfth, and thirteenth centuries to win the Holy Land.

Islamized: Forced to follow the faith of Islam.

Pogrom: Attacks on Jews.

Auschwitzed; Auschwitz: Site of one of the largest Nazi concentration camps used during World War II (1939–45).

Despicable: Appalling, disgraceful.

The Jews wanted to live. The Jews wanted their own armies, their own protection, their own home.

[. . .]

If the Arab is unhappy about this one can understand. It is never easy to be a lodger in someone else's home. But his unhappiness will not be resolved, for the Jew will not turn a lodger into an owner. If the Arab would rather live in his own home and atmosphere, he is welcome in any of the twenty-plus Arab states that exist. Israel cannot, and morally dare not, change its Jewish character. For Israel to change that Jewish character would be to turn those who created it on the basis of the Jewish historical right into liars and thieves.

*It would be more than admitting that "Jewishness" was used in the past only in order to take away Arab land. It would be a cynical slap in the face to world Jewry which gave of its energies, funds, and in many cases, lives for the dream of a Jewish state. It would be a **despicable** cutting off of all obligations to oppressed and persecuted Jews who see in today's Israel their trustee and defender. The Israeli who was once in need of a home and who found it in a state that was pledged to help him would now—no longer in need—selfishly cut the lifeline for others.*

The Jew has no moral right to an Israel that is a non-Jewish state. But in a Jewish state let no one insult the Arab by insisting that he is equal and that it is "his" state, too. It is this ultimate contradiction between the Jewish character of Israel and the democratic right of the Arab to aspire to all the rights that Jews have—including to have an Arab majority in the land—that will never give the Arab rest or allow him to accept the status quo.

What happened next . . .

After his six-month detention in 1981, Kahane resumed his political activities with great enthusiasm. He formed a right-wing political party called Kach. The Kach political goal was to establish a Jewish state in Israel for Orthodox Jews, those who followed a strict interpretation of the Torah, the Jewish holy book. Kahane spoke of the removal of Arabs from Israel as an apocalypse, or event that would end the rule of evil on earth. Kahane drew critics within Israel as well as from the international community. Calling his views racist, some compared his policies to those promoted by the Nazi Party in Germany in the 1930s and 1940s, which oversaw the Holocaust. But Kahane also gained supporters.

In 1984 he won a seat in the Israeli Knesset, or legislature. His victory spurred a national debate about whether or not Israel was a state made up of racists. Were Israelis really unable to compromise with Arabs as Kahane so strongly believed? As his critics worried, Kahane gained more political support. By 1988 polls indicated that his Kach Party had almost 6 percent of the vote, enough to seize a good deal of power in the Knesset. But before the elections, the Israeli Supreme Court removed Kahane from his Knesset seat and banned the Kach Party from the vote, claiming that the party was racist and anti-democratic.

Nevertheless, Kahane continued on his same path, speaking out even more frequently about the removal of Arabs from Israel as the only real way to secure a Jewish state. After one such speech, given on a fund-raising trip in New York in November of 1990, Kahane was shot and killed by an Arab named El Sayyid A. Nosair.

Did you know . . .

- To avenge Meir Kahane's death, an Israeli supporter gunned down two Palestinians the next day.

- The Kach Party remains active into the 2000s and is suspected of sponsoring attacks on Palestinians in the Occupied Territories, areas of land controlled by Israel after the Six-Day War of 1967.

- Kahane's son, Binyamin, founded a group similar to his father's Kach Party, called Kahane Chai (meaning "Kahane Lives") in 1990. Binyamin Kahane and his wife were killed in 2000.

- The U.S. State Department listed both the Kach Party and Kahane Chai as terrorist organizations in 2004.

Consider the following ...

- The atrocities committed against the Jewish people by the Nazis during World War II (1939–45; war in which Great Britain, France, the Soviet Union, the United States, and their allies defeated Germany, Italy, and Japan) are universally denounced by Jews and others. Kahane mentions in his text the violence brought against Jews throughout history, but argues for similar treatment of Arabs. Given this, try to decipher Kahane's justification for ridding Israel of Arabs. Use specific examples from the text.

- Several groups, both political and militant, worked to secure Israel's independence. If Kahane's *They Must Go* formed the basis of such a group, could it be considered a legitimate freedom fighting group or a terrorist group? Explain.

- Was Kahane's suggestion that Arabs could move to the twenty-plus Arab states of the world legitimate? Write two arguments: one that supports this suggestion as reasonable and another that argues that this suggestion is racist. Evaluate each argument. Is it possible to make each convincing? Why or why not?

For More Information

Books

Friedman, Robert I. *The False Prophet: Rabbi Meir Kahane, from FBI Informant to Knesset Member.* New York: Lawrence Hill Books, 1990.

Kahane, Meir. *Never Again! A Program for Survival.* New York: Pyramid Books, 1972.

Kahane, Meir. *They Must Go.* New York: Grosset & Dunlap, 1981.

Mergui, Raphael, and Philippe Simonnot. *Israel's Ayatollahs: Meir Kahane and the Far Right in Israel.* London and Atlantic Highlands, NJ: Saqi Books, 1987.

Periodicals

Hewitt, Bill. "After a Career of Preaching Hatred for Arabs, Rabbi Meir Kahane Is Cut Down by an Assassin's Bullet." *People Weekly* (November 19, 1990): pp. 65–66.

Web Sites

Kahane.org: The Official Kahane Website. http://www.kahane.org/home.html (accessed on June 24, 2005).

Shyovitz, David. "Rabbi Meir Kahane." *Jewish Virtual Library.* http://www.jewishvirtuallibrary.org/jsource/biography/kahane.html (accessed on June 24, 2005).

Letters from Tel Mond Prison

Excerpts from Letters from Tel Mond Prison: An Israeli Settler
Defends His Act of Terror
Written by Era Rapaport
Printed in 1996

"Where did I get the nerve to do what I did? I dislike any type of violence. . . . Here I was doing what I've abhorred."

Certain events in life inspire ordinary people to do extreme things. As Era Rapaport's prison memoirs, *Letters from Tel Mond Prison: An Israeli Settler Defends His Act of Terror,* attests, a threat against one's home can be one such event. Era Rapaport (1945?–) responded to a perceived threat on his homeland after six Jews were killed by Arabs in the town of Hebron on May 2, 1980. Although it was rumored that Palestinian mayors had given the order to kill these Jews, the Israeli government did not retaliate or punish the Palestinians. Feeling no support from the Israeli government, Rapaport and others planned and executed the bombing of several Palestinian mayors' automobiles on June 2, 1980. The bomb Rapaport planted destroyed the legs of Bassam Shaka, the mayor of Nablus, a town about thirty miles north of Jerusalem.

"How does a nice Jewish boy from East Flatbush, Brooklyn, a gifted social worker, a marcher for civil rights, a loving husband and father, end up blowing off the legs of the PLO mayor of Nablus?" William B. Helmreich asked in his introduction to *Letters from Tel Mond Prison*. Rapaport struggled with that very question, considering his actions and their consequences carefully in letters and musings he wrote during his two-year prison term for helping plant a bomb under the car of an influential Palestinian leader.

Things to remember while reading excerpts from Era Rapaport's *Letters from Tel Mond Prison: An Israeli Settler Defends His Act of Terror:*

- Era Rapaport was raised in an Orthodox Jewish family in New York, which impressed upon him a historical faith and devotion to the teachings of the Torah, the Jewish holy scripture. Additionally, his father had been born in Jerusalem, Palestine, and he instilled a great love of that land in his son.

- Rapaport first visited Israel in 1966 to study at a yeshiva (an Orthodox Jewish rabbinical seminary). But when the Six-Day War of 1967 broke out, Rapaport lent his hand as a medic for the wounded in Jerusalem.

- Although he returned to the United States to complete a master's degree in social work, Rapaport felt that his future was in Israel, and moved there permanently in 1971.

- After marrying an Israeli woman, he moved to the West Bank, land Israel acquired during the Six-Day War, to establish the first Jewish settlement on land he considered to be the ancient capital of the Jews nearly three thousand years before. In the settlement of Shilo, his family grew to include six children.

- Since taking part in the car bombing of Palestinian leader Bassam Shaka in 1980, Rapaport was a fugitive in Israel. In 1983 Rapaport fled to the United States with his family, where he tried to persuade more Jews to settle in Israel. Upon his return to Israel in December 1986, he was arrested for his part in the car bombing. He was tried and jailed in January 1987.

- Many of the letters in this section serve as a way for Rapaport to recount the events that lead to his time in prison, attempting to explain how he changed from a pacifist fighting for Israeli rights to one who used violence as a way to influence change.

- While Rapaport wrote most of these letters while serving his sentence in Tel Mond Prison, the first letter was written just after the car bombing in 1980. This letter was never sent but it does capture Rapaport's frame of mind shortly after the violent act.

Excerpts from Letters from Tel Mond Prison: An Israeli Settler Defends His Act of Terror

May 1980

Shilo

Dear Avi,

I don't know that I'll ever mail this to you. It may be too problematic to do so. But more than ever before, I need your advice.

It's Sunday night now, forty-eight hours after the murders in Hevron [also spelled Hebron]. Some of the funerals were today. Besides the anger and the public cries for revenge, you could hear the **recriminations**: *"Had we acted before, after the attack on Solomon, this never would have happened. Now we must react, we must prevent another attack."*

What can I tell you? Who knows when one is prepared for life-or-death decisions? Never in my days in the States, and never here, would I have imagined myself dealing with the problem before me. This is not a question of what kind of car to buy, or where to purchase a house, or to what school to send the kids. I remember when we hassled with the question of participating in marches for the freedom of Soviet Jewry, rabbis published positive and negative responses to the question. Yes, it was a difficult decision, but it wouldn't necessarily change your life. In this situation, Avi, I don't really have any illusions. My government is not going to act. That is a given fact. Yes, we'll try to persuade them, but we've had the experience in the past. So I know that I have to act.

But, Avi, there are huge **ramifications** *to such a decision, some personal and some national. Truthfully, I am not sure which is more*

Recriminations: Criticisms, accusations.

Ramifications: Consequences.

important. This is not pre-1948 when the **Underground** acted against the British. We are a sovereign government, and we are a sovereign state. Do I have the right to assume responsibility for what my government is doing? Would an action by myself and others not be a **desecration** of the honor of Medinat Yisrael (the State of Israel)? I couldn't do that, Avi; I love my country too much to disgrace it publicly. Even when I come to the States to talk about the situation here, I won't talk negatively about **Aretz**. You know better than I that there is a halachah [law] against speaking lashon harah [evil speech] about our land. If I were to act, I'd be doing more than speaking lashon harah. All my life I've been taught by my **Abba** and **Ema** about the special honor that one must have for Medinat Yisrael and its leaders and elders. Could it be that by one act of mine, I'll throw all of that out the window? Is it also possible that my action will be the basis for others to act as well? Who knows where it would end? Everyone has his "red line." My red line is the present situation, and therefore I feel that something has to be done. Someone else's red line can be something else, and then he'll act. It'll be a situation of no law and order. I have grown up to be a law-and-order person. What right do I have to possibly hurt our country on a national level?

Then there is the personal level. I know, Avi, that if I am to act, there is a good chance, almost guaranteed, that I'll be spending time in jail. Possibly even ten years or more. That will, to an extent, destroy our family. Do I have a right to force Orit [Rapaport's wife] into being a living widow? That's exactly what it would be. My kids will grow up basically without a father. Don't they have to be asked? You know that's a **rhetorical question** question; they're too young to understand. Who knows how many years this could take from my parents' lives? And myself? You know me, Avi. I love kids so much. Just the thought of being in jail without them for two weeks or a month, I go crazy. I can't even begin to imagine how I'll live without them. Also, I love the outdoors, working, being active, building Eretz Yisrael. All that will stop. . . .

March 1987

Tel Mond Prison

. . . Orit and I held each other tight, sensing, together, the seriousness of the action that we were going to undertake in just one short hour or so. I looked in her eyes and said to her, "Thank you for all you've given me."

Underground: Jews working in secret to agitate for a Jewish homeland in Palestine prior to 1948, when the land was under the control of the British.

Desecration: Violation of something that is sacred or holy.

Aretz: A reference to Aretz Yisrael, or the land of Israel.

Abba: Father.

Ema: Mother.

Rhetorical question: A question asked merely for effect with no answer expected.

I rechecked my gear to see if everything was in place and then went to the kids' room for two last kisses. Oh, how I love them! I told Orit to get some sleep. Then I slipped out the door.

Noos [Rapaport's accomplice] and I met some fifty yards from the entrance to Shilo. We walked swiftly to a waiting car. With us, in a plastic bag, was a wooden box carrying the bomb.

[After riding in a car for several miles Era Rapaport and Noos arrive close to the Arab village of Yutma.]

. . .[W]e asked Moshe [the driver] to turn onto a side road and turn off his motor and lights.

Quickly Noos and I jumped out and opened our army bags. We had practiced doing this over and over at night in the mountains surrounding Shilo. At any moment a car could pass by; we had to work fast. Three minutes, and we were on our way, dressed as soldiers in army fatigues, gloves on our hands, and knitted caps ready to be pulled over our faces.

[. . .]

*We guided Moshe to a side street about three blocks from the **Bassam** house. He parked between two cars about one-third of the way up the street. This way a passing car couldn't make out the Israeli license plate. We both quickly stepped out of the car. We told Moshe that if we were not back in twelve minutes he should leave, or if he heard shots and we were not back within three minutes, he should also leave. We checked our watches, and then Noos and I were on our way.*

[. . .]

*A small light was on in Shaka's house, but I detected no movement. My **M16** was loaded, cocked with the safety off. In all our stakeouts we never encountered a guard, but we didn't intend to be surprised by one now.*

Noos was under Bassam's car. A wrong move, and the bomb would go off with Noos beneath it. Seconds passed slowly. I squelched the need to ask him how things were going. Noos had attached the bomb by magnet to the car and was stretching the trip wire. The slightest mishap, and it was all over. I heard him placing the rock on the wire and slipping out from under the car. He had successfully attached the bomb. [. . .] Within a minute we had left the area and were heading, via side streets, toward south Shechem, on out way back to Shilo. From what we could tell, no

Bassam: Bassam Shaka is Rapaport's target.

M16: A gas-operated assault rifle.

one had seen us, and everything went off well. Now we had to wait and see if everything worked as well in the morning.

[...]

I was dead tired, but my mind was racing. The main thought and hope was that the explosive would go off. We had done intensive information gathering and knew that Bassam drove the car by himself to his office. The explosive was built to maim only. Would it go off? Would it do the job?

Now, I was a bit scared. The action was over. How long would it take until the police would find me? Yet, I said to myself, you made a decision. But I was floored at my action. Where did I get the nerve to do what I did? I dislike any type of violence. As a social worker, I constantly tried to influence youth to reject violence. Here I was, doing what I've **abhorred**.

Yet I know, as **Ecclesiastes** says, "There is a time for everything under the sky... a time to throw stones and a time to gather them... a time for war and a time for peace... a time to kill and a time to heal." We would all prefer to be nonviolent all the time, and that day will come.

[...]

April 1987

Tel Mond Prison

[...]

After services, around 7:00 A.M., a few of us gathered around, as usual, for a few moments of what's new. Noos and I acted quite normal. The bombs were set to go off at 8:00 A.M., and I was a bit anxious but was careful not to mention a word that could be misinterpreted.

At home, after getting Moriyah and David off to kindergarten, Orit and I took a short walk, and I filled her in. "Beep, beep, beep," began the radio. " ... It is 9:00 A.M. and here is the news. Bassam Shaka, the Mayor of Shechem, was seriously wounded this morning when a bomb blew up his car. Karim Chalef, Mayor of Ramallah, was injured when his car also blew up."

[...]

March 1988

Tel Mond Prison

Abhorred: Disliked, despised.

Ecclesiastes: A book of wisdom in Jewish and Christian holy scriptures.

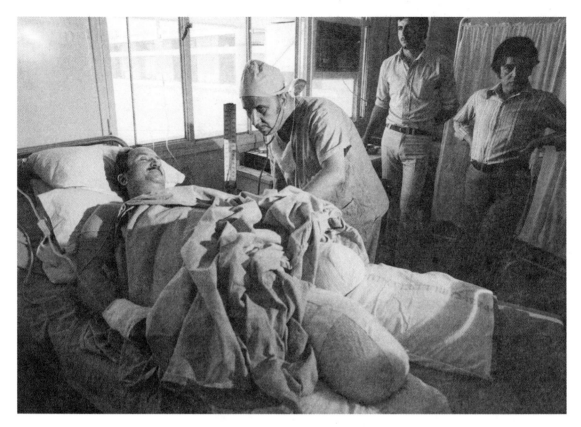

The mayor of Nablus, Bassam Shaka, lost both of his legs when the bomb that Era Rapaport set went off. *(© Davdid Rubinger/Corbis.)*

David and Goliath: A biblical story of a boy who successfully fights a giant.

Molotov cocktail: A crude bomb made by filling a bottle with a flammable liquid and using a rag as a fuse or wick.

Wild Wild West: The western frontier of the United States during the late nineteenth century when it was a rough, almost lawless, place to live.

*It seems to me that the newspapers are purposely not emphasizing that the Arabs are out to kill us. Their weapons are as deadly as ours. Your press presents it as a **David and Goliath** reversed. We are Goliath with modern arms and army, and the Arabs are David with slingshot and pebbles. What a lot of garbage! The roads that we drive are twisting and winding. Around every bend a terrorist with a **Molotov cocktail** or large stone can be waiting. They hide behind trees and boulders and wait until they see the "white of our eyes." There is no way to know where and when they'll appear.*

*If the situation sounds like the **Wild Wild West**, then, to an extent, it is. Yes, it's more dangerous than before to ride the roads. It is a difficult period. For me, also, it is a frustrating time—for many reasons. I acted against the same terrorist organization that is presently terrorizing a* *good part of our country and people. Yet I am sitting in prison, and they are free to continue their terrorist activities. Second, Orit and the children travel the roads often, and I can't even be out there to protect them if something happens. . . .*

I can only begin to imagine the difficult time that you people are going through: being bombarded by the terrible press, hearing such frightening reports of the situation here and seeing it all on TV. You are where it is really hard to be. I know that I have written this to you before, but I'll repeat it again. Being in Israel during these years has been an amazing experience, both difficult and happy. Above all is the fact and the feeling that we are continuing in the ways of our people. There is a weight on our shoulders—a weight of generations. It is as if the millions of Jews from all the thousands of years of our wandering are all standing around us watching, waiting to see our actions. I'm not imagining it, my Brother. I feel it.

[. . .]

Love ya,

Era

P.S. Come soon.

What happened next . . .

Upon his release from prison in 1989, Rapaport returned to the settlement he had started with eight other families; he eventually served as its mayor. But life in the settlement areas remained difficult, for Jews and Palestinians had yet to solve their differences. Even Jews were divided over the settlements in the Occupied Territories, the areas of land Israel captured during the Six-Day War. Some believed that the Occupied Territories could be used as offerings to the Palestinians in a "land for peace" deal. Rapaport and other religious settlers remained committed to the belief that the Occupied Territories were home to Jews in Biblical times and should remain theirs forever. He and other religious settlers steeled themselves against Palestinian and Israeli attempts to stop their efforts.

In 1992 the editor of *Letters from Tel Mond Prison*, William Helmreich, contacted Rapaport to arrange for a tour of the West Bank. Rapaport picked up his guest in a car with reinforced windows and an M16 rifle, saying "We don't take chances here." Little had changed by 2005. Jewish settlers continued to revolt against the Palestinians and the Israeli government. But in 2004 and 2005 Jewish settlers rose up in protest against Israeli prime minister Ariel Sharon's (1928–) proposal to evacuate all the settlements in the Gaza Strip and some in the West Bank by the end of 2005. It remains to be seen if Jewish settlers, Palestinians, and the citizens of Israel can find a compromise that will establish peace in the region.

Did you know . . .

- In 2005 there were approximately 21 Jewish settlements in the Gaza Strip and more than 140 in the West Bank.

- Rapaport had been an activist in an underground group known as the Machteret, which used the Bible as its guide as it planned to destroy Palestinian governing bodies and holy places.

- After the assassination of Israeli prime minister Yitzhak Rabin in 1995, twenty-seven members of the Machteret were identified. Israel and the world learned that terrorist acts had been committed by respected members of their society, including establishers of settlements, teachers, and war heroes.

Consider the following . . .

- Era Rapaport writes of loving his family and the pain he would feel without them in jail. Nevertheless he decides that his convictions outweigh the personal pain he would feel without his family. What specific examples does Rapaport use to justify his act of terror? Are they convincing? Explain why.

- Rapaport writes "We would all prefer to be nonviolent all the time, and that day will come." Explain how his actions helped or hindered the coming of this time of peace.

What other means could he have used to reach his objective?

- Rapaport based his decision to commit a violent act on a belief that the land of Israel belonged to Jews in biblical times and should again be theirs. Did this idea come across in his letters as he explained his actions? Explain using specific examples.

For More Information

Books

Gunderson, Cory Gideon. *The Israeli-Palestinian Conflict.* Edina, MN: Abdo Publishing, 2004.

Rapaport, Era. *Letters from Tel Mond Prison: An Israeli Settler Defends His Act of Terror.* New York: Free Press, 1996.

Web Sites

"Transcript: Troubled Lands." *PBS: NOW with Bill Moyers.* http://www.pbs.org/now/transcript/transcript_settlers.html (accessed on June 24, 2005).

Daughter of the Olive Trees

Excerpts from **Daughter of the Olive Trees**
Written by Sumaya Farhat-Naser
Published in 2003

"Everywhere . . . there are checkpoints. Soldiers bar the way and carry out inspections; they are a serious obstacle to everyone on the road."

What is life like for Palestinians living under the occupation of the Israeli government? Born in a tiny village called Birzeit near Jerusalem in 1948, the same year that the state of Israel declared its independence, Sumaya Farhat-Naser never experienced the freedoms of her ancestors who had lived in Palestine for centuries. The year she was born nearly 700,000 Palestinians fled their homes to escape the increasing Jewish population that forced them off their land and sometimes raided their villages and burned their homes.

Sumaya Farhat-Naser and her family did not flee. Her village was located in an area commonly called the West Bank. In 1948 the country of Jordan, then Trans-Jordan, assumed control of this land, including her village. But Israel took control of the area after the Six-Day War of 1967. Farhat-Naser never experienced life in her village without the presence of an occupying power.

Although her childhood was marked by poverty and hunger, Farhat-Naser grew up in a strong, loving family. Possessed of a quick mind and a strong will, Farhat-Naser rejected her grandfather's attempt to marry her off at age fourteen and

When Israel took over the West Bank, many families such as Sumaya Farhat-Naser's were forced to live in refugee camps like this one.

(© Hulton-Deutsch Collection/Corbis.)

instead persuaded him to allow her to earn an education. After completing her doctorate in botany at a German university, Farhat-Naser returned to teach at the Palestinian University in her hometown of Birzeit from 1982 to 1997. But she returned from Germany with an appreciation for her occupiers' position, for in Germany she learned of the Nazi Party's extermination of the Jews during the Holocaust of World War II (1939–45; war in which Great Britain, France, the Soviet Union, the United States, and their allies defeated Germany, Italy, and Japan).

Dismayed at the difficulties in finding peace with Israel, Farhat-Naser began a quest of her own in the 1980s; she sought out Israeli peace activists from whom she could learn the thoughts of her occupiers. In turn, she told the story of her people. In the following excerpts from *Daughter of the Olive Trees*, Farhat-Naser explains in detail what life has been like in her hometown.

Things to remember while reading excerpts from Sumaya Farhat-Naser's *Daughter of the Olive Trees:*

- At the time *Daughter of the Olive Trees* was first published in German in 2002, Farhat-Naser had not been able to contact the Israeli peace activists with whom she had discussed peace since the 1980s. The Palestinian uprising against Israel, called the Second Intifada, which began in 2000, ended their discussions.

- Farhat-Naser wrote in the introduction to her book that her decision to write it was an attempt to continue her efforts for peace in the Middle East.

- *Daughter of the Olive Trees* documents not only the difficulties of living under occupation, but also the successful steps toward peace she has experienced over the years.

Excerpts from Daughter of the Olive Trees

*In recent years I had seen from my balcony how the lights of Bet El were increasing. At first they were only on one hill, a few years later on two, and then they spread to three and today to four hills. The settlement has been built round the village of Doura, which is really surrounded by it. Doura is a breathtakingly beautiful village that used to live from terrace market-gardening. The village women used to work on the terraces every day, singing and telling stories, and the next day before the sun was up they would take the vegetables to market in Ramallah. I was often in this village working on projects for the women, for instance **literacy** courses. ... I often went to Doura to visit my friends Izz, Jamila, Umm Muhammad and others and to buy vegetables.*

Literacy: The ability to read and write.

When a large plot of land belonging to the village of Doura was **confiscated** five years ago, there was a big protest. I was among the demonstrators and had to look on with the others as **settlers** shot at students, killing two of them. One was Ibrahim, my friend Izz's cousin. After the deaths of the two students it was reported that a committee would investigate the incident. A week later we were told that it was only a water reservoir which was being built and the agitation over the confiscation of land was unnecessary. Today the second hill behind the water reservoir has already been built on. At the moment the settlement of Bet El is being connected with other settlements by a road. It runs through the fields of the farmers of Doura and is destroying the foundation of the village's life. I, too, can no longer go to Doura, although it is only three kilometres from Birzeit.

[...]

Separate roads are built for the settlers. Everywhere where the settlers' roads cross Palestinian roads there are checkpoints. Soldiers bar the way and carry out inspections; they are a serious obstacle to everyone on the road. ...

[...]

Sometimes there is a checkpoint in the middle of a Palestinian village or town where Israelis never come. For instance in Samiramis, the first checkpoint before Ramallah, soldiers block the road. On the 14-kilometre long stretch to Jerusalem there are also the checkpoints at Qalandia and al-Ram. It is pretty well impossible to drive round the checkpoints; any way round them is blocked off with concrete obstacles. Yet thousands of cars try to find another way, for instance across fields and through the labyrinth of streets in Kufr Aqab and the Qalandia refugee camp, between houses and along unasphalted roads. Cars often have to reverse back along the road from the point they have struggled to reach because a lorry or bus is coming from the other direction. There is a danger of plunging over the unfenced verge into the field below. And all the time we see before us the settlements which are expanding from one hill to the next. In the evening the increasing number of lights from the nearest confiscated hill proclaim their presence over a wide area.

One feels enormous pain and rage when one arrives back on the road beyond the soldiers' checkpoint, only fifty metres after all those detours. ...

[...]

One Friday I, my husband Munir and our daughter Ghada had to drive to Ramallah to do some shopping, get an exit visa, go to the bank

Confiscated: Taken without payment.

Settlers: Israelis who move into territory once occupied by Palestinians to form settlements.

and do other things which had been accumulating for weeks. We were glad that that day traveling by car was permitted. But on the way back there were hundreds of cars and people waiting at the checkpoint; no car was allowed to pass. I went over to one of the soldiers and said: "This morning you let us through. Now we want to go home." He replied that new regulations had arrived that the journey was only allowed in one direction. No argument helped, no entreaties. The people stood there furious. A few were weeping.

What happened next . . .

Sumaya Farhat-Naser offered a unique perspective on life for Palestinians living under Israeli occupation, and she has not stopped working for peace.

Although Palestinians and Israelis had yet to secure a lasting peace by 2005, several indications of progress emerged. Mahmoud Abbas (1935–), who was elected president of the Palestinian Authority, the government of the Palestinian people, on January 9, 2005, after the death of longtime Palestine Liberation Organization (PLO) chairman Yasser Arafat (1929–2004), instilled hope in both Palestinians and others for practical steps toward peace. Meanwhile, Israeli prime minister Ariel Sharon (1928–), who had spent most of his career supporting the establishment of settlements in the Occupied Territories, proposed a disengagement plan that would remove all the Jewish settlements from the Gaza Strip and some from the West Bank by the end of 2005.

Did you know . . .

- The **Oslo Accords** (see entry) of 1993 introduced an idea of "land for peace." Upon signing the agreement, Palestinians agreed that Israel existed within borders that comprised nearly 78 percent of the land of Palestine once governed by the British mandate, a system that gave Britain control of Palestine after World War I (1914–18; war in which Great Britain, France, the United States, and their allies defeated Germany, Austria-Hungary, and their allies). But Palestinians also hoped that Israel would turn over control of the Occupied Territories, which made up the remaining 22 percent of the mandate, to them. This idea of land for peace had yet to be resolved when Farhat-Naser wrote her book.

- Without an agreement with the Palestinians, Israeli prime minister Ariel Sharon decided to withdraw troops and evacuate settlements from some of the Occupied Territories in 2005.

- The Gaza Strip was home to nearly 200 Palestinians for every one Israeli in 2004.

- There were approximately 140 Israeli settlements in the West Bank in 2005.

Consider the following ...

- Farhat-Naser considers herself a peace activist. Given her account of life under occupation, what aspects of life for Palestinians are the most important ones for her to impress upon the Israeli peace activists she knows?

- Farhat-Naser describes the Israeli settlements as seen from the village of Doura. Imagine what a Jewish settler looking from the other direction at Doura would see. Explain in detail the scene from a Jewish settler's position and how he or she might feel about the situation.

- Farhat-Naser wrote her book in part because her dialogue with fellow peace activists had been cut off by the Second Intifada in 2000. What other means could she have used to continue to work for peace? Explain how they compare to the effectiveness of writing her book.

For More Information

Books

Farhat-Naser, Sumaya. *Daughter of the Olive Trees*. Basel, Switzerland: Lenos Verlag, 2003.

Periodicals

Derfner, Larry. "Sharon's Switcheroo." *U.S. News and World Report* (November 8, 2004): p. 40.

"Israeli Cabinet OKs Gaza Withdrawal." *Los Angeles Times* (February 21, 2005).

Weymouth, Lally. "No Guts, No Glory, No Peace." *Newsweek* (December 6, 2004): p. 32.

Den of Lions

Excerpts from Den of Lions
Written by Terry Anderson
Published in 1993

The impact of the ongoing conflicts in the Middle East has not been restricted to those living there. American journalist Terry Anderson learned firsthand that all people can be targets during times of war. Assigned to cover Beirut, the capitol of Lebanon, for the Associated Press (AP) in 1982 in the aftermath of the Israeli invasion to remove the Palestine Liberation Organization (PLO) from southern Lebanon, Anderson followed the U.S. Marine Corps throughout the country on a peacekeeping mission. He wrote a series of stories about Lebanon's attempts to rebuild itself after the destruction caused by Israel's attack. Anderson grew accustomed to moving freely through checkpoints as a member of the press. He recalled the late fall of 1982 and the early part of 1983 as a time of optimism, when "everyone saw an end to the war, an end finally to the bad times," as he wrote in his memoir *Den of Lions*.

But soon after Anderson was promoted to chief Middle East correspondent for the AP, violence in Lebanon surged once again. Religious factions within Lebanon fought for political power; the international peacekeeping force changed the focus

"My mind seemed to stall for a few seconds, and by the time I realized what was happening, one of the men was beside the driver's door of my car, yanking it open and pushing his pistol at my head."

of its mission and began to act in support of the Lebanese government; and Israeli troops occupied the south of Lebanon as Syrian troops increased from the north. As violence grew, reporters, once treated by all groups as neutral observers, were singled out and harassed according to their nationalities. Sometimes caught in the crossfire of others' battles and sometimes direct targets, journalists were no longer safe. Americans in particular were scorned by the Lebanese, as witnessed by the bombing of the 1983 U.S. embassy in Beirut and the kidnapping of American scholars and journalists.

The Lebanese government collapsed in February 1984 and in March the United States removed its Marines from Lebanon. On March 12, 1985, the United States ordered Americans working for international agencies to leave Beirut. Anderson and other journalists delayed, ignoring the call. Four days later Terry Anderson's life was forever changed. The following excerpts from his book *Den of Lions* recount his kidnapping and his years in captivity.

Things to remember while reading excerpts from Terry Anderson's *Den of Lions:*

- Terry Anderson was born on October 27, 1949, in Ohio, and had served with the U.S. Marines as a combat correspondent during the Vietnam War (1954–75).

- In the early 1980s the activist group Hezbollah received money from Iran to build its strength and to gain influence over the Shiites, a branch of Islam that regards Ali and his descendants as the true successors of Muhammad, in Lebanon in order to wrest political power from the Christians.

- Shiites in Lebanon were battling mostly with Christian factions, who were friendly with and supported by both Israel and the United States.

- On March 15, 1985, Anderson mentioned to his news editor that four men in a Mercedes had followed him during his lunch hour. He kept the incident quiet.

- On March 16, 1985, Terry Anderson was kidnapped. He was held by a terrorist organization for nearly seven years, during which time he was interrogated and treated as a prisoner of war, even though he knew very little information that could help his kidnappers.

- Anderson was able to communicate with several fellow hostages during his time in captivity. One such hostage was Terry Waite. Waite is a British humanitarian who was in Lebanon to help negotiate the release of four hostages when he was taken hostage himself.

Excerpts from Den of Lions

Beirut. 8 A.M. *March 16, 1985*

The green Mercedes, sparkling clean in the weak morning sunlight, drifted to a gentle halt in the narrow road, just a few yards up the hill from the graffiti-covered monument to **Gamal Abdel Nasser**. Don Mell, the young AP photographer I was dropping off at his apartment after our tennis game, had noticed it earlier at the sports club but hadn't mentioned it—it didn't seem important. Now, though, it struck him as odd, especially the curtains drawn over the rear window.

… [T]hree unshaven men threw open the doors and jumped out, each holding a 9mm pistol in his right hand, hanging loosely by his side.

My mind seemed to stall for a few seconds, and by the time I realized what was happening, one of the men was beside the driver's door of my car, yanking it open and pushing his pistol at my head. "Get out," he said fiercely. "I will shoot. I will shoot."

"Okay," I answered quickly. I pulled the keys from the ignition and dropped them between the seats. "Okay, no problem. No problem."

He reached in and pulled the glasses from my face. As I slid out of the seat, half crouched, he put his hand around my shoulders, forcing me to remain bent over.

"Come, come quickly."

I glanced up at Don, just a vague blur on the other side of the car, willing him to run, but not daring to shout the words. He just stood, frozen.

Gamal Abdel Nasser (1918–1970): The longtime president of Egypt and champion of Arab causes.

The young man, dark and very Arab-looking, perhaps twenty or twenty-five, pulled me along beside him toward the Mercedes, just four or five yards away, still forcing me to remain half bent.

"Get in. I will shoot," he hissed at me, pushing me into the backseat. "Get down. Get down."

I tried to crouch in the narrow space between the front and back seats. Another young man jumped in the other door and shoved me to the floor, throwing an old blanket over me, then shoving my head and body down with both his feet. I could feel a gun barrel pushing at my neck. "Get down. Get down."

The car lurched into gear and accelerated madly up the hill....

[...]

After fifteen or twenty minutes, the car turned off the main highway straight into what seemed to be a garage. A metal door clanged down, cutting off the street noise. The doors were yanked open and hands grabbed at me, pulling me upright, but careful to keep the blanket over my head. There were mutterings in Arabic, short, guttural, incomprehensible.

Someone slipped the blanket away, slipping a dirty cloth around my head at the same time, then wrapping plastic tape around and around. Other hands grabbed at my tennis shoes, yanking them off....

[...]

"What is your name?" a voice asked, heavily accented.

"Terry Anderson. I am a journalist."

"Your company?"

"The Associated Press. A wire service."

The man seemed uninterested in my answers.

[...]

Beirut. April 1985.

Hours, days, nights, weeks. Blank nights. Gray dawn after gray dawn.

An English-speaking man came in today and dictated a short letter to me. At least I know why I've been kidnapped, or at least what the "official" reason is. He was abrupt, but not threatening. Simply gave me a pen and a piece of paper, then told me what to write:

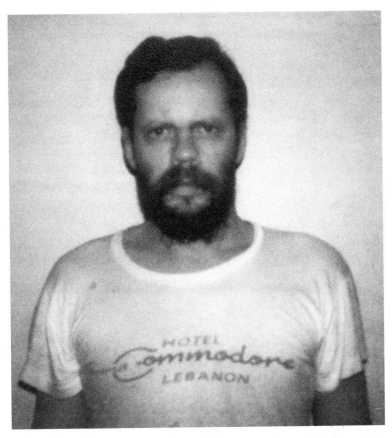

This photograph of Terry Anderson was released in April 1988, proving that he was still alive. Anderson would not be released for another four years. *(© Sygma/Corbis.)*

"I am fine. I received your message. You should know that I am a victim of the American policy that favors Israel and which forced the detained persons in Kuwait to do what they did. My freedom is tied to the freedom of the detained over there. The American government still does not care about us. I ask you to do your best to pressure the American government to release the detained people over there because we are very close to being hanged in the case that this term is not met." . . .

[. . .]

The days begin to settle into a kind of routine: Sleepless nights, watching the dawn light grow slowly on the ceiling, shifting and turning, trying to ease the stiffness and pain of lying on a bed twenty-fours hours a day. Listen to the roaches, occasionally watch one or two or three, two inches long, crawl slowly up the wall. Hear the stirring and muttering in Arabic as the guards awaken. Food—usually a sandwich of Arabic bread and dry, yellow cheese. Brief trip down the hall to the filthy bathroom. One guard unlocks the chains. Another stands against the wall holding a small automatic pistol with a silencer. Back to the cot. Read the Bible for a while. Lunch—perhaps a bowl of soup, or cold rice with canned vegetables dumped on top. The evenings are sometimes enlivened by short visits from one or two of the young men, sometimes to ask questions in broken English, sometimes just to amuse themselves. Occasionally, one or two will kneel or sit on my chest, poke their guns in my ear or neck, and hiss threats: "You dead. I kill you." [. . .]

[. . .]

Beirut. April 1990.

All good, but we're still chained to the wall in this dammed room.

[. . .]

I pray a great deal, mostly at night, and read the Bible, in English or French. It helps keep me calm, and able to accept whatever happens.

[. . .]

Beirut. August 1990.

Brian's gone home! And we're back with John. No warning, no indication that something was going to happen. The guards just came in, ordered us to stand up, taped our arms and around our eyes, then dumped us in a car trunk for a ten-minute ride, apparently just a few blocks.

When we were unwrapped in our new abode, another apartment in the southern suburbs of Beirut, John was sitting against the wall, bearded and grinning with relief.

It seems Brian and he had been together, along with Frank Reed, for more than a year. Suddenly, Reed was taken out nearly four months ago; then two days ago, they came for Brian.

[. . .]

The apartment is the same one I was kept in with Fontaine, and again later. The blood mark from beating my head on the wall is still there, a little faded but obvious.

John says Reed was in very bad shape when they were put together with him, and didn't get much better. He had been abused badly, and was being treated with contempt by the guards until John and Brian protested. They said he had gone off his head—believed he had a radio in his head and could talk with the U.S. embassy in East Beirut.

John also said there was another prisoner in the apartment, in the next room, and both he and Brian believed it was Terry Waite. They had communicated sporadically and vaguely with knocks on the wall, but couldn't really exchange information. Both he and Brian were chained on the opposite side of the room from the wall between the two rooms, and could tap on it only during exercise periods.

[...]

September 5, 1990. My two thousandth day.

I've established contact with Terry Waite. He is next door, as John and Brian thought. I began by tapping on the wall and, when he tapped back, painstakingly tapped out the series 1-2-3-4-...to 26. Then, using numbers for the alphabet (1 = a, 2 = b, and so on) I tapped out our names. It took a while, but he caught on. I spent all one night tapping out a summary of all the news: Brian's release, Frank's release; the comments and promises of Iran, Syria, and others on hostages over the past year. Then the world news: the Berlin Wall's falling, communism's demise in eastern Europe, free elections in the Soviet Union, work toward multiracial government in South Africa. All the incredible things that have happened since he was taken nearly three years ago. He thought I was crazy.

He's been in isolation all that time, without even a scrap of news.

[...]

Baalbek, Lebanon. December 4, 1991.

The 2,454th day, and the last. The two new subchiefs came in this morning to say that I would be going home tonight. They talked with me awhile about various things. Strangely, they seemed mostly concerned with justifying themselves, and the last seven years. They said that their group now realized that this had all been a mistake, and they had gotten little out of it. They knew that the release last year of their brothers in Kuwait, the main goal they'd had in the beginning and for all those years, had nothing to do with the hostages they had held so long. "This tactic [kidnapping] is not useful. We will not do it again," one of them said. "We are not giving up. But we will use other means."

He did not explain what that meant, and I was not interested enough to pursue the subject.

[...]

It's dark outside now. They always prefer to wait for darkness to fall before making any move. The door opens. Several guards come in. I'm already dressed—I put on my new clothes two hours ago. Mahmoud says, as he has so many times, "Stand up."

No tape this time. Just the blindfold. The new subchiefs are there. One of them hands me a small bouquet. Half a dozen carnations. "Give this to your wife, and tell her we're sorry."

Someone takes my arm, guides me through the door, outside, and into a car. Another Mercedes, just like the one they forced me into so long ago. [...]

The car stops. I'm pulled out. Someone puts his hand on my shoulder. "I'm a Syrian colonel. You're free."

What happened next ...

On December 4, 1991, Terry Anderson was released, the last of the American hostages to be freed in Lebanon. Greeted by his love, Madeleine, and their six-year-old daughter Sulome, Anderson regained his life. After a recuperation period spent on the island of Antigua, Anderson resumed a "normal" existence. About his terrible years in captivity, Anderson concluded, as German philosopher Friedrich Wilhelm Nietzsche (1844–1900) once wrote, "That which does not destroy me, makes me stronger."

Following his release, Anderson eagerly sought out new opportunities. He took a professorship at Ohio University in Athens, from which he retired in 2002. He opened a restaurant in Athens called the Blue Gator and bought a 200-acre horse ranch. He also married Madeleine on April 18, 1993. And in 2004 he ran for a seat in the Ohio senate. His goal: to be remembered as more than "the guy who was kidnapped," as he told the *Akron Beacon Journal*.

Did you know . . .

- Throughout Anderson's captivity the American government and other international organizations tried to secure the release of the American hostages. The American government's attempts to free American hostages even included a secret arms deal with Iran in 1986, but no American hostages were released from Lebanon between 1986 and 1989.

- The Shiite group Hezbollah, which was responsible for Anderson's kidnapping, hoped to establish Lebanon as an Islamic state.

- Anderson attributed his survival in captivity to the Bible and to writing poetry.

- While Anderson emerged from captivity in relative good health, some of the other American hostages suffered permanent nerve damage and hearing loss. One hostage had a dented skull from torture endured in captivity.

Consider the following . . .

- The American government refused to negotiate directly with Anderson's kidnappers. It is the policy of the American government not to give in to terrorist demands. Is this policy valid? Based on what happened to Anderson, explain why such a policy should stand or why it should be revised.

- Anderson realized that life in Lebanon was growing increasingly dangerous in the months before his capture. What was Anderson's rationale for staying in such a violent, chaotic area? Offer specific reasons why Anderson might have chosen to stay in a region that was so unsafe to Americans.

- Should journalists be able to move freely throughout areas of conflict? Consider how a journalist's job might be compromised if he/she is not allowed access to firsthand information.

For More Information

Books

Anderson, Terry. *Den of Lions*. New York: Crown, 1993.

Periodicals

Bugeja, Michael J. "Terry Anderson and The Truth." *Editor & Publisher* (June 26, 2000): p. 18.

"Delivered from Evil." *Time* (December 16, 1991): p. 16.

Gersh, Debra. "Journalists Recall the Allure of Beirut." *Editor & Publisher* (April 6, 1991): p. 9.

Smolowe, Jill. "Lives in Limbo." *Time* (December 16, 1991): p. 18.

"Terry Anderson Seeks Legacy of Rural Public Servant Over Foreign Hostage." *Beacon Journal* (Akron, Ohio) (October 18, 2004).

Web Sites

Congressional Record. "Terry Anderson Begins Sixth Year of Captivity." *(Senate—March 20, 1990), p. S2709.* http://www.fas.org/irp/congress/1990_cr/s900320-anderson.htm (accessed on June 24, 2005).

7

Artists' Perspectives on the Middle East Conflict

U nited Nations Security Council resolutions, memoirs of prisoners and terrorists, declarations of war, statements of political vision, reports from British Royal commissions—these are the documents that historians and students typically use to understand the complicated issues relating to the long-standing and ongoing Middle East conflict. In most cases, these documents are attempts to establish the truth, to state a political program, to promote change, or to account for past actions. They tell a large part of the story...but not the whole story.

Artists have also sought to interpret the political problems that exist in the Middle East. Through their sculptures and paintings, poems and novels, and even graphic novels, they offer different perspectives on the major events in the region. Artists bring a unique approach to understanding the world: they emphasize the use of the senses, such as sight, sound, and touch; they examine the emotional elements of issues; and urge people to open themselves to the difficulty and complexity of human problems. In the documents in this section, two distinct ways of understanding and representing the nature of conflict in the Middle East are explored.

An artistic representation of Palestinian president Yasser Arafat. Arafat was often used by artists as a symbol for Palestinian nationalism.

(© Suhaib Salem/Reuters/Corbis.)

The excerpts from Joe Sacco's graphic novel *Palestine* and selections from the poetry of Mahmoud Darwish both focus on the conflict between Palestinians and Israelis over who should claim sovereignty, or political control, over the territory that was once known as Palestine and is today known as Israel and the Occupied Territories (Israeli-occupied territories in the West Bank and Gaza Strip). Like most works of art, however, these selections present the viewpoints of Sacco and Darwish, and do not represent a balanced perspective.

Palestine

Excerpts from **Palestine**
Written and illustrated by Joe Sacco
Published originally as individual comics between 1993 and 1996
Republished as a collection by Fantagraphics Books in 2001

D uring the winter of 1991–92, Maltese-American comic artist Joe Sacco (1960–) traveled to the Middle East, where he spent several months in Israel and in the Occupied Territories of Gaza and the West Bank. (The Occupied Territories are portions of land bordering on Israel that are claimed by Palestinians but occupied and ruled by the Israeli army ever since the Six-Day War of 1967.) Sacco arrived near the end of the First Intifada, an Arabic word for "uprising." The First Intifada was a Palestinian effort to use street protests, strikes, and small-scale violence to draw international attention to the unjust ways they had been treated by their Israeli occupiers.

In January 1993 Sacco published his first comic book about his experience in the Middle East. He went on to publish a total of nine issues between 1993 and 1996, eventually combining them to create the graphic novel called *Palestine*. Through black-and-white illustrations, a strong plot, and plenty of dialogue from the dozens of characters who are included in the book, Sacco explored

"Look, on your side there are some extremists, and on our side there are some extremists."

his arrival in the Occupied Territories, a visit to Israel, and the encounters he had with Palestinians, Arabs from other countries, Israelis, and Americans and Europeans traveling in the region. Along the way, Sacco offered a history of the Palestinian-Israeli conflict, bringing readers into the complicated world of Middle Eastern politics. In each new issue, Sacco focused more closely on the nature of the Palestinian experience, using a wide range of characters to tell different aspects of the story.

Palestine was unlike any other work published on the Israeli-Palestinian conflict, an ongoing battle between the Jewish country of Israel and the Arab Palestinians over the control of land and government of the territory once known as Palestine. Other works on the conflict have been the product of journalists, scholars, or people who wanted to persuade others of their position on the conflict. Sacco provided an entirely different approach. He let his characters speak, and they reported all sides of the story (though Sacco did have great sympathy for the Palestinians living in the Occupied Territories). According to the well-known Palestinian scholar Edward Said's writing in *Palestine,* readers see these stories "through the eyes and persona of a modest-looking ubiquitous [all knowing] crew-cut young American man who appears to have wandered into an unfamiliar, inhospitable world of military occupation, arbitrary [random] arrest ... torture ['moderate physical pressure'] and sheer brute force generously, if cruelly applied."

Sacco's work was immediately praised for its imaginative approach to understanding the complex conflict. An *Utne Reader* reviewer wrote that "Sacco uses the comic book format to its fullest extent, creating bold perspectives that any photojournalist would envy," and *Entertainment Weekly* wrote that "It figures that one of the first books to make sense of this mess would be a comic book." Sacco won the 1996 American Book Award for his work. In 2001, all nine volumes of the series were collected in the graphic novel *Palestine.*

In the excerpts below, Sacco offers his unique artistic perspective on the clashes between Israelis and Palestinians in the Occupied Territories. In the first excerpt, Sacco visits a village

Joe Sacco

Comic book artist Joe Sacco was born in 1960 on the island nation of Malta and lived in Australia as a child before settling permanently in the United States. He studied journalism at the University of Oregon. After graduating from college he worked in several journalistic jobs, but spent more of his time working on comic books. In addition to *Palestine,* Sacco has published another piece of comic book war journalism, *Safe Area Gorazde: The War In Eastern Bosnia, 1992–1995* (2000), and a collection of his works called *Notes from a Defeatist* (2003).

In a *January* magazine interview with Rebecca Tuhus-Dubrow, Sacco referred to himself as "Just a cartoonist, I mean, doing journalism in comics form." Critics have praised Sacco's ability to use an artist's attention to physical detail to highlight specific elements of the stories he tells, yet they have also noted that his works provide a good understanding of the nature of the issues he covers. Sacco has said that his biggest hero was the British journalist and novelist George Orwell (1903–1950), who had a unique ability to insert himself into the nonfiction stories that he told without compromising his ability to describe events. Asked what his goals were in writing *Palestine,* Sacco told Tuhus-Dubrow that he hoped people would "just pay a little more attention to the news, or just understand a little more from reading the book what's going on, or get involved in activism, or get involved in reading, you know, really get involved in the subject itself."

that he calls in *Palestine* a "veritable gold mine of Palestinian misery" to hear one family's story of how Israeli soldiers cut down their family's beloved olive trees. In the second excerpt, Sacco allows a Palestinian man to tell the story of his interrogation by Israeli soldiers.

Things to remember while reading excerpts from Joe Sacco's *Palestine*:

- Joe Sacco has said that *Palestine* was written primarily for an American audience.

- Palestinians are Arabs, usually Muslims, who claim historic roots to the region known as Palestine, which now makes up most of the nation of Israel.

- Israel took control of the Occupied Territories following the Six-Day War of 1967, when it occupied lands previously held by Egypt and Jordan. The war forced many thousands of Palestinians to live in refugee camps in countries such as Jordan and Syria, or temporary shelters for people forced to relocate because of war. By the 2000s, many of these refugee camps had become permanent homes for Palestinians.

- The narrator makes reference to Greek Orthodox Christmas. The Orthodox religion is a Christian religion that split from the Catholic church over issues of religious law. While the religions share many aspects, including holidays, each religion follows its own religious calendar which tells which days specific religious holidays are celebrated on. Hence, Greek Orthodox Christmas and Catholic Christmas might occur on different days depending on the year.

- Olive trees are a symbol of Palestinian land ownership.

- Hebrew is a language commonly spoken by Jews in Israel, though many also speak English. Arabic is a language commonly spoken by Palestinians.

- A Molotov cocktail is a crude bomb made by filling a bottle with a flammable liquid and using a rag as a fuse or wick.

- The Homestead Act was a nineteenth-century American law that gave pioneers the right to claim Western lands that appeared unoccupied, though they were often home to Native American tribes.

Excerpts from Palestine

And speaking of settlements, Sami drives us to the village outskirts...

ALL THE LAND ON THIS SIDE OF THE ROAD HAS BEEN CONFISCATED BY THE ISRAELIS FOR SETTLEMENT...

It's scores of acres of farmland and pasture we're looking at... again, just drops in the bucket... Israel has expropriated two-thirds of the West Bank for its own use, including the settlement of Jews... (and I'm not counting annexed "Greater Jerusalem")...but like Prime Minister Shamir says:

IF WE ESTABLISH A SETTLEMENT HERE OR EXPAND A SETTLEMENT THERE, THIS IS ONLY NATURAL. WE ARE OPERATING ACCORDING TO THE UNDERSTANDING THAT THE LAND BELONGS TO US.

And with that "understanding" in mind, the World Zionist Organization's 'Master Plan 2010' points out that only five percent of the West Bank is "problematic for settlement..."

I suppose what makes it "problematic" is that hundreds of thousands of Palestinians still live here ... in the countryside, though, they're mostly confined within village boundaries set under British rule in 1942 ... and the Israelis routinely reject rural building applications, forcing tens of thousands of Palestinians to build and live in "illegal" dwellings, hundreds of which are leveled every year... in fact, according to some official Israeli figures, in '87 and '88 the Israelis demolished more Palestinian homes than they granted building licenses...

But if a Jew wants to join a settlement on occupied Arab land, it's full steam ahead! Incentives to make your head spin! A government grant to offset moving expenses! Eligibility for higher loans at lower interest! Cheaper housing than in Israel! A seven percent income tax deduction! You get the idea — the yuppie version of the Homestead Act...

63

What happened next . . .

Near the conclusion of *Palestine,* Sacco depicts three Israeli soldiers questioning a thirteen-year-old Palestinian boy who is forced to stand in the rain. Sacco wonders what will happen to the Palestinians and Israelis, caught in a seemingly unending conflict, as a result of the violence and hatred that characterize their relationship. He wonders "what can happen to someone who thinks he has all the power . . . [and] what becomes of someone when he believes himself to have none?"

In July 2001, when he wrote the preface to the collected edition of *Palestine,* Sacco was still unsure about the prospects for peace: "As I write these words, a second Intifada is taking place because, in short, Israeli occupation, and all the consequences of the domination of one people by another, has not ceased." Since 2001, some progress has been made between the Palestinians and Israelis. Palestinians elected a new president, Mahmoud Abbas (1935–), early in 2005, and serious peace talks were renewed between the two sides. Perhaps even more importantly, Israel began to withdraw settlers from some parts of the Occupied Territories. Yet the questions raised by *Palestine* remain: how will the Palestinians and Israelis whose entire culture has been shaped by years and years of conflict learn to set aside their anger and hostility and live in peace?

Did you know . . .

- The Second, or al-Aqsa, Intifada began in 2000 and may have ended in 2005 with the election of Mahmoud Abbas to the presidency of the Palestinian Authority, the governing body for Palestinians living in the Occupied Territories.

- There were approximately 3.9 million Palestinians living in the Occupied Territories in 2005, as well as about 370,000 Jews and 50,000 Christians.

Consider the following ...

- In the introduction to *Palestine*, Edward Said wrote, "Joe Sacco can ... transmit a great deal of information, the human context and historical events that have reduced Palestinians to their present sense of stagnating [unchanging] powerlessness." Point to several instances in Sacco's work where he uses visual images to convey information about people and events.

- One of the things that makes art different from regular journalism is that it uses such artistic devices as metaphors, similes, and imagery to help the reader or viewer understand the story. Locate examples of these devices in Sacco's work and explain how they help to heighten the effect of the story.

- Compare Sacco's work on Palestine with more standard historical or journalistic sources. What are the strengths and weaknesses of both types of work? Is one better at conveying the "truth" about a situation? Explain in detail.

- Identify some of the important questions raised by Sacco's work. What are other sources that can be used to further explore these issues?

For More Information

Books

Sacco, Joe, with introduction by Edward Said. *Palestine*. Seattle, WA: Fantagraphics Books, 2001 (previously published in nine comic books, 1993–96).

Periodicals

Blincoe, Nicholas. "Cartoon Wars." *New Statesman* (January 6, 2003): p. 26.

Burr, Ty. "Palestine: A Nation Occupied." *Entertainment Weekly* (October 7, 1994): p. 71.

Utne Reader (March–April 1995): p. 111.

Web Sites

"Joe Sacco." *Fantagraphics Books*. http://www.fantagraphics.com/artist/sacco/sacco_bio.html (accessed on June 24, 2005).

Tuhus-Dubrow, Rebecca. "Joe Sacco." *January*. http://www.january magazine.com/profiles/jsacco.html (accessed on June 24, 2005).

Poetry of Mahmoud Darwish

Select poems from Unfortunately, It Was Paradise
Includes the poems "On This Earth"; "I Belong There"; "Athens Airport"; and "I Talk Too Much"
Printed in 2003

Poem from The Adam of Two Edens
Includes the poem "As He Walks Away"
Printed in 2000

Palestinian poet Mahmoud Darwish (1942–) is widely considered to be the most significant Palestinian poet, and one of the most important poets to write in the Arabic language. According to Munir Akash and Carolyn Forché, editors of Darwish's poetry collection *Unfortunately, It Was Paradise,* he is "beloved as the voice of his people, he is an artist demanding of his work continual transformation and a living legend whose lyrics are sung by fieldworkers and schoolchildren." Darwish has spoken about Palestinian issues throughout the world, and he is cheered by huge crowds when he appears in the Middle East. His poems are considered some of the most moving to emerge from the clash between Jews and Arabs over who will control the territory once known as Palestine.

Darwish writes poems about olive trees, women that he loves or has loved, bread, an airport, speaking at conferences, and many other subjects. Yet in his best-loved

"Our flutes would have played a duet / if it weren't for the gun."

Select poems from Unfortunately, It Was Paradise

"On This Earth"

*We have on this earth what makes life worth living: April's
hesitation, the aroma of bread*

at dawn, a woman's point of view about men, the works of
Aeschylus, *the beginning*

*of love, grass on a stone, mothers living on a flute's sigh and
the invaders' fear of memories.*

*We have on this earth what makes life worth living: the final
days of September, a woman*

*keeping her apricots ripe after forty, the hour of sunlight in
prison, a cloud reflecting a swarm*

*of creatures, the peoples' applause for those who face death
with a smile, a tyrant's fear of songs.*

*We have on this earth what makes life worth living: on this
earth, the Lady of Earth*

*mother of all beginnings and ends. She was called Palestine.
Her name later became*

Palestine. My Lady, because you are my Lady, I deserve life.

"I Belong There"

*I belong there. I have many memories. I was born as everyone is
born.*

*I have a mother, a house with many windows, brothers,
friends, and a prison cell*

*with a chilly window! I have a wave snatched by seagulls, a
panorama of my own.*

*I have a saturated meadow. In the deep horizon of my word, I
have a moon,*

a bird's sustenance, and an immortal olive tree.

I have lived on the land long before swords turned man into prey.

*I belong there. When heaven mourns for her mother, I return
heaven to her mother.*

And I cry so that a returning cloud might carry my tears.

*To break the rules, I have learned all the words needed for a
trial by blood.*

Aeschylus: An ancient Greek
dramatist.

*I have learned and dismantled all the words in order to draw
from them a single word:* Home.

An armed guard patrols Athens Airport, which is the connection point for many flights to the Middle East and the site of some terrorist attacks associated with Palestine. *(© Reuters/Corbis.)*

"Athens Airport"

> *Athens airport disperses us to other airports. Where can I*
>   *fight? asks the fighter.*
> Where can I deliver your child? *a pregnant woman shouts back.*
> Where can I invest my money? *asks the officer.*
> This is none of my business, *the intellectual says.*
> Where did you come from? *asks the customs' official.*
> *And we answer:* From the sea!
> Where are you going?
> To the sea, *we answer.*
> What is your address?

A woman of our group says: My village is the bundle on my
　　　　　back.
We have waited in the Athens airport for years.
A young man marries a girl but they have no place for their
　　　　　wedding night.
He asks: Where can I make love to her?
We laugh and say: This is not the right time for that question.
The analyst says: In order to live, they die by mistake.
The literary man says: Our camp will certainly fall.
What do they want from us?
Athens airport welcomes its visitors without end.
Yet, like the benches in the terminal, we remain, impatiently
　　　　　waiting for the sea.
How many more years longer, O Athens airport?

"I Talk Too Much"

*I talk too much about the **slightest nuance** between women*
　　　　　and trees,
about the earth's enchantment, about a country with no pass-
　　　　　port stamp.
I ask: Is it true, good ladies and gentlemen, that the earth of
　　　　　Man is for all human beings
as you say? In that case, where is my little cottage, and
　　　　　where am I?
The conference audiences applaud me for another three
　　　　　minutes,
three minutes of freedom and recognition.
*The conference approves our **right of return**,*
like all chickens and horses, to a dream made of stone.
I shake hands with them, one by one. I bow to them. Then I
　　　　　continue my journey
to another country and talk about the difference between a
　　　　　mirage and the rain.
I ask: Is it true, good ladies and gentlemen, that the earth of
　　　　　Man is for all human beings?

Slightest nuance: Romantic
subjects.

Right of return: Right,
claimed by Palestinians, to
return to homes they say were
stolen from them by Israel.

Poem from The Adam of Two Edens

"As He Walks Away"

The enemy who drinks tea in our hovel
has a horse in smoke, a daughter with

thick eyebrows, brown eyes and long hair
braided over her shoulders
like a night of songs.
He's never without her picture
when he comes to drink our tea,
but he forgets to tell us about her nightly chores,
about a horse of ancient melodies
abandoned on a hilltop.
Relaxing in our shack, the enemy
slings his rifle over my grandfather's chair,
eats our bread like any guest,
dozes off for a while on the wicker couch.
Then, as he stoops to pat our cat on the way out,
says: "Don't blame the victim."
"And who might that be?" *we ask.*
"Blood that won't dry in the night."
His coat-buttons flash as he walks away.
Good evening to you! Say hello to our well!
Say hello to our fig trees! Step gingerly
on our shadows in the barley fields.
Greet our pines on high. But please
don't leave the gate open at night.
And don't forget the horse's terror of airplanes.
And greet us there, if you have time.
That's what we want to say at the doorstep.
He hears it well enough,
but muffles it with a cough,
and waves it aside.
Then why does he visit the victim every evening,
memorize our proverbs by heart, as we do,
repeat our songs about our
specials holidays in the holy place?
Our flutes would have played a duet
if it weren't for the gun.
As long as the earth turns around itself inside us
the war will not end.
Let's be good then.
He asked us to be good while we're here.
He recites **Yeats's** *poem about the* Irish Airman*:*
"Those that I fight I do not hate,
Those that I guard I do not love."
Then he leaves our wooden ramshackle hut

Yeats: Irish poet William Butler Yeats (1865–1939).

and walks eighty meters to our old stone house
on the edge of the plain.
Greet our house for us, stranger,
The coffee cups are the same.
Can you smell our fingers still on them?
Can you tell your daughter
with the braid and thick eyebrows
she has an absent friend
who wishes to visit her, to enter her mirror
and see his secret.
How was she able to trace his age in this place?
Say hello to her, if you have time.
What we want to tell him
he hears well enough, but muffles with a cough
and waves aside.
His coat buttons flash
as he walks away.

What happened next . . .

Poetry does not have consequences in the same way that a declaration of war or a peace treaty has consequences. No one has ever claimed that one of Darwish's poems sparked a military victory or encouraged a soldier to lay down his weapon. Yet many who read Darwish's poetry remark that they emerge from that reading with a different sense of the world, that they feel a new compassion for the Palestinian sense of injustice at being removed from their land. Salma Khadra Jayyusi, editor of the anthology *Modern Arabic Poetry*, writes that "poetry is the main vehicle for expressing the emotional experience of a people, and for revealing their deeper consciousness of the world, and it may bring the reader into a more intimate knowledge of other people's actual life situations." In this subtle way, poetry can have consequences of its own.

"I thought that poetry could change everything, could change history and could humanize, and I think that the illusion is very necessary to push poets to be involved and to believe, but now I think that poetry changes only the poet," Darwish told *The Progressive* in 2002. For Darwish personally, his poetry certainly has had very real consequences. He was punished for writing a poem as a schoolboy, imprisoned for his poetry and protest as a young man, and revered for his work and heralded as a spokesman for his people as an adult.

Did you know . . .

- Darwish won the Lannan Foundation Award for Cultural Freedom in 2001, which included a $350,000 prize. He also received the Sultan bin Ali al Owais Cultural Award for cultural and scientific achievement. Some critics suggest that he will be considered for the literary world's most prestigious prize, the Nobel Prize for literature.

- Darwish is not the only poet writing about the Israeli-Palestinian conflict. Many poets and writers on both sides of the conflict such as Kemal Nasir and Aharon Shabtai have offered their own unique perspective.

Consider the following. . .

- Darwish is often considered to be making political statements in his poetry, though in a very subtle way. Select one of Darwish's poems and write a short essay pointing out how the poem engages with political issues.

- Pick one of Darwish's poems and discuss the ways he uses figures of speech such as metaphor or simile to enhance the meaning of his poems.

- Salma Khadra Jayyusi, editor of *Modern Arabic Poetry*, writes that "poetry is the main vehicle for expressing the emotional experience of a people." In what ways does Darwish's poetry express the emotional experience of his people?

- Locate and read the work of another poet who has written about politics in the Middle East. How is his or her view of the situation different from that of Darwish?

For More Information

Books

Contemporary World Writers. Detroit: St. James Press, 1993.

Darwish, Mahmoud. *The Adam of Two Edens: Selected Poems.* Syracuse, NY: Syracuse University Press, 2000.

Darwish, Mahmoud. *Unfortunately, It Was Paradise: Selected Poems.* Translated and edited by Munir Akash and Carolyn Forché. Berkeley: University of California Press, 2003.

Jayyusi, Salma Khadra, ed. *Modern Arabic Poetry: An Anthology.* New York: Columbia University Press, 1987.

Periodicals

Progressive (May 2002): pp. 24–27.

Web Sites

"Mahmoud Darwish." *Khalil Sakakini Culture Centre.* http://www.sakakini.org/literature/mdarwish.htm (accessed on June 24, 2005).

"Mahmoud Darwish." *Poets from Palestine.* http://www.barghouti.com/poets/darwish/bitaqa.asp (accessed on June 24, 2005).

Where to Learn More

Books

Altman, Linda Jacobs. *The Creation of Israel*. San Diego, CA: Lucent Books, 1998.

Brand, Laurie A. *Palestinians in the Arab World: Institution Building and the Search for State*. New York: Columbia University Press, 1988.

Bratman, Fred. *War in the Persian Gulf*. Brookfield, CT: Millbrook Press, 1991.

Carew-Miller, Anna. *The Palestinians*. Philadelphia: Mason Crest, 2004.

Choueiri, Youssef M. *Arab Nationalism—A History: Nation and State in the Arab World*. Malden, MA: Blackwell Publishing, 2000.

Ciment, James. *Palestine/Israel: The Long Conflict*. New York: Facts on File, 1997.

Cipkowski, Peter. *Understanding the Crisis in the Persian Gulf*. New York: John Wiley and Sons, 1992.

Cleveland, William L. *A History of the Modern Middle East*. 3rd ed. Boulder, CO: Westview Press, 2004.

Cobban, Helena. *The Making of Modern Lebanon*. London: Hutchinson, 1985.

Diller, Daniel, ed. *The Middle East*. 8th ed. Washington, DC: Congressional Quarterly, 1995.

Drummond, Dorothy. *Holy Land Whose Land? Modern Dilemma Ancient Roots.* Seattle, WA: Educare Press, 2002.

Dudley, William, ed. *The Middle East: Opposing Viewpoints.* San Diego: Greenhaven Press, 2004.

Encyclopedia of the Modern Middle East. 4 vols. New York: Macmillan Reference USA, 1996.

Farah, Tawfic E., ed. *Pan-Arabism and Arab Nationalism: The Continuing Debate.* Boulder, CO: Westview Press, 1987.

Farsoun, Samih K., with Christina E. Zacharia. *Palestine and the Palestinians.* Boulder, CO: Westview Press, 1997.

Freedman, Robert O., ed. *The Middle East and the Peace Process: The Impact of the Oslo Accords.* Gainesville: University Press of Florida, 1998.

Gilbert, Martin. *The Arab-Israeli Conflict: Its History in Maps.* 5th ed. London: Weidenfeld and Nicolson, 1992.

Gomaa, Ahmed M. *The Foundation of the League of Arab States: Wartime Diplomacy and Inter-Arab Politics, 1941 to 1945.* New York: Longman, 1977.

Gunderson, Cory Gideon. *The Israeli-Palestinian Conflict.* Edina, MN: Abdo Publishing, 2004.

Haneef, Suzanne. *What Everyone Should Know about Islam and Muslims.* N.p.: Library of Islam, 1996.

Hourani, Albert Habib. *The Emergence of the Modern Middle East.* Berkeley: University of California Press, 1981.

The Israeli-Palestinian Conflict: Crisis in the Middle East. Upper Saddle River, NJ: Prentice Hall, 2003.

Katz, Samuel M. *Jerusalem or Death: Palestinian Terrorism.* Minneapolis, MN: Lerner, 2004.

Kepel, Gilles. *Jihad: The Trail of Political Islam.* Cambridge, MA: Belknap Press of Harvard University Press, 2002.

Khalil, Muhammad, ed. *The Arab States and the Arab League: A Documentary Record, Vol. II International Affairs.* Beirut, Lebanon: Khayats, 1962.

Kort, Michael. *The Handbook of the Middle East.* Brookfield, CT: Twenty-First Century Books, 2002.

Lesch, David W., ed. *The Middle East and the United States: A Historical and Political Reassessment.* Boulder, CO: Westview Press, 2003.

Lewis, Bernard. *From Babel to Dragomans: Interpreting the Middle East.* New York: Oxford University Press, 2004.

Lewis, Bernard. *The Middle East: A Brief History of the Last 2,000 Years.* New York: Scribner, 1995.

Lewis, Bernard. *What Went Wrong? The Clash Between Islam and Modernity in the Middle East.* New York: Perennial, 2003.

Luciani, Giacomo, and Ghassan Salam&é, eds. *The Politics of Arab Integration.* New York: Croom Helm, 1988.

Long, Cathryn J. *The Middle East in Search of Peace.* Brookfield, CT: Millbrook Press, 1996.

Louis, W. Roger. *The British Empire in the Middle East, 1945–1951: Arab Nationalism, the United States and Postwar Imperialism.* New York and London: Oxford, 1984.

Marr, Phebe, and William Lewis, eds. *Riding the Tiger: The Middle East Challenge after the Cold War.* Boulder, CO: Westview Press, 1993.

Maswilili, Ahmad. *Historical Dictionary of Islamic Fundamentalist Movements in the Arab World, Iran, and Turkey.* Lanham, MD: Scarecrow Press, 1999.

Miller, Debra A. *The Arab-Israeli Conflict.* San Diego, CA: Lucent Books, 2005.

Ojeda, Auriana. *The Middle East: Current Controversies.* San Diego: Greenhaven Press, 2003.

Pasachoff, Naomi. *Links in the Chain: Shapers of the Jewish Tradition.* New York: Oxford University Press, 1997.

Raider, Mark A. *The Emergence of American Zionism.* New York: New York University Press, 1998.

Shpiro, David H. *From Philanthropy to Activism: The Political Transformation of American Zionism in the Holocaust Years, 1933–1945.* New York: Pergamon Press, 1994.

Simpson, Christopher. *The Splendid Blond Beast: Money, Law, and Genocide in the Twentieth Century.* New York: Grove Press, 1993.

Smith, Charles D., ed. *Palestine and the Arab-Israeli Conflict: A History with Documents.* 4th ed. Boston and New York: Bedford/St. Martin's, 2001.

Urofsky, Melvin I. *American Zionism from Herzl to the Holocaust.* Lincoln: University of Nebraska Press, 1995.

Vatikiotis, P.J. *The Middle East: From the End of Empire to the End of the Cold War.* New York: Routledge, 1997.

Vital, David. *The Origins of Zionism.* Oxford: Clarendon Press, 1975.

Wagner, Heather Lehr. *Israel and the Arab World.* Philadelphia: Chelsea House, 2002.

Watson, Geoffrey R. *The Oslo Accords: International Law and the Israeli-Palestinian Peace Agreements.* New York: Oxford University Press, 2000.

Worth, Richard. *Israel and the Arab States.* New York: F. Watts, 1983.

Web Sites

Beinin, Joel. "Is Terrorism a Useful Term in Understanding the Middle East and the Palestinian-Israeli Conflict?" (originally published in *Radical History Review* no. 85 [Winter 2003]: 12–23), *Why War?* http://www.why-war.com/files/85.1beinin.pdf (accessed on July 8, 2005).

"Guide to the Middle East Peace Process." *Israeli Ministry of Foreign Affairs.* http://www.mfa.gov.il/mfa/peace%20process/guide%20to%20the%20peace%20process/ (accessed on June 24, 2005).

"Gulf Wars I and II: A Comparison of the Two Wars Between the U.S. and Iraq." *Time.* http://www.time.com/time/covers/1101030331/wgw1.html (accessed on July 8, 2005).

Internet Islamic History Sourcebook. http://www.fordham.edu/halsall/islam/islamsbook.html#Islamic%20Nationalism (accessed on July 8, 2005).

"Is Islamism a Threat?: A Debate." *The Middle East Quarterly* (December 1999). http://www.meforum.org/article/447 (accessed on June 24, 2005).

The Islamic World to 1600. http://www.ucalgary.ca/applied_history/tutor/islam/ (accessed on July 8, 2005).

Jewish Virtual Library. http://www.jewishvirtuallibrary.org/ (accessed on July 8, 2005).

League of Arab States. http://www.arableagueonline.org/arableague/index_en.jsp (accessed on June 24, 2005).

MEMRI The Middle East Research Institute. http://memri.org/index.html (accessed on July 8, 2005).

"Middle East: Land of Conflict." *CNN.* www.cnn.com/SPECIALS/2003/mideast (accessed on July 8, 2005).

"Muslim Brotherhood." *FAS Intelligence Resource Program.* http://www.fas.org/irp/world/para/mb.htm (accessed on July 8, 2005).

"The Origins and Evolution of the Palestine Problem: 1917–1988." *United Nations Information System on the Question of Palestine.* http://domino.un.org/UNISPAL.NSF/561c6ee353d740fb8525607d00581829/aeac80e740c782e4852561150071fdb0!OpenDocument (accessed on June 24, 2005).

"Palestine Facts & Info." *PASSIA: Palestinian Academic Society for the Study of International Affairs, Jerusalem.* http://www.passia.org/index_pfacts.htm (accessed on July 8, 2005).

"Palestine, Israel and the Arab-Israeli Conflict: A Primer," *Middle East Research and Information Project.* http://www.merip.org/palestine-israel_primer/occupied-terr-jeru-pal-isr.html (accessed on July 8, 2005).

"Patterns of Global Terrorism." *U.S. Department of State.* http://www.state.gov/s/ct/rls/pgtrpt/ (accessed on June 24, 2005).

The Question of Palestine and the United Nations. http://www.un.org/Depts/dpi/palestine/ (accessed on July 8, 2005).

Shah, Anup. *The Middle East.* http://www.globalissues.org/Geopolitics/MiddleEast.asp (accessed on July 8, 2005).

"Sunnis vs. Shiites." *Islam Web.* http://islamicweb.com/beliefs/cults/shia.htm (accessed on July 8, 2005).

The Washington Institute for Near East Policy. http://www.washington institute.org/ (accessed on July 8, 2005).

"Zionism and the Creation of Israel." *MidEast Web.* http://www.mideastweb.org/zionism.htm (accessed June 24, 2005).

Text Credits

Following is a list of the copyright holders who have granted us permission to reproduce excerpts from primary source documents in *Middle East Conflict: Primary Sources*. Every effort has been made to trace copyright; if omissions have been made, please contract us.

Copyrighted excerpts reproduced from the following books:

Anderson, Terry A. From *Den of Lions: Memoirs of Seven Years*. Crown Publishers, Inc., 1993. Copyright © 1993 by TMS Corporation. Reproduced by permission of the author.

Bechara, Soha. From "Excerpts from Resistance," in *Resistance: My Life for Lebanon*. Edited by Gabriel Levine. Soft Skull Press, 2003. Copyright © 2003 Soha Bechara. Translation © 2003 Gabriel Levine. Reproduced by permission.

Darwish, Mahmoud. From "On This Earth," in *Unfortunately, It Was Paradise*. Edited by Munir Akash and Carolyn Forche. University of California Press, 2003. Copyright © 2003 by The Regents of the University of California. Reproduced by permission.

Index

Boldface indicates primary
sources, primary source
authors, and primary source
page numbers.

Illustrations are marked
by (ill.).

V

Vietnam War 67, 72, 204
Violence, calls to 6–7, 74–80,
    99–101, 156–161. *See also*
    Terrorists and terrorism; Wars

W

Wahhabism 161
Wailing Wall. *See* Western Wall
Waite, Terry 205, 209
War of Attrition 86
War of Independence. *See*
    Arab-Israeli War of 1948
Wars
    Arab-Israeli War of 1948 (War of
        Independence) 44, 54–55
    Gulf War 63, 156–157
    Korean War 63
    Six-Day War of 1967 57–60, 67
    Vietnam War 67, 72, 204
    War of Attrition 86
    World War I 1, 5, 25, 35, 38, 125,
        141, 154, 200–201
    World War II 14, 18, 21–23, 26,
        36–37, 39, 48, 184, 197
    Yom Kippur War 66, 86
Weizmann, Chaim 19
Wellesley, William Robert 7,
    7 (ill.)

West Bank. *See* Occupied territories
Western Wall 6
White Paper 3, 14, 19–20
Wilson, Woodrow 20
Women's rights 124
World Islamic Front 156
World Zionist Organization 3, 19,
    20, 138

Y

Yemen 31, 152
Yom Kippur War 66, 86

Z

Zionism
    Arab statements against 72, 77,
        146–151
    Biltmore Program 4, 17–24
    Jewish immigration 14–15
    The Jewish State (Herzl) 128–138
    origin of 2–4, 125, 128–138
    Palestinians unifying against 26
    reaction to White Paper 19–20
    They Must Go (Meir) 177–184
Zionist Congress 137–138
Zionist Organization. *See* World
    Zionist Organization